AGENDA 21:

The Earth Summit Strategy To Save Our Planet

Introduction by Senator Paul Simon

Edited by Daniel Sitarz

Boulder, Colorado

Printed on
recycled paper

Library of Congress Cataloging-in-Publication Data

AGENDA 21: The Earth Summit Strategy To Save Our Planet/
    Introduction by U.S. Senator Paul Simon; Edited by Daniel Sitarz
        p.   cm.
    The main text of this abridged version of AGENDA 21 is based
    on the final official United Nations document AGENDA 21 and
    the United Nations Guide to AGENDA 21: The Global
    Partnership for Environment and Development.
    Includes index.
    ISBN 0-935755-11-X   : $24.95
    1. Economic development--Environmental aspects.
    2. Environmental policy--International cooperation.
    3. Sustainable development. I. Sitarz, Dan 1948- II. United
    Nations Conference on Environment and Development (1992 :
    Rio de Janeiro, Brazil)
    HD75.6.A37 1993
    363.7--dc20   92-74303   CIP

ISBN 0-935755-11-X
Library of Congress Catalog Card Number 92-074303

EarthPress would like to thank the National Oceanic and Atmospheric Administration for the use of the NASA satellite photgraph of Planet Earth for the cover of this book.

Schools, Organizations and Corporations:

Multiple copies of this book are available at a substantial discount. If you would like to order multiple copies of this book for your school, private organization or company, please contact:

    EarthPress   Toll-free: (800)748-1175
    Special Sales   FAX: (303)545-9901
    4882 Kellogg Circle
    Boulder CO 80303

Table of Contents

Chapter 5

The Management of Human Settlements

Chapter 6

Chemicals and The Management of Waste

Acknowledgements

This work would not have been possible without the assistance and encouragement of many people. Most importantly, I would like to thank my wife and partner, Janet Harris Sitarz, for her dedicated and professional editing of this enormous project. I could not have completed this book without her love and support. Thanks also to Nancy Jane Cottom for her patient and scholarly editing; to United Nations Publications for their permission to undertake this project and for their assistance and support; to the United Nations Conference on Environment and Development for the materials from which this version of *AGENDA 21* has been prepared; to UNCED Secretary-General Maurice Strong for his encouragement; to the EcoNet computer network; to the Global Tomorrow Coalition for background information on sustainable development; to Dr. Donella Meadows, Dr. Dennis Meadows and Dr. Jorgen Randers for background information on sustainable development; to Dr. James Garbarino for background information on sustainable development; to Herman Daly for background information on environmental economics; to Drs. Paul and Anne Ehrlich for background information on global environmental problems; to George Roche of Concepts 3 in Boulder, Colorado for his cover design; to the National Oceanic and Atmospheric Administration for their permission to use the NASA satellite photograph on the cover; to the Haddon Craftsmen for printing; to Michael Haldeman for indexing; and to all of the individuals and groups worldwide who participated in the preparation of the official United Nations document AGENDA 21 and attended the Earth Summit or the Global Forum in Rio de Janeiro, Brazil. I would particularly like to thank Senator Paul Simon for his preparation of the Introduction to this book.

Dedication

This book is dedicated to my children, Justin and Jessica Sitarz,
and all the other children of the world.

Introduction

June 13, 1992 may mark the beginning of an environmental renaissance. On that date in Rio de Janeiro, Brazil, the world's leaders met to plan the prevention of our Earth's environmental death. This momentous gathering, the Earth Summit, held on the twentieth anniversary of the first United Nations Conference on the Environment was a watershed Event; never had so many heads of state gathered together. All were united in recognition of the fact that what happens in one part of the world has a definite and dramatic impact on the rest of the planet. Clearly, the Rio Summit confirmed that all nations stand to benefit when we work together to protect the Earth.

What has also become clear is that business and commercial activity must be undertaken with respect for the fragility of our land, our air, and our water; a healthy environment and a healthy economy can no longer be exclusive pursuits. "Sustainable development" practices are crucial if the Earth is to continue supporting life as we know it. In the blind rush toward economic prosperity, mankind has placed a tremendous strain on our environment. Much of this environmental deterioration is caused by the process of production and consumption; especially in the industrialized world. Although the industrialized nations comprise 25 percent of population, they account for three-quarters of the global carbon dioxide emissions.

If we are going to ask other countries to change their ways, the United States must set an example. As the leader of the free world, we bear a special responsibility. Given our country's effect on the world economy, the United States should lead the worldwide effort for a better environment. Unfortunately, American leadership prior to and during the Earth Summit was anemic. It will require courage, vision and leadership on the part of *all* nations to make the changes we need. If the U.S. can't take the steps necessary to protect the environment, it can not expect other nations to do so.

For reforms to begin, the political reality is that policy-makers need to know that people are aware and concerned. *AGENDA 21: The Earth Summit Strategy To Save Our Planet* is an important tool in educating the public on the environmental challenges we face. Given the amount of critical information contained in *AGENDA 21*, Daniel Sitarz has performed an important public service. His clear, concise analysis and summary presents the essential elements in a manner easily accessible to the public.

Several months have now passed since the Earth Summit. The responsibility to preserve our natural resources for future generations must become one of our highest priorities. Reversing the damage we have wrought will be difficult, expensive, and achievable only over a long period of time, but with a concerted worldwide effort, it can be done. The Earth's future requires it.

U. S. Senator Paul Simon
January 8, 1993

Chapter 1

Understanding AGENDA 21

AGENDA 21 is, first and foremost, a document of hope. Adopted at the Earth Summit in Brazil by nations representing over 98% of the Earth's population, it is the principal global plan to confront and overcome the economic and ecological problems of the late 20th century. It provides a comprehensive blueprint for humanity to use to forge its way into the next century by proceeding more gently upon the Earth. As its sweeping programs are implemented world-wide, it will eventually impact on every human activity on our planet. Deep and dramatic changes in human society are proposed by this monumental historic agreement. Understanding those changes is essential to guide us all into the future on our fragile planet.

Humanity is at a crossroads of enormous consequence. Never before has civilization faced an array of problems as critical as the ones now faced. As forbidding and portentous as it may sound, what is at stake is nothing less than the global survival of humankind.

The effects of human impact upon the Earth have been accelerating at a rate unforeseen even a handful of decades ago. Where once nature seemed forever the dominant force on Earth, evidence is rapidly accumulating that human influence over nature has reached a point where natural forces may soon be overwhelmed. Only very recently have the citizens of Earth begun to appreciate the depth of the potential danger of human impact on our planet. The equilibrium of the planet is in

1

jeopardy, as judged by forces as profound as the global climate and the atmospheric protection from the Sun's damaging rays. Major changes in the ecological balance of the world are occurring very rapidly, more rapidly in many cases than humanity's ability to assess the dangers.

Despite perceived feelings of superiority over nature, humanity remains fully and totally dependent upon the natural world. We need the bounty of nature to survive on this planet. We need the fresh air to breathe, the clean water to drink, the fertile soil to provide our sustenance. Human impact upon these vital substances has reached the point of causing potentially irreversible damage. Scientists around the world, in every country on Earth, are documenting the hazards of ignoring our dependence upon the natural world.

There is strong evidence from the world's scientific community that humanity is very, very close to crossing certain ecological thresholds for the support of life on Earth. The Earth's ozone layer, our only protection from the harmful rays of the Sun is being depleted. Massive erosion is causing a rapid loss in the fertile soil of our planet and with it a potentially drastic drop in the ability to produce food for the world's people. Vast destruction of the world's forests is contributing to the spread of the world's deserts, increasing the loss of biodiversity and hampering the ability of the Earth's atmosphere to cleanse itself. The planet's vast oceans are losing their animal life at a staggering rate and are fast reaching the limit of their ability to absorb humanity's waste. The land animals and plants of our planet are experiencing a rate of extinction unseen on Earth since the time of the dinosaurs; extinctions brought on not by cataclysmic events of nature but by the impact of a single species: *homo sapiens*. The increasing pollution of air, water and land by hazardous and toxic waste is causing wide-spread health problems that are only now beginning to be understood. All of these problems are being intensified by the explosive growth in the sheer numbers of human beings in the last half of the 20th century.

For the first time in history, humanity must face the risk of unintentionally destroying the foundations of life on Earth. The global scientific consensus is that if the current levels of environmental deterioration continue, the delicate life-sustaining qualities of this planet will collapse. It is a stark and frightening potential. To prevent such a collapse is an awesome challenge for the global community.

As serious as these environmental dangers are to the equilibrium of life on Earth, the human effects of poverty, hunger, poor health and illiteracy also threaten the human race. Famine and malnutrition are claiming ever more lives even as the absolute quantity of food on Earth increases. Poor health is causing greater world-wide suffering even as our knowledge of medicine increases. Pandemics of communicable diseases threaten to devastate entire regions of the Earth. The deepening gaps between the rich and poor on Earth are creating explosive situations of social strife. The very fabric of civilization on Earth is at risk when 1 billion people live in abject poverty, without adequate food, shelter, health care or education.

Until very recently, the problems of environmental degradation and poverty were viewed as unrelated. Each was also seen as a localized problem, with little if any global impact. Water pollution in a particular area was not seen as impacting on a wider realm. Soil erosion in one country appeared to have no effect on its neighbors. Lack of health care or sanitation in the slums of a great city was assumed to be a localized problem.

Increasingly, however, irrefutable evidence has mounted that there is an intricate interdependence of both the world's economy and the world's ecology. Seemingly local problems are now known to have global effects. Pollution in one locality can affect an enormous area. The loss of soil fertility in one country can cause a world-wide impact on food prices and availability. Poverty and lack of basic human needs can create the potential for enormous social upheaval with global impact of far-reaching dimensions. Gradually, it is being understood that the issues of poverty, population growth, industrial development, depletion of natural resources and the destruction of the environment are all very closely interrelated. Solutions to any of these problems can not be achieved in a vacuum. The development of the Earth to provide a basic level of comfort for all humanity and the protection of the global environment are two sides of the single coin of human survival.

The seeds of the global response to these problems were planted over a span of many years. Some of the first of these were planted by scientists, researchers, artists and writers who began to observe and quantify the effects of human civilization on nature. Thirty years prior to the signing of *AGENDA 21*, Rachel Carson, in her somber and epic book *"Silent Spring"*, produced one of the most powerful and eloquent warnings to humanity of the consequences of its actions. A decade after Ms. Carson's alarm, the United Nations convened the Conference on the Human Environment in Stockholm, Sweden, the first global response to the enfolding environmental crisis. The Stockholm Conference documented the growing threat that human existence posed to the continued health of the planet and outlined strategies to begin to deal with the problems identified.

In the twenty years since that conference, there has been a progression of notable conferences and meetings regarding the perils that the growth and activities of humanity have created. In those same twenty years, however, concern has steadily mounted over the continuing deterioration of the global environment and the declining quality of life for vast portions of humanity.

In 1987, the U.N. World Commission on Environment and Development linked the issue of environmental protection to the seemingly unrelated topic of global economic growth and development. Headed admirably by Norwegian Prime Minister Gro Harlem Brundtland, this commission produced a stunning report entitled *"Our Common Future"*, which carefully documented the status and future of the global economic and ecological situation. Perhaps the most lasting accomplishment of the Brundtland Commission, however, was to thrust the concept of "sustainable development" into the mainstream of world debate. Although this concept had been the focus of discussion in the world scientific community for some time, its introduction into international dialogue elicited an almost instant response.

The concept of sustainable development was immediately seen by many as the only rational manner by which to confront the interrelated problems of environmental destruction and necessary economic development. To conquer those two problems, the types and levels of production and consumption of goods on a global level must be brought into line with the finite ability of the Earth to sustain them. The Earth cannot long support the types of production and consumption that the industrialized countries now enjoy. Yet the developing countries of the world are racing forward to achieve such production and consumption for its citizens.

The concept of sustainable global development is based on two central questions. First, is it possible to increase the basic standard of living of the world's expanding population without unnecessarily depleting our finite natural resources and further degrading the environment upon which we all depend? and, second: can humanity collectively step back from the brink of environmental collapse and, at the same time, lift its poorest members up to the level of basic human health and dignity? Largely unheralded by the world press, in recent years the nations of the Earth have taken positive steps to ensure that the answer to both of these questions is a resounding "yes".

In December of 1989, the General Assembly of the United Nations confronted this daunting task. The urgency of the problems of development and environment prompted the nations of the world to call for an unprecedented meeting—a meeting of all of the nations on Earth—an Earth summit. The United Nations Conference on Environment and Development was set for June of 1992 in Rio de Janeiro, Brazil.

The scope of attendance at this historic meeting clearly defines the importance of its task. It was, very simply, the largest gathering of heads of state in the history of life on Earth. On June 13th, 1992, nearly 100 world leaders met around a single table in Rio de Janeiro in the largest face-to-face meeting of national leaders in the history of international diplomacy. However, it is the background leading up to the Earth Summit by which its true magnitude can be appreciated.

In the years prior to the Earth Summit, people around the world came forward in meetings to voice their concerns about the future of our planet. Participation ranged from gatherings of the Council of Elders on the tiny Pacific island nation of Tokelau to meetings of the Parliament of the United Kingdom; from assemblies of the Swaziland Boy Scouts to conventions of business people in the upper echelons of multinational corporations; from meetings of private organizations around the globe to conferences at the highest levels of the largest governments on Earth. People representing all walks of life met, discussed and prepared extensive national reports which became the background reports from which the main agreement of the Earth Summit was drafted. Never in history have so many individual human beings been able to effectively convey their concerns in an effort to influence the direction of humankind. Never before have so many governments, private organizations and individuals collaborated on a single monumental task. This prelude to the Earth Summit was a global effort of enormous historical, political and social significance.

Against this backdrop of unprecedented participation by the citizens of the world, the latest technical information and projections from leading scientists around the world were also compiled for use by the Preparatory Committee of the Earth Summit. In four pre-conference sessions of this Committee, the central tenets of a coordinated global approach to confronting the problems of the Earth were formulated. It is these tenets which have evolved to become the central agreement of the Earth Summit—*AGENDA 21*.

AGENDA 21 is not a static document. It is a plan of action. It is meant to be a hands-on instrument to guide the development of the Earth in a sustainable manner. Recognizing the global nature of the environmental problems that face humanity, it is based on the premise that sustainable development of the Earth is not simply an option: it is a requirement—a requirement increasingly imposed by the limits of nature to absorb the punishment which humanity has inflicted upon it. *AGENDA 21* is also based on the premise that sustainable development of the Earth is entirely feasible. The transition to a global civilization in balance with nature will be an exceedingly difficult task, but *AGENDA 21* is the collective global alert that there is no alternative. We must align human civilization with the natural equilibrium of our planet and we must do so very rapidly if we are to prevent an irreversible decline in the quality of life on Earth.

AGENDA 21 proposes an array of actions which are intended to be implemented by every person on Earth. The actions are specific and concrete proposals which are meant to address the sustainable and efficient use of our global natural resources, the effective management of pollution and the waste products of development and the achievement of a basic standard of living for all humanity. The bold goal of *AGENDA 21* is to halt and reverse the environmental damage to our planet and to promote environmentally sound and sustainable development in all countries on Earth. It is a blueprint for action in all areas relating to the sustainable development of our planet into the 21st century. It calls for specific changes in the activities of all people. It includes concrete measures and incentives to reduce the environmental impact of the industrialized nations, revitalize development in developing nations, eliminate poverty world-wide and stabilize the level of human population.

Effective execution of *AGENDA 21* will require a profound reorientation of all human society, unlike anything the world has ever

6

experienced—a major shift in the priorities of both governments and individuals and an unprecedented redeployment of human and financial resources. This shift will demand that a concern for the environmental consequences of every human action be integrated into individual and collective decision-making at every level.

The successful implementation of the far-ranging actions proposed by *AGENDA 21* will require active participation by people throughout the world, at the local, national and global levels. There are measures that are directed at all levels of society—from international bodies such as the United Nations and the World Bank to local groups and individuals. There are specific actions which are intended to be undertaken by multi-national corporations and entrepreneurs, by financial institutions and individual investors, by high-tech companies and indigenous people, by workers and labor unions, by farmers and consumers, by students and schools, by governments and legislators, by scientists, by women, by children—in short, by every person on Earth.

To cope with the enormous global changes which are proposed, *AGENDA 21* provides a myriad of opportunities. Suggestions are furnished for individuals and companies world-wide to develop new industries, pioneer innovative technologies, evolve fresh techniques and institute novel trade arrangements. *AGENDA 21* offers a broad range of actions for educators, scientists and researchers to use to expand human understanding of the concepts and actions contemplated. Government officials and public servants on every level are provided with specific and concrete guidance on how to foster the proposals of this historic international agreement. Numerous specific personal actions are outlined and intended to be undertaken by individual citizens throughout the world.

AGENDA 21 does not presume to propose solutions to all of the problems confronting humankind, but rather it introduces a series of actions by which local, regional and global solutions can be identified and implemented. An entirely new relationship between and among nations is envisioned: a global partnership based on common interests, mutual needs and common yet differentiated responsibilities. The relationship proposed is one in which developing and industrialized countries will have both the incentive and the means to cooperate in protecting the global environment while meeting the needs and aspirations of its citizens for economic growth.

Although the environmental devastation of the developing countries of the world is most often highlighted in the world press, the roots of global environmental deterioration are now recognized as primarily a result of activities initiated by the industrialized countries of Earth. It is in the industrialized regions of the world that certain unsustainable patterns of consumption have developed, supported by production processes that place enormous stress on the natural balance of the Earth. It is in these industrialized countries that the largest proportions of the world's current emissions of pollutants and hazardous waste are produced. To correct the global problems that the process of industrialization has brought about, the industrialized countries of the world must bear the main responsibility. It is these same industrialized countries that have the capacity, technological prowess and education to lead the effort to combat the global impacts of environmental decay.

The developing countries of the world also have a very important responsibility in the careful management of their growth and development. An enormous internal effort must be made to increase the ability of these countries to use the technology and knowledge gained in the industrialized world to avoid the mistakes of the past. Environmental concerns must be linked irrevocably with the future development of these countries. International cooperation on all levels will be necessary to successfully manage our planet's future.

The comprehensive approach of *AGENDA 21* provides a blueprint for action in all areas of human activity. Virtually every aspect of human civilization is addressed by some potion of *AGENDA 21*. Specifically, 40 separate sections of concern are addressed and 120 separate action programs are outlined. All of these areas and programs are inter-connected in a myriad of ways, reflecting the inter-related nature of the problems. In each of the action programs, specific activities are proposed for confronting the particular problem which is addressed. For ease of understanding, the main program areas are grouped around seven central themes.

The Quality of Life on Earth

The first major theme of *AGENDA 21* relates to the quality of life on Earth. In many portions of the world, the day-to-day quality of life is deteriorating due to a combination of poverty, malnutrition, unemployment, population growth, lack of health care and pollution. At the same time, a minority of humanity continues to sustain a lifestyle which is based on highly wasteful consumption patterns and pollution-generating production processes. To confront these two problem areas, a dual approach is necessary.

People in the developing regions of the world must be encouraged and enabled to achieve sustaining livelihoods which do not destroy the environment or undermine the resource base upon which they rely. To do so, the inefficient consumption patterns in the industrialized countries which encourage resource waste must be drastically modified. This will entail fundamental and difficult changes in consumer preferences and practices. It will also require major shifts in the manufacturing base of the industrialized countries.

The overall levels and patterns of human consumption and production must be compatible with the finite capacities of the Earth. As the human population on Earth increases, there will be ever greater pressure for people throughout the world to attain a higher standard of living. If the model lifestyle for this increasing populace is based on the current excessive consumption levels and inefficient production methods of the industrialized countries, the thresholds of economic and environmental disaster will soon be reached. Sustainable patterns of consumption and efficient methods of production must be developed and encouraged in all societies.

One of the most important root causes of the intensifying human impact on our planet is the unprecedented growth in the sheer numbers of human beings in the last 50 years. The world's population is now growing by nearly 100 million people every year. Population pressures are placing increasing stress on the ecological systems of the planet. All countries must improve their ability to assess the environmental impact of their population growth rates and develop and implement appropriate policies to stabilize populations.

The general levels of health in many regions of the world have been deteriorating, in many cases due to environmental damage. Poverty is often a direct determinant of the health and disease levels in local populations. Achieving primary health care for all humanity requires sustainable social and economic development. Sustainable development and improved health are reciprocal. The general health of a particular population will be enhanced by developing reliable sources of food and energy; by encouraging safe and environmentally sound methods of resource use; and by implementing safe practices into the process of development.

The fundamental goal of this portion of *AGENDA 21* is to achieve a sustainable living for all of the inhabitants of our planet for many generations to come. This lofty, but achievable, goal entails the eventual eradication of poverty world-wide, the availability of healthy and equitable livelihoods for all and the implementation of consumption patterns that drastically reduce damage to the environment. *AGENDA 21* offers a wide-ranging set of actions to accomplish these major goals; actions which are intended to be implemented by governments, businesses, private organizations and consumers world-wide. The educational community must also be a full member of this partnership. Access to the necessary information to allow participants to act from a strong foundation of knowledge is essential.

Efficient Use of the Earth's Natural Resources

The efficient use of the world's natural resources forms the basis for the second theme of *AGENDA 21*. The finite resource base of our world is being depleted and degraded at an increasingly rapid rate. Altering consumption patterns and containing population growth will reduce some of the demand for these resources. It is essential, however, that more efficient and environmentally sound methods of utilizing our precious resources be developed. Both the Earth's renewable and non-renewable resources must be managed much more carefully in order to sustain their yield far into the future.

In the past, the Earth's seemingly unlimited supply of natural resources and its ability to assimilate waste were taken for granted. The enormous increase in human numbers and activities in this century has placed profound stress on these capacities. Fundamentally, it must be accepted that there are finite limits to both the Earth's resources and the Earth's capacity to handle the waste of human society. The carrying capacity of the Earth must be valued as an economic resource if it is to be assured of protection.

The actions in this area focus on the necessity to reverse the destruction of our renewable resources and implement strategies to conserve and provide for the sustainable use of our non-renewable resources. The protection of the global resources of land, fresh water, biological and genetic resources and energy must be paramount. Development of the Earth's resource base must be accomplished in a manner which raises productivity and meets rising global demands, while ensuring protection of the fragile ecosystems of our planet. The deserts, mountains and forests of the Earth must be afforded special protection as resource demand increases. Concern for environmental protection must be intimately incorporated into the process of resource development.

The challenge of sustainable agricultural development is to raise productivity and incomes without irreversibly depleting or degrading global soil and water resources. Without damaging the environment, there must be sufficient production, distribution and access to affordable and nutritious food supplies for all humanity. Again, in areas of the most fragile global ecosystems, special attention must be paid to providing access to ecologically sound farming techniques and alternative livelihoods.

Water is an essential ingredient to life on Earth. With the explosive growth in the world population and rapidly increasing economic activities, demand for water has already outstripped supply in many areas. This has lead to critical water management problems and, in some areas, to potential sources of severe conflict. These global water supply problems have been intensified in many areas by increasing levels of water pollution. Coherent water resource policies must be developed as an integral part of sustainable development. These policies must be flexible enough to take into account local and regional constraints and demands, as well as anticipated needs and opportunities for future growth.

Energy use is at the heart of some of the principal environmental problems faced by humanity. The unprecedented economic growth that has occurred during this century in the industrialized countries has depended to a great extent on the easy availability of low-cost energy—principally fossil fuels. Although oil is a non-renewable resource which will eventually be depleted, it is still the dominant global energy source and will remain so for the foreseeable future. Coal is the most environmentally damaging of all the fossil fuels. It is also in abundant supply and is the most available source of new energy in many major developing countries. Special efforts must be made on a world-

11

wide basis to find ways to reduce the environmental impact of the use of these two major fossil fuels.

Curbing the global appetite for fossil fuels is the single most important action that must be taken to reduce the adverse impacts of energy use on the atmosphere. This will necessitate a dramatic shift in consumer and industrial practices that are deeply entrenched. It will require rapid change toward a pattern of energy production and consumption that relies more heavily on efficiency and environmentally sound energy systems, particularly clean and renewable energy sources. This transition will be one of the most difficult to accomplish. Most of the industrial and transportation foundations of modern human society are based on the production and use of fossil fuels. To establish the basis for the transition to a new energy economy, efforts must be concentrated in those areas where economic and environmental considerations reinforce each other. The complete transition will require a major redeployment of research and development efforts towards new and renewable sources of energy.

The forests of the world play a number of critically important environmental and developmental roles. They are essential for the absorption and storage of carbon dioxide and as a primary source of biodiversity. Forests also play an important role in stabilizing watersheds and tempering local climates. Trees and forest lands also have significant economic development value. They are sources of habitat and livelihoods for millions of people, particularly traditional and indigenous communities. Many of these local populations have long understood the benefits of sustainable livelihoods obtained from forests. Only recently, however, have the developmental and environmental value of forests become apparent at the global level. The realization that forests significantly affect the lives of both local and global populations has helped place forest-related issues on the international agenda.

Each year large areas of the Earth are transformed into desert areas. Although desertification is a natural process, in recent years human activity has greatly accelerated the rate at which productive lands are being converted to deserts. Particularly in sub-Saharan Africa, desertification has lead to dramatic decreases in agricultural production causing widespread famine and human suffering. Slowing the process of desertification and coping with drought are problems of immediate concern in many regions of the world.

The biological diversity of plants and animals is one of the principal assets of the Earth. The vital environmental and developmental roles of this diversity are crucial to the future of humanity, yet it is presently accorded no value. The true social and economic values of biological resources are vastly underestimated and poorly appreciated. Too often, only their short-term commercial value is taken into account, leading to over-exploitation and destruction. The potential contributions of global biodiversity to human health and welfare are enormous. The benefits of deriving new and improved food crops, developing innovative pharmaceutical products and improving biotechnological processes can not be overstated. Urgent measures are required to halt the current trends of species loss and declining global biodiversity. To accomplish this, close international cooperation is essential. Most of the world's remaining biodiversity exists in the developing world, while the technological and financial capacity to develop and conserve these genetic resources exists in the industrialized world.

Biotechnology has wide applications of great economic relevance for both developing and industrialized countries. New biotechnological techniques can substantially increase the economic values available from the Earth's living resources. Sophisticated biotechnological tools and products are now being developed which offer an impressive array of possible applications for global development. These technologies should be made widely available to all countries to increase their food, animal feed and fiber production—and enhance their overall quality of life. These new techniques must be applied, however, in a manner that is both environmentally sound and in step with traditional methods of resource use. There is an immediate need for programs which use biotechnology for development, while providing mechanisms to insure that such use is safe for human health and the environment.

A wide array of actions is presented in this section of *AGENDA 21* to begin a global transition to a more efficient and environmentally sound use of the Earth's resources. These actions are intended for use by the farming, manufacturing and resource development industries (mining, forestry, oil production, etc.) as well as by local and national governments and individual citizens. As with all phases of *AGENDA 21*, private organizations and educational institutions must play a decisive role in promotion of the principles of *AGENDA 21*.

The Protection of Our Global Commons

Related to the efficient use of resources is the third central theme of *AGENDA 21*: the protection and management of our global commons—the atmosphere and the oceans. Global climate and weather and the physical processes which give rise to life on Earth are directly influenced by the atmosphere and oceans. Adverse human impact on these once-pristine domains has now reached perilous levels.

The Earth's capacity to sustain and nourish life depends primarily on the quality and composition of the atmosphere. Human activities have now reached the stage where the delicate balancing mechanisms of the atmosphere are being effected. The depletion of the ozone layer, climate change, acid rain, forest destruction, desertification and air pollution are some of the critical and complex atmospheric problems facing humanity. One of the principal difficulties in dealing with these complicated problems is that the time frames involved tend to separate the causes from the effects. Traditional economic and political decision-making is not accustomed to dealing with time spans that stretch beyond a human lifetime. New and innovative methods of dealing with these problems must be developed and put into action. The risks involved are of a critical, perhaps even decisive, nature to the future of humanity. Precaution must be the dominant principle applied in correcting these global problems.

The world's oceans play a dominant role in the life-sustaining processes of our planet. The oceans are also a vast source of food and mineral resources. Huge increases in marine catches in the last two decades have resulted from the introduction of new fishing technologies. Some of these new techniques, however, have caused the dramatic depletion of many fish, bird, reptile and mammal populations. Many seal and whale species have been overexploited, some to the verge of extinction. A fundamental cause of this exploitation is the status of marine life as common property—owned by no one—with no legal protection or appropriate global management plans. This common-property status encourages the over-exploitation of our marine resources by the use of such wasteful techniques as: habitat destruction, dynamite and chemical fishing, incidental capture and destruction of non-target species, unselective seining, wide-range driftnetting and indiscriminate trawling.

Marine pollution can be observed from the poles to the tropics and from the beaches to the abyssal depths. High-seas waste dumping and maritime activities each contribute around 10 percent to the total pollution load of the oceans. It is land based activities which add the bulk of the contaminants: 40 percent from river run-off, 30 percent via airborne pollution from land sources and an additional 10 percent from direct land-based dumping of wastes. The last few decades have seen a dramatic decline in catches of numerous marine fish species through both overfishing and marine pollution. The oceans are fast approaching their capacity to tolerate this environmental abuse.

The physical and ecological degradation of coastal areas is also accelerating. The root cause of the destruction of coastal marine habitat is the explosive growth of human numbers and activities. The rapid development of coastal settlements, an expansion of recreational areas and a concentration of industrial development along fragile coastal areas all have resulted in increasing coastal destruction.

Small island nations are at particular risk involving problems related to oceans and marine life. Their isolation, small size and dependance on the sea for sustenance place them in direct jeopardy whenever levels of marine life decline. Climatic changes which may cause increased tropical storms, hurricanes or sea-level rise threaten their very existence.

Regional and global agreements must be developed to ensure the fair and responsible use of global resources which are outside of national boundaries. Local and regional activities which cause environmental damage to these common areas must be understood and controlled. Immediate steps must be taken to reverse the perilous trends that have arisen in the past few decades. This portion of *AGENDA 21* outlines actions in which all levels of society must participate. Specifically, industries involved in development, the fishing industry, chemical manufacturing concerns and all other industries which impact upon the common areas of the globe must become more deeply involved with both the protection and management of these shared areas.

The Management of Human Settlements

The fourth central theme addressed in *AGENDA 21* involves the management of human settlements. The quality of human life depends, in large part, on the physical, social and economic conditions of the settlements where people live—whether those communities are villages, towns or cities. Today, some 2.5 billion people live in urban settlements.

This number is expected to increase rapidly in the years to come. Over 3 billion people are expected to inhabit urban areas by the year 2000 and over 5 billion by the year 2025. Thus, in the span of one generation, the urban population of the world is expected to double. The repercussions of this rapid and often uncontrolled urban expansion are profound. In many countries, the breakdown of urban services, the spread of slums and the accompanying social decline may well pose the most immediate threat to human well-being and the environment.

A fundamental challenge facing humanity is to develop coherent methods of managing human urban areas in order to reduce these risks. The quality of water supplies must be insured. Adequate shelter must be provided. The careful management of increasing quantities of solid waste and sewage must be established. Energy distribution and transportation systems must be expanded. Adequate health care, education and other essential services must be provided. All of these demands must be handled in a manner which reduces rather than increases the toll on the environment.

Most urban municipal systems in developing countries cannot meet this demand. Their fragile economies are often heavily burdened by external debt. They must deal with unfavorable trade terms, importation of most food and energy supplies and inadequate institutions with which to cope with explosive urban growth. The resulting environmental deterioration quickly translates into economic decline and human suffering.

The industrial activities, energy plants, transportation systems and municipal waste management of many of the world's urban areas were developed with little or no regard for environmental protection. While cities in industrialized countries have made great progress in upgrading their infrastructure to higher environmental standards, this is not generally the case in most developing countries. Urban pollution is at dangerous and increasing levels throughout the developing world. A priority must be to develop the capacities of urban settlements to deal with rapid growth while reducing the basic levels of pollution. A broad, preventive approach to environmental protection must be adopted and instituted for the management of both industrialized and developing urban areas. Pollution prevention at the source, waste minimization and cleaner technologies must be made available in urban areas on a broader basis.

This section of *AGENDA 21* offers plans for both the environmental and developmental management of urban areas throughout the world. These plans are designed to be put into effect by local, state and national officials and fostered by local and regional business, financial and educational communities.

Chemicals and the Management of Waste

The use of chemicals and the management of human and industrial waste is the focus of the fifth central theme of *AGENDA 21*. The use of resources and the process of production necessarily generates waste. If industrial production continues to increase world-wide and excessive consumption patterns remain in place, economic development may well be overwhelmed by the amount of waste and pollution that it produces. There has been a recent increase in the amount of residue waste products that are not or cannot be reintegrated into the world's ecosystems. These ultimate waste products are causing significant problems for human health and environmental quality. The volume and complexity of waste materials has also accelerated in recent years, overpowering efforts to effectively control and manage their disposal.

Inadequate waste disposal severely affects national wealth and productivity in many ways. The impact on human health is perhaps the most significant. Over 80 percent of all disease and over one-third of deaths in developing countries are caused by the ingestion of waste-contaminated food and water. As much as 10 percent of each person's productive time in developing countries is sacrificed to waste-related diseases. The economic burden and human suffering caused by this problem has substantial consequences for any attempts at progress in developing countries.

The use of chemicals has become essential to the development process and to the promotion of human well-being. Chemicals are extensively used in all societies, regardless of the stage of development. Their misuse, however, can have adverse effects on human health and cause extensive damage to the environment. It is extremely important that the properties of chemicals are sufficiently known and that adequate precautions are taken in their manufacture, handling, use and disposal.

The action programs adopted in this section of *AGENDA 21* include plans to reduce waste generation, recycle waste materials into useful products, find safe methods of human and chemical waste disposal and eliminate the illegal trade in hazardous waste. All businesses and industry have a part to play in implementing the necessary activities in this area. The chemical and waste management industries in particular must become closely involved with the proposals included in this division of *AGENDA 21*. Local, regional and national governments must cooperate closely to implement successful waste management programs and monitor global chemical use.

Sustainable Economic Growth

The sixth theme is global economic growth based on sustainability. Most of the environmental problems in the world have their origins in the processes of industrialization and development. Much of the world has been affected in recent years with declining standards of living. Income levels are stagnant or falling. The infrastructures and levels of public services throughout the world are declining. Air and water pollution are increasing, bringing with them greater health hazards. People throughout the world are gradually losing the economic resilience necessary to combat these difficulties. This deterioration in the quality of life is of particular concern in the developing world where debilitating poverty severely affects over 1 billion people.

The goal of this portion of *AGENDA 21* is to accelerate the correction of these economic problems and yet do so on a basis which is sustainable well into the future. Sustainable development and environmental soundness must be integrated into all levels of political and economic decision-making. The system of incentives and penalties which motivates economic behavior must be re-oriented to support sustainability. Corporate and national accounting practices must be amended to reflect the true impact of development on the environment and the real value of natural resources. This alteration in basic systems of accounting will promote greater efficiency in the use of natural resources and serve to reduce global pollution. It is wholly consistent with market economy principles for economic transactions to reflect their true costs, including their full environmental costs. By re-orienting the system of economic accounting to reflect the true costs of development and resource use, market forces can act as a powerful stimulant for the global transition to a sustainable society. By insuring that the environmental costs of projects and policies are considered, the protection of the environment can be given a proper place in the market economy of the world. This fundamental change in economic accounting has wide implications.

At present, the industrialized countries import products and resources from developing countries at costs which reflect neither the loss of the resource base in the developing country nor the environmental damage incurred. In recent years, many developing countries have encountered a substantial fall in the price of commodities which they export. The falling prices earned by commodity export has had three primary effects. First, it has severely affected the foreign exchange earnings of the exporting countries. Second, the lower purchase prices in the importing countries have fostered wasteful patterns of consumption of the commodities. Finally, it has encouraged the developing countries to export ever greater quantities of their natural resources in order to earn an equivalent income, often leading to over-exploitation of the resources and damage to the environment. International trade policy can ensure that the price of goods reflects the true value of the natural resources and the costs of necessary environmental protection measures.

AGENDA 21 provides a comprehensive plan of activities to coordinate this economic transition; a plan which applies to economists, entrepreneurs, big businesses, financial institutions, the international trade community, individuals and governments alike. As with virtually all aspects of *AGENDA 21*, there will be a difficult and wrenching period of change incurred in implementing these plans. The support and backing of the international trade community is crucial to enable this transition to take place.

Implementing AGENDA 21

The above six themes form the basis of the core of *AGENDA 21*: the action programs designed to foster the sustainable use of natural resources for human development while ensuring a basic and healthful standard of living for all humanity. An essential ingredient for the success of these programs is the active and full participation of all groups in society. Business and industry, the scientific and technological communities, the educational community, workers and trade unions, farmers, local, state and national administrative and government officials, women, children and indigenous people must all become involved in the process. The diverse backgrounds, skills and experiences of these groups are essential to the global transition to sustainable development. A genuine commitment and broad public participation in all aspects of the decision-making process will be critical to the successful implementation of *AGENDA 21*. The seventh and final theme of *AGENDA 21* revolves around the active participation and responsibility of all people on Earth for implementing the six action sections.

Strengthening the roles of each of these major groups in helping to achieve a sustainable global society will involve deep and fundamental changes in education, public awareness and training. It will require far greater public participation in the decision-making process at all levels. Full accountability by government and industry for its actions is also a high priority. All of the actions of *AGENDA 21* are aimed at placing the issues of environment and sustainable development at the heart of decision-making at all levels. The actions are also directed towards ensuring the maximum possible participation and contribution by all groups of society. Only through a truly universal response to the global environmental and developmental challenges can progress toward the goals of *AGENDA 21* be achieved.

In order to successfully implement the broad *AGENDA 21* program, modern data and information systems must be made available to every nation on Earth. The availability of accurate and timely information to decision-makers and the general public is essential to the planning, implementation and monitoring of the actions. The final portion of *AGENDA 21* details the means and methods of implementation which are relevant to all other portions.

The industrialized countries of the world have far greater access than the developing countries to the information required to make informed decisions about environmental and economic activities. This information gap is growing wider daily. Many developing countries lack sufficient capability to collect, assess and distribute data. To ensure that the necessary plans and actions are based on reliable and pertinent information, a number of measures to strengthen data collection are proposed.

Building the capacity of all countries to implement the necessary changes for the transition to a sustainable world is crucial to the success of *AGENDA 21*. The capacity of developing countries to assimilate knowledge, apply appropriate technologies and build a workable institutional framework must be enhanced. Industrialized countries must strengthen not only their own internal sustainable development programs, but also increase their efforts to provide support to the developing nations of the world. Unprecedented cooperation on all levels of society will be required.

A monumental and sustained commitment will be imperative to build the human and technological capacity to save our planet. World-wide, in all societies, there are deeply-entrenched patterns of behavior which collectively threaten life on Earth. These patterns must be changed. Development strategies since the Industrial Revolution have been based on an extravagant use of energy and resources that can no longer be sustained. Environmentally sound technologies must be developed and made available on a world-wide basis. In the wave of industrial development that has swept over the Earth in the past century, pollution has been seen as an inevitable by-product. This can no longer continue. Effective pollution abatement and recycling technologies must be developed. The Earth's natural systems cannot provide infinite natural resources nor an endless capacity to assimilate waste.

There is a critical global need for environmentally sound technology. Meeting this need will require much greater international scientific cooperation. The transfer of this technology to the developing countries of the world is crucial in order to prevent outmoded and environmentally destructive technologies from being put into place. The Earth, very simply, cannot support a global civilization which consumes and pollutes at the current levels of the industrialized world. The burgeoning populations of the developing countries of Earth are clamoring for a greater standard of living. These desires for an improved life must be met with technology that does not further destroy the environment. The scientific and technological knowledge available in the industrialized countries must be made easily available and on favorable terms. The application of modern and safe technology, however, must be carefully made in keeping with the cultural heritage and traditions of developing countries.

The legal and regulatory framework of the Earth, as it relates to environment and development, must be also restructured and streamlined in order to effectively promote sustainable development. Five guiding principles are identified which should be the basis for changes and progress in this area. The improvements should foster democracy, participation, openness of the decision-making process, cost-effectiveness and accountability. The current and future laws and regulations necessary to implement *AGENDA 21* must be based on all of these basic principles.

A substantial flow of new and additional financial resources to developing countries must be made to achieve global environmentally sound and sustainable development. The current cost estimates of international financing and aid from industrialized countries to implement all of the actions of *AGENDA 21* is an annual average level of $125 billion through the year 2000. This level of funding amounts to only 0.7 percent of the Gross National Product of the industrialized countries on Earth. In addition to this funding, the required national expenditures of the governments and industry in the developing and industrialized countries is estimated at approximately $400 billion annually through the year 2000. Thus, the total estimated expenses for implementing all of the comprehensive and dramatic action programs envisioned by *AGENDA 21* amounts to less than $100 per person per year on a global basis.

International cooperation on all of these final aspects of *AGENDA 21* is an essential requirement for success. Negotiations prior to and during the Earth Summit in Rio regarding financing and technology transfer proved the most difficult of all. Agreement on the broad aspects of *AGENDA 21* was reached with relatively little major dissension. In a world shaken by recession, unemployment and famine, however, allocating the financial resources necessary to implement the full range of actions contemplated in *AGENDA 21* will be, by far, one of the most difficult tasks facing humanity. Individual initiative and boldness will provide much of the needed stimulus to begin the process of preparing the world for a sustainable society, both through innovative business enterprise and courageous political leadership.

The overall thrust of *AGENDA 21* is that the global community must be set on a bold new course—a course which strives for a sustainable future for humanity—a course which fully implements an understanding of the impact of humanity on the natural world.

The world scientific community has seen into the abyss of environmental collapse and has sounded an urgent alarm. The leadership of the world has finally grasped the consequences of the failure to heed the warning to step back from the brink. *AGENDA 21* is the call for an unprecedented global partnership among all nations and all citizens to confront and overcome the problems. It is now up to individual citizens to understand and grasp the crucial nature of the twin global problems of environmental destruction and poverty.

The responsibility for our common future is in our own hands. The prospect of inevitable global environmental disaster or world-wide social upheaval must not be the legacy which we leave our children. Within the lifetime of a child born today, we have the opportunity to create a world in which concern for life is paramount—a world in which suffering is not taken for granted—a world in which nature is revered and not exploited—a world which is just, secure and prosperous—a world in which our children's children are assured of enjoying the bounty of nature and the splendor of life.

This particular point in history offers a unique opportunity for humanity to make the transition to a global community which provides a sustainable living for all. The end of the Cold War, the world-wide thrust for democracy and other recent political events have created an atmosphere of hope that positive and productive change can occur and occur very rapidly. The fundamental changes necessary to make the global transition to a sustainable global society are admittedly difficult, but they are possible. By postponing the difficult choices proposed in *AGENDA 21*, humanity will not manage to avoid such choices. It will only narrow the already limited options available. It will only magnify the extent of action needed to overcome the unavoidable problems which it faces. It will only increase the dangers of passing the irreversible thresholds of ecological and social catastrophe. More so than at any other time in history, the collective decisions that humanity makes in the next few years will irrevocably determine the future of life on Earth.

AGENDA 21 is the blueprint for a future of hope for the human family. Our response to this universal challenge will be our legacy.

Editor's Note

The following chapters of this book have been abridged from the final official text of *AGENDA 21*, as adopted by all 172 nations (including the United States) in attendance at the United Nations Conference on Environment and Development in Rio de Janeiro, Brazil on June 14th, 1992. The entire official text of *AGENDA 21* is contained in United Nations document E.92-38352; A/CONF.151/26 (Volumes I, II and III). The United Nations documents 92-1-100481-0/E.92.I.15 The Global Partnership for Environment and Development: A Guide to *AGENDA 21*; Earth Summit Press Summary of *AGENDA 21* (Final Text) DPI/1298 October 1992; and the final Earth Summit Press Release DPI/1296 July 1992 were also consulted in the preparation of this text. Various draft versions of *AGENDA 21* were also referred to in the editorial process.

Most of the final text of *AGENDA 21* was finalized prior to the Earth Summit in Rio de Janeiro. The basic negotiations and drafting of *AGENDA 21* took place during sessions of the Preparatory Committee for the United Nations Conference on Environment and Development, which met four times between March 1991 and April 1992. Approximately 15 percent of the text of *AGENDA 21* was disputed and agreement on this portion of the text was reached during extensive negotiation sessions at the Earth Summit.

The most politically difficult issues to be resolved were aspects of *AGENDA 21* regarding financing and the transfer of environmentally sound technology to developing nations. Most of the funding for the programs of *AGENDA 21* is expected to come directly from public and private sources within each country. However, new and additional external funding is also considered necessary for many of the programs to succeed. The basis for this external funding is expected to be as grants, aid and loans in the form of official development assistance from industrialized countries to developing countries. After very difficult negotiations, agreement was reached on a target figure for the amount of total official development aid from industrialized countries. This target amount was set at 0.7 percent of the Gross National Product of each industrialized country. Many countries supported achieving this amount of development assistance by the year 2000, including most of the Nordic states, the Netherlands and France. Germany and the United Kingdom agreed in principle to the amount but not the deadline of the year 2000 for reaching that amount of aid. The United States was not involved in these discussions since it had never made a commitment to fund development based on a percentage of its Gross National Product.

All of the financing estimates which are contained in *AGENDA 21* were made by the Secretariat of the United Nations Conference on Environment and Development. These cost estimates are order-of-magnitude estimates and have not been specifically reviewed by each individual government which approved *AGENDA 21*. The actual costs and financial terms for the implementation of *AGENDA 21* programs will depend upon the specific strategies and programs which the individual governments decide upon for the execution of the *AGENDA 21* activities.

Regarding the transfer of technology, it was agreed in principle prior to the Earth Summit that developing countries need to have access to environmentally sound technology which has been developed in the industrialized nations of the world. There was, however, intense disagreement regarding the terms of such technology transfer. Essentially, the disagreement centered on whether such transfer would be on commercial terms—by sale to developing countries—or on concessional and preferential terms—by grant to developing countries. At Rio, it was agreed that governments should promote and finance access to environmentally sound technology on favorable terms "as appropriate" for developing countries, which would include concessions and preferences. However, exact details of such transfers and methods to protect intellectual property rights (patents and copyrights) continue to be explored.

In a number of important areas in *AGENDA 21* the negotiations regarding specific wording of the agreement proved difficult. Several countries pressed for softening certain portions of the language. Although several of these language changes were approved for the final version of *AGENDA 21*, it is important to remember the historical significance of this document. It is a document which encompasses agreements on the direction the world community has chosen to pursue in solving many of the most pressing global problems. It is also essential to bear in mind that *AGENDA 21* was unanimously adopted by every nation in attendance at the Earth Summit.

In several instances, for the sake of clarity, the order of the certain sections of the original text of *AGENDA 21* has been rearranged. Additionally, for the sake of clarity, certain technical phrases and language have been revised. In a few instances, common terms have been substituted for the actual negotiated language of the original official text.

Those individuals and groups that wish to fully understand the specific activities proposed by *AGENDA 21* and desire to comprehend the official negotiated language are urged to consult the text of the official United Nations document, which is available from United Nations Publications, 2 United Nations Plaza, New York NY 10017 USA.

Additionally, all of the participants in the Earth Summit also unanimously adopted two other agreements. The first, The Rio Declaration on Environment and Development, is a set of 27 principles which outline the rights and responsibilities that all nations have in the areas of environment and development. The other document which all nations agreed to at the Earth Summit is a statement of 15 principles regarding the management of global forests. This Statement of Forest Principles, although not legally-binding, is the first global consensus on the protection and development of forests. These documents are available from United Nations Publications.

Two other documents were also part of the negotiations prior to and during the Earth Summit in Rio: a convention on biodiversity and a convention on climate change. These important agreements were signed by only 153 of the nations participating in the Earth Summit. These documents are also available from United Nations Publications. In addition, the entire unedited Preamble to *AGENDA 21* as adopted at the Earth Summit is included immediately following this Editor's Note.

As you read through this abridged version of *AGENDA 21* you will notice that some program areas contain proposals for relatively general activities, while other programs contain more extensive and detailed activities. This reflects the content of the original document and the outcome of the actual negotiations that took place both before and during the Earth Summit.

Finally, as you read through the programs and activities proposed by *AGENDA 21*, it is important to bear in mind that these proposed actions are not simply obscure and dubious proposals. The comprehensive programs and far-ranging actions in *AGENDA 21* have all been approved and accepted by virtually every single nation on Earth. *AGENDA 21* is the universal blueprint for the future of life on Earth.

Preamble to AGENDA 21

Note: This is a final unedited version of the Preamble to Agenda 21, as adopted at the United Nations Conference on the Environment and Development in Rio de Janeiro, Brazil, on June 14, 1992.

1.1.   Humanity stands at a defining moment in history. We are confronted with a perpetuation of disparities between and within nations, a worsening of poverty, hunger, ill health and illiteracy, and the continuing deterioration of the ecosystems on which we depend for our well-being. However, integration of environment and development concerns and greater attention to them will lead to the fulfillment of basic needs, improved living standards for all, better protected and managed ecosystems and a safer, more prosperous future. No nation can achieve this on its own; but together we can—in a global partnership for sustainable development.

1.2.   This global partnership must build on the premises of General Assembly resolution 44/228 of 22 December 1989, which was adopted when the nations of the world called for the United Nations Conference on Environment and Development, and on the acceptance of the need to take a balanced and integrated approach to environment and development questions.

1.3.   Agenda 21 addresses the pressing problems of today and also aims at preparing the world for the challenges of the next century. It reflects a global consensus and political commitment at the highest level on development and environment cooperation. Its successful implementation is first and foremost the responsibility of Governments. National strategies, plans, policies and processes are crucial in achieving this. International cooperation should support and supplement such national efforts. In this context, the United Nations system has a key role to play. Other international, regional and subregional organizations are also called upon to contribute to this effort. The broadest public participation and the active involvement of the nongovernmental organizations and other groups should also be encouraged.

1.4.   The developmental and environmental objectives of Agenda 21 will require a substantial flow of new and additional financial resources to developing countries, in order to cover the incremental costs for the actions they have to undertake to deal with global environmental problems and to accelerate sustainable development. Financial resources are also required for strengthening the capacity of international institutions for the implementation of Agenda 21. An indicative order of magnitude assessment of costs is included in each of the programme areas. This assessment will need to be examined and refined by the relevant implementing agencies and organizations.

1.5.   In the implementation of the relevant programme areas identified in Agenda 21, special attention should be given to the particular circumstances facing the economies in transition. It must also be recognized that these countries are facing unprecedented challenges in transforming their economies, in some cases in the midst of considerable social and political tension.

1.6.   The programme areas that constitute Agenda 21 are described in terms of the basis for action, objectives, activities and means of implementation. Agenda 21 is a dynamic programme. It will be carried out by the various actors according to the different situations, capacities and priorities of countries and in full respect of all the principles contained in the Rio Declaration on Environment and Development. It could evolve over time in the light of changing needs and circumstances. This process marks the beginning of a new global partnership for sustainable development.

Official Notes: Throughout Agenda 21 the term "environmentally sound" means "environmentally safe and sound", in particular when applied to the terms "energy sources", "energy supplies", "energy systems", or "technology/technologies". When the term "Governments" is used, it will be deemed to include the European Economic Community within its areas of competence.

Chapter 2

The Quality of Life on Earth

The central purpose of development is to improve the quality of life on our planet—to enable all of humanity to enjoy long, productive and fulfilling lives. A balanced and healthy environment is equally crucial to allow humanity to achieve a standard of living which provides comfort, security and satisfaction. Currently, the quality of human life on Earth embraces dramatic extremes. A level of bare subsistence living is the day-to-day reality for nearly one-fifth of the world's population. This vast contingent of humankind is plagued by continual hunger and malnutrition. Inadequate shelter from the elements is prevalent. Substandard or nonexistent health care is the norm. Illiteracy and unemployment are rampant. As the world approaches the 21st century, the very basic needs of this enormous portion of humanity are not being adequately met.

Poverty, malnutrition and health ailments currently afflict more than 1 billion people worldwide. Every day, over 800 million people go hungry, many of them children. Some 1.5 billion people do not have access to basic health care and are threatened by a host of diseases, many of them easily avoidable. As the world's population continues to increase, meeting the needs of all the world's inhabitants will become an ever greater challenge. The nations of the world have agreed that alleviating poverty world-wide is a moral imperative and is essential for the sustainable development of our planet to be successful.

At the other end of the spectrum, a minority of humanity enjoys a standard of living that is based on a staggering level of wasteful consumption. Extravagant energy use, throw-away consumer products and lavish use of seemingly abundant resources has become standard practice in the upper levels of human society around the world, particularly in industrialized countries.

This century has seen a massive increase in the world's production and consumption, particularly in these industrialized countries. Although this increase has stimulated economic growth in the short term, the nations of the world now recognize that this globally unsustainable use of the Earth's resources has degraded the environment and generated unmanageable amounts of waste and pollution.

The nations of the world have begun to realize that the Earth's carrying capacity is finite. There is also a broad consensus that the current levels and rates of growth of consumption, production and population are simply not sustainable. If future generations are to live healthy, prosperous and satisfying lives, these patterns must be rapidly brought into balance with the limits of the Earth's resources and its ability to handle waste.

Natural resources and living standards are often the direct casualties of population growth. The impact of population on environment and development issues is profound. The consequences of human population growth must be thoroughly grasped and this understanding must be incorporated into planning, policy and decision-making at every level. Population programs must be developed and instituted to enable the world to stabilize human population levels. Improvements in global living standards and continued progress in development will also contribute towards achieving stable populations.

Making primary health care available to everyone is a key aspect of alleviating poverty. Standards of health care for those now receiving poor or moderate services must be increased. Specialized health care for environmentally related problems must be provided. People must be assisted in achieving access to affordable health care. There should be a focus on encouraging health care facilities that communities can maintain on their own.

Achieving a sustainable standard of living for all people requires a bold new approach—an environmentally responsible global approach to confront these problems. A large variety of techniques can be utilized to accomplish this goal. Greater efficiency in the use of the Earth's limited resources, minimization of waste and fundamental changes in production processes are some methods that can be employed. Encouragement of less wasteful consumption, a drive to ensure universal access to health care and major efforts to reduce population growth are also required to meet this challenge.

In the decade of the 1990's, it is important that the world community make a social transition to a civilization in which the alleviation of poverty is a priority. In order to achieve this in a manner which does no further damage to our fragile environment, sustainable patterns of consumption must be instituted. A world in which poverty is endemic will always be susceptible to ecological and human crises. Global cooperation and a reinforcing international partnership are essential to achieving the fundamental goal of improving human welfare throughout the world.

This section of *AGENDA 21* addresses four key areas relating to the quality of life on Earth: eradicating poverty, changing resource consumption patterns, controlling population growth and raising the levels of human health.

Eradicating Poverty

Of the roughly 4.2 billion people in the developing world, about 25 percent live in conditions of intolerable poverty; lacking adequate food, basic education and even rudimentary health care. In many cases, they are deprived of basic human dignity and their very cultural identity. Even in the industrialized countries, there are as many as 100 million poor people, many of whom are homeless and unemployed. The poor in the industrialized world, generally at least, have access to some social security benefits and limited health care.

Poverty in rural areas around the world forces people to cultivate ever more marginal lands to survive. This results in soil erosion, depletion of shallow water resources and consequently lower crop yields, leading to greater poverty. In their attempts to merely survive on a daily basis, the world's poor often have little choice but to continue to over-exploit their resources. This destruction of the resource base in turn reduces the chances of their children ever escaping from the poverty cycle. Of the estimated 1 billion poor people living in developing regions, some 450 million live in agricultural areas with a low potential for food production. A similar number live in ecologically vulnerable areas which are highly susceptible to soil erosion, land degradation, floods and other ecological disasters. About 100 million poor reside in urban slums in the developing countries.

The poor are often the victims of environmental stresses caused by the actions of the rich. They are forced to live in areas more vulnerable to natural disasters, industrial hazards and air or water pollution. There is a growing migration from rural poverty to urban squalor. This increasing concentration of poverty in cities often leads to the breakdown of urban services and social systems, resulting in increased crime and an ever lower standard of living.

The global effects of poverty contribute to a reduction in the quality of life throughout the planet. The struggle against poverty is the shared responsibility of all nations. Any efforts to protect the Earth's environment must take the poverty of the world into full account. An environmental policy that focuses mainly on the conservation and protection of resources without consideration of livelihoods of those who depend on the resources is unlikely to succeed. Equally, any development policy which focuses mainly on increasing production without concern for the long-term potential of the resources on which such production is based will sooner or later run into problems. An effective and sustainable strategy to tackle the joint problems of poverty and environmental degradation should simultaneously focus on resources, production and people.

Sustainable Livelihoods

The long-term objective of *AGENDA 21* is to enable all people to achieve livelihoods which are sustainable well into the future. This objective provides a central factor that allows policies to simultaneously address the issues of development, sustainable resource management and the eradication of poverty. The activities proposed in *AGENDA 21* to confront the problems of poverty are directed at many levels of society and government. The programs envisioned should contain immediate steps to alleviate extreme poverty as well as long-term strategies for sustainable national development to eliminate mass poverty and reduce inequalities.

Programs and Activities

Governments, at the national and international level, need to provide the means and the commitment to combat poverty in all countries. National governments, with the aid of private organizations and local community groups need to actively establish the following programs and measures to confront the problems of poverty.

- A comprehensive strategy which targets the causes of poverty and focuses on vulnerable groups and fragile, low-potential ecosystems will require considerable funding and manpower resources. It should feature imaginative programs to generate employment opportunities but also provide essential social services such as health, nutrition, education and safe water.

- Programs should cover a wide range and should be geographically and ecologically specific. Effective programs must be aimed at specific vulnerable groups and take into consideration the physical characteristics of the ecosystem concerned.

- The participation of local communities in the planning, formulation and implementation of such programs is essential. Local and community groups must be given more power to adopt programs that are appropriate both geographically and ecologically. Power must be delegated to such groups to allow them to take immediate steps to alleviate poverty in their particular locale.

- Women, children, indigenous people, minority communities, landless households, refugees and migrants often suffer disproportionately from the effects of poverty. There must also be a priority in improving the social and economic conditions of the most vulnerable groups in society.

- In order to effectively alleviate poverty, sustainable development must be achieved at every level of society. Peoples' organizations, women's groups and other private organizations are important sources of innovation and action at the local level. Such local groups have a strong interest and proven ability in promoting sustainable livelihoods.

- Governments must support a community-based approach to sustainability which will provide women with full participation in any decision-making. Such an approach must also respect the cultural integrity and rights of indigenous people and their communities.

- Grass roots mechanisms must be promoted or established to allow for the sharing of experience and knowledge between similar communities.

- Communities must be allowed to participate directly in the management and protection of the local natural resources.

- A network of community-based learning centers for sustainable development must be developed.

- Methods must be put into place which will allow community-based groups to share their experiences and knowledge at national and international levels.

- By the year 2000, poor households world-wide should be provided with an opportunity for paid employment and productive job opportunities as well as access to essential services.

- The scale of job creation must be sufficient to take care of prospective increases in the labor force of the local areas. This will entail improving the collection of information on poverty target groups and areas in order to design specific local employment programs.

- The local programs should work to develop an infrastructure which will promote sustainable livelihoods. Marketing systems, technology use systems and credit systems must also be developed and implemented.

- Facilities for issuing lines of credit to poor people must be established in order to allow them to begin to create their own means of employment. In this area, strict appraisals of the risk for impoverished borrowers will be needed to avoid debt crises.

- High priority must be given to providing basic education and professional training of people to support such systems.

- Full public participation must be encouraged to widen sustainable options for households in resource-poor areas. Research must be conducted to identify traditional methods of production that have been shown to be environmentally sustainable.

- Sustainable methods of agriculture must be improved, with the aim to provide food self-sufficiency and food security for local populations.

35

- The legal frameworks for land ownership and access to land resources must be strengthened or developed. The rights of tenants and women must be given a higher priority. The landless poor must be given increased access to the means of production and natural resources.

- Measures to rehabilitate degraded resources must be encouraged, as well as policies to promote the sustainable use of resources for basic human needs.

- Community-based mechanisms which enable the poor to have access to resources for livelihoods must be enhanced. Regulations and hindrances that discriminate against informal types of livelihoods should be eliminated.

- Effective primary health care and maternal health care systems which are accessible to all must be set up.

- Matters of poverty and sustainable livelihoods must embrace the issue of responsible parenthood. As a matter of urgency, measures to ensure that women and men have the same right to decide freely and responsibly on the number and spacing of their children is imperative. Both women and men must have access to the information, education and means to exercise this right.

- The poor of the world must be provided with access to fresh water and effective sanitation systems.

- A basic level of primary education must be provided to all children throughout the world.

- Each of these aspects in the eradication of poverty will increase the opportunities of the poorest people to develop employment and livelihoods which will be more in balance with the environment on which they depend. There is a critical need for technical and professional assistance in all of these areas.

- In order to provide 1 billion poor with sustainable livelihoods, a cooperative global action program on poverty and sustainable development should be fully implemented within the next 5 years.

- A central focal point in the United Nations system should be established to facilitate the exchange of information. Technical cooperation between developing countries must be promoted.

- Pilot projects which can be duplicated must be developed and tested. In degraded and ecologically vulnerable areas, intensive efforts should be made to rehabilitate resources and alleviate poverty. This should involve development activities of lasting value, such as food-for-work programs to build infrastructure. A special emphasis should be placed on providing employment and income-generating activities for the poor.

- There must be increasing international cooperation in addressing the root causes of poverty. The development process will not gather momentum if the developing countries of the world are weighted down with external indebtedness, if development financing is inadequate, if trade barriers restrict access to markets and if commodity prices and the terms of trade in developing countries remain depressed.

- The international economic framework must be examined carefully to ensure that social and environmental concerns are addressed more fully.

- The policies of international and financial institutions must be reviewed to guarantee that there are adequate provisions made for basic services to the poor and needy of the world. This must be made an international priority.

Many of the general *AGENDA 21* activities in the area of alleviation of poverty are covered in more detail in the individual sections which pertain directly to the particular topic involved. For example, while the alleviation of poverty entails improving the general health of humanity, the details of confronting the issue of human health are contained in the sections relating to health later in this chapter.

The broad objective of this section of *AGENDA 21* is to eradicate world poverty. This ambitious goal must be seen as an important and central issue in any global efforts to protect the Earth's environment. Human desperation in the struggle to survive is placing enormous pressure on the Earth's natural resources. Only by renewing and increasing the global efforts to combat chronic poverty can the natural resources of our planet be truly protected.

Financing

The estimated total annual cost of implementing the activities in this program area are $30 billion, including approximately $15 billion as direct grants from the international community.

Changing Resource Consumption Patterns

While poverty results in certain environmental stresses, one of the most serious problems now facing the planet is the excessive levels of consumption and production in the industrialized countries of the world. Economic growth is essential to meeting basic human needs and achieving acceptable levels of personal well-being. However, the modern industrial economy has led to the unprecedented use of energy and raw materials and the generation of enormous amounts of waste. Industrialized countries consume most of the world's energy and many other resources, far surpassing the consumption levels in developing countries.

Present levels of certain kinds of consumption in industrialized countries are already giving rise to serious environmental problems. The unrestrained use of global energy resources is placing tremendous stress on the Earth. Such levels of consumption cannot be sustainable over the long term. Sustainable thresholds will be passed much more rapidly if similar consumption patterns take hold in the developing countries. The growing economies, incomes and populations in the developing world are currently striving to achieve similar levels of consumption and production. Such aspirations seem destined to push global human activities well beyond sustainable levels.

At the same time, however, consumption remains important as a driving force for development. It is consumption that drives the creation of income and export markets desperately needed to promote worldwide growth and prosperity. It is the consumption of the Earth's natural resources that affords humanity with a basic standard of living.

There is an immediate need for a practical strategy to bring about a fundamental transition from the wasteful consumption patterns of the past to new consumption patterns based on efficiency and concern for the future. In this respect, new understandings and partnerships between industrialized and developing countries are critical.

Since the mid-20th century, world production of energy has increased twenty-fold. World industrial production has increased four-fold. Over the same time, world population has more than doubled from 2.5 billion to 5.5 billion. This rapid growth in production has, for some, resulted in increased resource consumption and higher living standards. However, most of this growth has occurred in the industrialized countries. These industrialized portions of the world, although containing only about one-fifth of the total world population, account for about four-fifths of the consumption of fossil fuel and metal mineral resources. Even with regard to the world's basic food commodities, such as cereals, meat and milk, the industrialized countries consume between 48 and 72 percent. Continuing these consumption levels in the industrialized countries while at the same time adopting them in developing countries would not only be unsustainable, but would gravely threaten the Earth's ecology. The world community must move quickly to assess and curtail wasteful and inefficient consumption patterns, particularly those that risk seriously and irreversibly damaging the common environment.

Changing Consumption Patterns

Altering consumption patterns is one of humanity's greatest challenges in the quest for environmentally sound and sustainable development. Given the depth to which such consumption patterns are rooted in the basic values and lifestyles of industrial societies, this transition will be very difficult to achieve. Such wasteful lifestyles are now, by virtue of global advertising and media, increasingly sought after throughout much of the developing countries of the world. To achieve a transition to a more basic level of consumption will require the combined efforts of governments, individuals and industry. New concepts of growth and prosperity must be developed which rely less on the flow of energy and natural resource materials through the economy. These new concepts of prosperity must take into account the availability and true value of our precious natural resources. Such concepts must allow for higher standards of living through lifestyles that are more in harmony with the Earth's finite resources and carrying capacity.

Programs and Activities

- Industrialized countries must take the lead in promoting sustainable patterns of consumption. The governments and industries of many industrialized countries are already intensifying their efforts to reduce the amount of resources used in the generation of economic growth. By reducing the amount of energy and materials used per unit, productivity can be measurably increased. These countries have recognized that this can both reduce environmental stress and contribute to greater economic and industrial competitiveness. Such positive trends must be encouraged and strengthened.

- Consumer pressure can play a large role in encouraging this basic shift in production values.

- All phases of industrialization must be examined and reoriented to emphasize optimal resource use. Current methods of production must be altered to require far greater efficiency. Some progress has been achieved in making energy and raw material use more efficient through the adoption of environmentally sound technologies and re-cycling. These advances should be continued and expanded.

- The environmentally sound use of renewable resources and energy must be encouraged. Research and development into the use of any environmentally sound technologies must be promoted. The experiences gained by these actions must be passed on to developing countries. The developing countries must be assisted in their efforts to acquire these technologies and to develop other ones suited to their particular circumstances.

- At the same time, society needs to develop effective ways of dealing with the problem of disposing of mounting levels of waste products. Governments, industry and the public need to act to encourage the introduction of more environmentally sound products. Pressure must be applied to reduce the wasteful packaging of products. At both the consumer level and in industrial processes, increased recycling of waste and resources must be encouraged.

- The recent emergence in many countries of a more environmentally-conscious consumer public is a significant development that should be encouraged at all levels.

- In addition, there is an increased interest on the part of some industries in providing environmentally sound consumer products. These trends must be encouraged and promoted.

- Methods should be developed to determine the full environmental impact of products—from the initial extraction of the resource, through the production process and on to its disposal or recycling.

- Results of these assessments should be transformed into clear indicators to inform consumers and decision-makers of the true environmental impact of products. Information on the real environmental costs and consequences of various production processes and services can be critical in influencing consumers and enabling them to make environmentally conscious product choices. These changes in demand will, in turn, also induce industry to adopt more efficient and environmentally sound production processes.

- The expansion of such environmental labeling and other environmentally-related product information should be encouraged. New information programs should be developed to assist consumers in their efforts to make informed choices. The emerging environmentally-conscious consumer must be provided with information on the consequences of consumption choices. Environmentally sound products should be encouraged at all levels. Consumers should be made aware of the health and environmental impact of products through consumer legislation, advertising and labeling programs. Specific consumer-oriented programs such as recycling and deposit/refund systems should also be developed and encouraged.

- Governments themselves also play a role in consumption, particularly in countries where government plays a large role in the economy. Governments can wield considerable influence over both corporate decisions and public perceptions. Purchasing policies of government agencies and departments should be reviewed in an effort to improve the environmental soundness of procurement policies. Government agencies and departments should lead the way in increasing demand for environmentally sound products and services.

- While the need to examine the role of consumption in dealing with environment and development is widely recognized, it is not yet matched by an understanding of the full nature of the issue or how to effectively address it. Governments, economic and environmental organizations, as well as private research and policy institutes, should make concerted efforts to compile basic data on consumption patterns.

- The complex relationship between production, consumption, technological adaptation and innovation, economic growth and development and population dynamics must be carefully analyzed. A priority in such research must be understanding how modern economies can grow and prosper while reducing energy and material use and the production of harmful wastes.

41

- Methods must be identified by which the basic structure of modern industrial societies can be shifted away from economic growth which relies heavily on the use of natural resource materials. Efforts must be made to identify balanced patterns of consumption worldwide which the Earth can support over the long term.

- The costs and consequences of wasteful and environmentally damaging consumption are generally not borne fully by the producers and consumers who cause them. Clear market signals and pricing are a prerequisite to ensuring that producers and consumers understand the environmental costs of production and consumption.

- It is essential to design and implement market policies and sound environmental pricing that explicitly take into account the costs and consequences of consumption and waste generation. These may comprise environmental charges and taxes, deposit/refund systems, emission standards and charges and "polluter pays" principles. Governments should consider the adoption of such measures on a widespread and effective scale.

- Positive attitudes towards sustainable consumption should be promoted through education, public awareness programs and advertising. The positive advertising of products and services that utilize environmentally sound technologies should be bolstered. Industries which use or encourage sustainable production and consumption patterns should be fostered. The significant role of women and households as consumers and the potential impact of their combined purchasing power should be fully taken into account in promoting sustainable consumption.

The duplication throughout the developing world of the present consumption patterns of industrialized countries is simply not a viable option. Such an expansion of wasteful resource use would place a tremendous and unbearable stress on the Earth's environment. At the same time, levels of consumption in developing countries must be increased in order to improve general living standards. This increase must be achieved through improving industrial efficiency as well as through reducing wasteful consumption and the related waste generation. Without the immediate implementation of responsible attitudes and rational measures, both the consumption needs and the living environment for future generations will be severely compromised.

As humanity begins to comprehend the full effects of human activities on the Earth, a deeper understanding of the repercussions of our own consumption patterns must develop. Each person must be encouraged to grasp the consequences of his or her own personal actions which impact on our environment. The simple daily choices made in business, at home and in government have a direct relationship on the global quality of life. If our children are to enjoy a healthy and prosperous world, environmentally sound patterns of resource consumption must be achieved. The current patterns of resource consumption simply cannot continue. The challenge to this generation of humanity is to make the global transition to patterns of production and consumption which are sustainable well into the future.

Financing

The set of activities relating to changing resource consumption patterns is concerned primarily with changes in values. Although it will require the combined efforts of consumers, producers and governments, it is estimated that actual implementation of the activities will not require significant new financial resources.

Controlling Population Growth

The world's population reached 5.5 billion in mid-1992. Of these, 77 percent lived in developing countries and 23 percent in industrialized countries. During the 1960's, the global population was growing at about 2.1 percent annually. Currently, this rate of growth has declined slightly to some 1.7 percent per year. The number of people added to the world's population each year, now amounting to 92 million, is higher then ever before. It is projected that world population will reach some 6.3 billion people in the year 2000 and 8.5 billion in the year 2025.

Over 90 percent of the population increase today occurs in developing countries, having risen from 1.7 billion in 1950 to 4.2 billion in 1991. The population in the developing countries is expected to reach nearly 5 billion people in the year 2000, a mere seven years from now.

Under all possible future scenarios, explosive urban population growth will continue. Rapidly growing cities, unless well-managed, face major environmental problems. By the year 2000, some 2.0 billion people in the developing world will be living in urban areas, with over 40 percent of Africans and Asians (excluding Japan) and 76 percent of Latin Americans urbanized. Of the world's 20 largest cities, 17 will be in the developing regions. At present, over 40 percent of the urban population in the developing world lives in squalor, without access to essential services such as health care or education. Coping with these projected urban populations poses major challenges to sustainable development.

The spiraling growth of world population fuels the growth of global production and consumption. Rapidly increasing demands for natural resources, employment, education and social services make any attempts to protect natural resources and improve living standards very difficult. There is an immediate need to develop strategies aimed at controlling world population growth. There is an urgent demand to increase awareness among decision-makers of the critical role that population plays in environmental protection and development issues.

Education and Population Information

An increased awareness of population issues is required at all levels. The interaction between the rational use of resources, consumption patterns and population must be fully understood.

Programs and Activities

- The exchange of research and population program information must be increased between research institutions, government agencies and local community organizations. The information generated must be distributed to decision-makers at all levels through technical reports, scientific journals, forums and workshops.
- There must be more training of population specialists and demographic professionals.
- Educational materials for all levels of society should be developed, including guides/workbooks for planners and decision-makers.
- Culturally-based advertising and education programs which transmit reproductive health information to both women and men must be developed. Special care must be taken to ensure that the messages are clear and easily-understood by the populations to whom the information is directed.

- Better *population literacy*, a recognition of population/environment issues, should be developed among decision-makers, parliamentarians, journalists, teachers and students, civil and religious authorities and the general public.

- The results of all research into the impact of population growth on the Earth must be disseminated as widely as possible. Public awareness of this issue must be increased through distribution of population-related information in the media.

- Education programs which provide information on population must be given particular attention. Worldwide dissemination of educational material, particularly to women, is crucial in confronting population growth.

Financing

The estimated costs of funding all of the *AGENDA 21* programs which relate to developing and disseminating relevant information regarding population are $10 million annually. It is proposed that all of the funding for these programs come from grants and aid from international sources in the industrialized world.

National Population Policies

Existing plans for sustainable development have generally recognized that population is a vital factor which influences consumption patterns, production, lifestyles and long-term sustainability. Far more attention, however, must be given to the issue of population in general policy formulation and the design of global development plans. All nations of the world have to improve their capacities to assess the implications of their population patterns. The long term consequences of human population growth must be fully grasped by all nations. They must rapidly formulate and implement appropriate programs to cope with the inevitable increase in population numbers. At the same time, measures must be incorporated to bring about the stabilization of human population. The full consequences of population growth must be understood and taken into account at all levels of decision-making.

Programs and Activities

- The recognition of women's rights must accompany the development of any population policies and programs. Awareness must be increased of the fundamental link between improving the status of women and population stabilization.

- For population stabilization efforts to succeed, it is vital to improve women's access to education, provide better primary and reproductive health care, promote women's economic independence and ensure their equal participation in all levels of decision-making.

- Promoting education, literacy and social and economic gains for women is fundamental in controlling population growth.

- Improving women's right's, their access to assets, labor-saving measures and job opportunities are necessary steps in any efforts to influence population trends.

- Population programs must be developed which integrate these issues and allow women to mobilize themselves to improve their social and economic positions.

- The relationships between population growth and environmental degradation must be analyzed more thoroughly. We must have a better understanding of the implications of population levels on natural resource demand.

- Research must also be undertaken to determine each country's population carrying capacity—what are the population limits that a country can adequately sustain? This assessment must take into account the satisfaction of basic human needs, water use, land use and the health and diversity of local ecosystems.

- The full impact of population growth on traditional livelihoods and land use patterns must be understood. Methods must be developed to identify those areas where population growth will place the most pressure on the environment.

- Promoting an understanding of the crucial link between population and sustainable development must be a priority. Population dynamics must be fully incorporated into the research and global analysis of environment and development issues.

- Current computer modelling technology must be expanded to attempt to identify the possible outcomes of human activities. Such computer projections of the future should take into account population growth, per capita resource use, wealth distribution and migration trends.

• Another priority is to formulate comprehensive national policies for population, environment and development. Population issues must be integrated into the national planning and decision-making process.

• Governments should enhance their capacities to deal with integrated population/environment/development issues by strengthening population committees and commissions, population planning units and advisory committees on population. These planning groups must be given the authority to elaborate population policies consistent with national strategies for sustainable development.

• Government policies and programs should combine environment and development issues with population concerns to foster a cohesive view of sustainable development.

• This integrated view of sustainable development must hold as its goal a number of fundamental issues: the alleviation of poverty, secure livelihoods, integrated health care, the reduction of maternal and infant mortality, education and services for the responsible planning of family size, the improvement of the status and income of women, the fulfillment of women's personal aspirations and individual and community participation.

• These policies and programs should be people-centered, aimed at increasing the quality and capacity of people to achieve environmental conservation and economic development in their own local communities.

Financing

The amount of estimated annual costs of implementing all of the programs and activities in the area of formulating comprehensive national population policies is $90 million. All of this amount is proposed to be made available from international sources in the form of grants or direct aid.

Local-Level Programs

Implementing population, environment and development programs at the local level is also a critical priority. Local-level programs require a new framework that examines population dynamics in conjunction with environmental and resource development factors. These programs should work to improve the quality of life, ensure the sustainable use of natural resources, enhance environmental quality and stabilize local populations.

Programs and Activities

- Local population/environment programs should closely correlate action on population with activities on resource management and development. Community-based groups, particularly women's organizations, can assist in providing the information to ensure that the local level efforts are successful.

- The direct involvement of the local groups affected is imperative. Women, the poor and people living in the most vulnerable areas must become intimately involved in the planning and implementation of population programs.

- Demonstration projects should be developed and reports on the results shared with other local groups. Local educational efforts to raise awareness of the issues must be intensified.

- Reproductive health programs must be developed and enhanced worldwide. They must have the resources and capacity to reduce maternal and infant mortality. Such programs must also provide the information and resources to enable men and women to fulfill their personal aspirations in terms of family size.

- Governments worldwide should take active steps to ensure that women and men have the same right to decide freely on the number and spacing of their children.

- Governments must also act to ensure that both women and men have access to the information, education and means to enable them to effectively exercise this right.

- Governments should take active steps to implement programs to develop health facilities which include women-centered, women-managed, safe and effective reproductive health care. These facilities should focus on providing comprehensive family health care; including pre-natal care, information on responsible parenthood and measures aimed at allowing all women to breast-feed fully for the first four months after birth. These programs should fully support both women's productive and reproductive roles and well-being.

• Special attention must be paid to the need for providing equal and improved health care for all children and the need to reduce the risks of maternal and child mortality and sickness.

There must be a global as well as local understanding of the dire consequences of unrestrained human population growth. The nations of the earth must strive for a worldwide effort to reduce the effects of human population on our finite natural resources. There must be a universal recognition of the crucial impact of population on the success of any programs which are necessary to build a sustainable global society.

Financing

The estimated total cost to implement all of the local-level activities in the population-related program areas of *AGENDA 21* is approximately $7 billion per year for the years 1993 through 2000. $3.5 billion of this annual total is expected to be provided as grants from the international community.

Raising the Level of Human Health

Human health, development and the environment are intimately related. Meeting the primary health needs of the world's population is integral to achieving the goals of sustainable development and protection of the environment.

Lack of development is often linked to poor levels of general hygiene and sanitation and inadequate management of the environment. This lack of hygiene and sanitation is directly related to the occurrences in the developing world of many parasitic diseases, such as malaria, schistosomiasis, onchocerciasis (*river blindness*) and other diseases. Due to inaction, African trypanosomiasis (*sleeping sickness*) continues to take a heavy toll. Efforts to reduce communicable diseases in these countries may have no effect, or even backfire, if development efforts aggravate the local environmental problems. Deforestation, the alteration of hydrological systems, soil erosion, desertification and the ensuing changes in population movements and habitats—all can have a significant influence on the health of the local population. The spread of these diseases is determined by the social, cultural and economic activities of the people and the ecosystems they inhabit. The public health importance of each disease varies from one developing country to another and lack of development will have different impacts on the progression, spread and control of these diseases.

The poor health and disease situation in developing countries, most of which are situated in tropical environments, is to a large extent the result of poverty. This poverty leads to the lack of basic health services, crowded and poorly serviced housing, low levels of literacy and rapidly increasing populations. Poverty remains the most significant predictor of urban and rural disease and death. The strong association between poverty and poor health is evident in the widespread incidence of communicable and non-communicable diseases among the poor, especially in the developing countries.

Health ultimately depends on the ability to successfully manage our physical, biological, economic and social environment. The condition of local provisions and facilities for health care both helps determine and is dependent on the overall social and economic conditions of the community. It is also dependent on a healthy environment, including the provision of clean water, sanitation, adequate food supplies and proper nutrition. These criteria require the building of a health care infrastructure which is coordinated with an overall concern for environmental care and is supported by a general increase in the economic well-being of the local population.

Primary Health Care Needs

Although sound development is impossible without a healthy population, most developmental activities to some degree harm the environment and so indirectly cause or intensify many health problems. Conversely, underdevelopment is both the cause and effect of inadequate health in developing countries. Meeting basic health needs thus goes hand in hand with the alleviation of poverty and the development of human potential. Health care must be seen as a contribution to such efforts. The fundamental objective for governments should be to meet the basic health needs of all of the world's people by the year 2000. As a matter of priority, health service coverage should be achieved for those population groups that are in greatest need.

Programs and Activities

- Particular attention must be directed towards eliminating contamination of food supplies, providing safe water supplies, developing adequate sanitation systems and enhancing the nutritional content of diets.

- Health education, immunization programs and access to essential medicine is also a high priority in achieving universal access to health care.

- Providing information and resources regarding responsible family planning is crucial to elevating the levels of human health.

- In order to meet basic health needs, health care technologies which are practical, scientifically sound, socially acceptable and geared towards the needs of individual countries should be delivered.

- Coordination among the public health, environmental protection and development planning agencies should be strengthened at local and national levels.

- Health facilities, aided by mechanisms for local community involvement, should be established and monitored. Their medical and social services staff must be trained for basic health care delivery. Traditional knowledge of preventive and curative health practices can often support modern health care services for local communities.

- The self-management of health care facilities by local communities should be encouraged. The emphasis in developing health care should be on community-based systems.

- Preventive health care information must be distributed on a much wider basis. Health education in schools should be increased and should be provided by community-based health-care workers.

- Local social services that support health care must also be increased.

- Community-based rehabilitation services for the rural handicapped should be enhanced.

- Short but practical and intensive training programs must be initiated to develop localized management of health care delivery. The training of personnel to develop the managerial skills necessary to provide efficient organization of health care systems is also required.

- Research regarding health care delivery must be increased with a goal of finding affordable methods of increasing health care coverage and services for women, children and other vulnerable groups.
- New and innovative approaches to planning and managing health care delivery should be tested.
- There is a critical need for the development of affordable health care technology that can be easily used, maintained and repaired in rural community-based settings.
- Programs to share health care information and transfer health care technology to developing countries must be developed and supported.

Financing

The costs of funding all of the *AGENDA 21* programs relating to global primary health care needs is estimated to be approximately $40 billion annually, including $5 billion from international grants or aid from the industrialized world to the developing world.

Communicable Diseases

Advances in vaccines and medicines have brought many communicable diseases under control. However, there remain many important communicable diseases that are rampant throughout the developing world. Many of these diseases are directly related to environmental causes, particularly water safety and sanitation. Such diseases include malaria, cholera, diarrheal diseases, leishmaniasis and schistosomiasis. Health and hygiene education to control these diseases is critical. To conquer these killers, environmental measures to provide safe water and sanitation are a crucial element for success and are integral to the issue of health care.

Programs and Activities

- National plans and monitoring mechanisms should be established for the control of communicable diseases, including malaria, diarrheal diseases, hepatitis, sleeping sickness, soil-transmitted helminths, schistosomiasis and acute respiratory diseases.

- Specific targets to be achieved by the year 2000 include the eradication of polio and Guinea worm disease and the effective control of onchocerciasis and leprosy.
- By 1995, the goal is to reduce measles deaths by 95 percent.
- The objective is to reduce childhood diarrheal deaths by 50-70 percent in developing countries by the year 2000 and reduce parasitic infections by 25-40 percent in the same period.
- A global monitoring system for endemic diseases, in particular those with a potential for international spread, should be established by the year 2000.
- With HIV-infection levels estimated to increase to 30-40 million people by the year 2000, the social and economic impact of the AIDS pandemic is expected to be devastating for all countries. Women and children are increasingly becoming infected with HIV. While the direct health care costs to care for the infected patients will be enormous, they will be dwarfed by the indirect costs of this pandemic. These indirect costs include the loss of income to impoverished groups and significant decreases in the productivity of humanity. This worldwide pandemic will inhibit growth in service and manufacturing industries and considerably increase the costs of human education and training. Because farming is very labor-intensive in the developing world, the agricultural segment of human production will be particularly affected—with potentially dramatic effects on food production.
- Coordinated national and international efforts against AIDS are essential to prevent and reduce the social impacts of HIV infection.
- National and regional institutions should promote broad approaches to prevent and control all communicable diseases. These measures should include applying new vaccines and chemotherapeutic agents and providing professional training in immunology, molecular biology, epidemiology and community prevention and control.
- Developing information for public awareness and education regarding the risks and prevention of communicable disease is extremely important.
- Disease-specific health education materials which are easily understood must be developed and disseminated.
- Preventative and early treatment programs must be put into action.

- Research must continue into the social and cultural factors which inhibit control of these diseases.

Financing

The estimated annual funding necessary to implement all of the *AGENDA 21* programs relating to communicable diseases is approximately $4 billion for the years from 1993-2000. This total is expected to include about $900 million in annual grants or aid from the international community.

The Health of Women, Children and Indigenous People

Specific health measures must be initiated to protect the most vulnerable groups in human society, particularly infants, youth, women, elderly, disabled and indigenous people. Approximately one third of the world's population are children under 15 years old. At least 15 million of these children die each year from preventable diseases—15 million each year and this tragic number is increasing. Deaths from birth trauma, birth asphyxia, acute respiratory infections, malnutrition, communicable diseases and diarrhea can be averted. The health of children is affected more severely than other population groups by malnutrition and environmental factors. Many children also face health problems due to exploitation as cheap labor or in prostitution.

Currently more than half of all people alive are under 25 years old and 4 out of every 5 of these youth live in developing countries. Youth are particularly vulnerable to problems associated with economic development, which often weakens traditional forms of social and family support. Rapid urbanization has increased substance abuse, unwanted pregnancy and sexually-transmitted diseases, including AIDS.

Despite health gains in the industrialized world, in developing countries the health status of women remains relatively low. During the 1980's, poverty, malnutrition and disease levels in women were actually rising. The majority of women in developing countries do not have adequate health care, sufficient educational opportunities, the rights to control their reproductive lives or the means to improve their social or economic status. Pre-natal health care is a particularly pressing need.

Indigenous people make up a significant portion of the global population. In many countries, the number of indigenous people is growing faster than the general population. Indigenous people tend to fare worse than other populations in terms of health care, employment and adequate food and housing. Their customary reliance on their local habitat is under increasing pressure. Fundamental changes in traditional lifestyles can have dramatic and often disastrous effects on their cultures. Better health care is crucial to the safety and existence of indigenous people.

The elderly and disabled in all societies merit increasing attention. Their needs are often overlooked in efforts to raise the health care standards of the general population.

The objective in protecting all vulnerable groups is to ensure that all individuals worldwide are allowed to develop to their full potential.

Programs and Activities

Active measures must be undertaken to protect and nurture those portions of the world population who are more susceptible to the pressures of modern society.

- Such measures should include: strengthening immunization and nutrition programs for women and children; treating and preventing communicable and diarrheal diseases; and providing social services for the education, counselling and treatment of specific health problems, including drug abuse.

- Other initiatives should include incorporating health issues into national action programs for women, and development and utilization of women's groups at the community and national level in all aspects of health care.

- Specific measures aimed at reducing the vulnerability of women and children to HIV infection must be implemented.

- The development of human resources to protect the health of children, youth, women and indigenous people should include strengthening the role of educational institutions in promoting health education and increasing the use of mass media in disseminating information to target groups.

- Concrete incentive programs must be developed which encourage attendance of women of all ages in school and health education classes.

- Adult education and training in child, home and maternal health care is vital. The training of more community health workers, nurses, midwives, physicians, social scientists and educators will also be required to extend the current level of services.

- Women's groups must be involved in decision-making at all levels to identify specific health risks and issues which impact primarily on women and children.

Financing

Funding to implement all of the programs and activities proposed in this section of *AGENDA 21* is estimated to be approximately $3.7 billion annually, including about $400 million from the international community in the form of grants or aid.

Urban Health Problems

For hundreds of millions of people, the poor living conditions in urban areas are destroying lives, health and social and moral values. Urban growth has outstripped society's capacity to meet basic human needs in the world's cities—leaving millions with inadequate incomes, diets, housing and services. Overcrowding and inadequate shelter contribute to respiratory diseases, tuberculosis, meningitis and a host of other diseases.

Rapid urban growth exposes millions to serious environmental health hazards and has surpassed the ability of governments to provide necessary health care services. All too often, urban development is associated with destruction of the local environment and natural resource base. In urban environments, many of the factors that affect health are outside the domain of traditional health care.

The health and well-being of all urban dwellers must be improved so that they can contribute meaningfully to the social and economic development of the Earth. The global objective is to improve overall health by 10-40 percent by the year 2000. The measurements for overall health include the percentage of low birth weight newborns, tuberculosis (indicative of crowded housing), diarrheal diseases (indicative of poor water and sanitation) and the social problems of drug abuse and violent crime.

Programs and Activities

- Local authorities and community-based groups must be encouraged to actively participate in developing urban health plans.

- Urban religious, medical, business and social institutions must become directly involved with the prevention and control of urban health problems.

- An emphasis must be placed on education and training of community-based workers to provide local health care services. The development of personal health care skills is also crucial.

- Basic training of health care personnel is also necessary to confront the mounting problems of urban health.

The plight of urban areas, including health care problems, is more fully discussed in Chapter 4: The Management of Human Settlements.

Financing

The estimated annual total costs of implementing all of the programs in the area of urban health are approximately $222 million. $22 million of this total is estimated to be required from grants and aid from international sources.

Environmental Health Problems

In many locations around the world, the air, water and land which surrounds workplaces and individual dwellings is so badly polluted that the health of hundreds of millions of people is in serious jeopardy. This is, in most cases, due to past and present development, production and consumption patterns that have little or no regard for environmental protection. There have been notable improvements in some countries, but globally the deterioration of the Earth's environment continues at an accelerating rate. Significant environmental health hazards are developing in the newly industrialized countries of the world. The ability of many countries around the world to tackle environmental health problems is greatly hampered by lack of financial and technical resources. Pollution control and health protection measures most often do not keep pace with economic development.

The overall objective of this section is to minimize environmental hazards to a degree that human health and safety is not endangered, yet encourage safe methods of development to continue.

Programs and Activities

- Specifically, by the year 2000, environmental standards and safeguards should be established in all countries of the world.

- Environmental protection, surveillance and abatement programs should be adopted in every country on Earth by 2000.

- Health education campaigns to inform people in developing countries of the environmental health risks in local areas must be established. Such programs should also concentrate on providing information on how to reduce the health risk of domestic use of wood and coal for cooking and heat.

- National action on this front should include development of pollution control technology and the introduction of environmentally sound production processes.

- Environmentally safe mass transit will be critical in reducing urban environmental pollution.

- Pesticide use must be controlled in order to minimize health risks.

- Solid waste disposal systems must be implemented. Noise pollution must be abated.

- The effects of ultraviolet radiation on the ozone layer must urgently be addressed.

- Fossil fuel energy use must be made more efficient and cleaner.

- Safe production, transportation and uses of chemicals must be made a priority.

- Clean and environmentally sound technology must be developed in all industries and transferred to the developing world.

Each of these areas related to environmental health matters will be further discussed in the specific *AGENDA 21* action programs which encompass the particular topics.

Financing

The cost of implementing all of the activities related to dealing with environmental health problems is estimated at approximately $3 billion per year, with $115 million required from international sources.

* * *

Concern for the global environment must necessarily encompass compassion for all of the human inhabitants of our planet. Attempts to protect the Earth's environment which do not address the human element of life on our planet will be doomed to failure. It is an equilibrium in the balance of nature that must be sought—an equilibrium which must embrace all of the natural world, including humanity. To successfully confront the challenges of environmental destruction, the root causes of poverty, poor health, overconsumption and population growth must be addressed. These massive fundamental problems seem intractable. Progress towards forging a sustainable and environmentally sound world civilization demands that these difficult challenges be faced.

Chapter 3

Efficient Use of the Earth's Natural Resources

Human activities on Earth have increased dramatically in the last half of the 20th century. Fed by explosive population growth and fueled by low-cost energy, industrial and agricultural development has accelerated at a rate unforeseen in the past. This rapid spurt of human influence on the planet has begun to place increasing pressure on the delicate ecosystems of the Earth—the intricate web of life upon which all living things must rely. Environmental changes normally occur over long periods of geological time under the influence of natural forces. However, the intensifying level of human activities has placed an additional burden on these natural forces, considerably stressing the environment and threatening the Earth's fertility. Growing demands on land resources have led to soil erosion, salinization and waterlogging, desertification, deforestation and the disruption of many precious and economically vital ecosystems. The pollution and overuse of the world's finite freshwater resources threaten us all.

This section of *AGENDA 21* encompasses the very broad topic of the use and protection of the Earth's natural resources; specifically land-use, fresh water, energy, agriculture, forests, deserts, mountains, biological diversity and the use of biotechnology. Objectives and actions in each of these 9 areas are introduced and discussed.

An integrated approach to land use must be adopted by all nations—an approach which recognizes the importance of conserving resources and protecting the natural environment. This type of land-use program should be used at all stages of decision-making, from the initial setting of goals to the actual implementation of action. Legislation, regulations and economic incentives should be used to encourage the rational use of land. Research is also important to determine the capacity of land and the interaction among various land uses and environmental processes.

Overdependence on non-renewable fossil fuels as our primary source of energy has contributed to air pollution, acid rain, greenhouse warming, marine pollution and other adverse global impacts. The level of the pollutants in the environment stemming from the use of fossil fuels poses a threat to human health and is damaging the forests, lakes, rivers and fragile ecosystems of the Earth. Despite these problems, fossil fuels will remain the dominant energy source for the foreseeable future. However, significant improvements can be made in the efficiency of fossil fuel use while making a long-term transition to environmentally safe and sound energy systems.

Fresh water is a finite resource and, in many parts of the world, is becoming increasingly scarce. Deforestation, urbanization and poor farming and mining practices are causing increasing sedimentation in water reservoirs. Over-pumping of ground water is threatening the natural balance in many aquifer systems. Excessive use of agricultural chemicals, acid rain from industrial pollution and the dumping of untreated sewage and factory wastes—all contribute to the deteriorating quality of water resources. An estimated 80 percent of all diseases in developing countries and one-third of the deaths are related to contaminated water.

World food production must more than double over the next four decades to meet the needs of a growing population. Since more than 80 percent of the global population will be living in the developing world, most of the new production will need to occur there. The challenge is to apply the most efficient possible food production methods to high potential lands while withdrawing destructive agriculture practices from marginal areas.

Forest resources are essential to both development and the preservation of the global environment. Mismanagement of forests is linked to degradation of soil and water, loss of wildlife and biological diversity, pollution and global warming. Each year some 17 million hectares of tropical forests are lost as a result of agricultural and industrial expansion, overgrazing, excessive or poorly managed tree-cutting for lumber or fuel and other similar human pressures. Meanwhile, air pollution and fires are depleting the wooded lands of many developed countries. A comprehensive approach to forest conservation and sustainable forest development must be developed which addresses all of the related issues. Population pressures, unsustainable agricultural and industrial practices, land ownership, employment opportunities and external debt are all relevant to coping with the problems which confront the world's forests.

The desert areas of the Earth are increasing, often as a direct result of human activity. Desertification affects one-fourth of the Earth's land areas and one-sixth of its people. To combat desertification, improved land and water use and reforestation are critical. Increased research and the provision of alternative livelihoods for subsistence farmers and herders are also needed. More emphasis on preparing for drought emergencies is also essential.

Population growth and the rapid development of high altitude areas are placing unprecedented stress on the mountainous regions of the Earth. The rapid deterioration of mountain ecosystems threatens the planet's biological diversity and the well-being of many people. Proposals focus on halting erosion and replanting damaged areas, preparing natural disaster plans and offering alternative employment to people whose livelihoods are linked to harmful environmental practices.

Sustaining the diversity of biological species—plant, animal and insect life—is a key element in the sustainable development of the planet. Today, however, short-term economic development rarely takes into account the conservation of biodiversity and usually works against it. At present, national and international policies do not encourage sharing the benefits of biodiversity. Current market and accounting practices also often equate economic gain with resource depletion. Commitments to conserve biodiversity must be included in national development strategies. Policies on financing, technology transfer, debt, trade and environmental accounting must begin to take into account the value of maintaining the Earth's biodiversity.

Conserving the world's natural resources and biodiversity and protecting the overall biosphere, while at the same time substantially increasing their productive yield, is one of civilization's greatest challenges. Halting and then reversing the current environmental degradation will require the mobilization of both progressive and valuable traditional technologies. It demands alternative and innovative approaches in the energy, agricultural and forestry industries. Increased awareness of the need for pioneering technology and specific training in the responsible use of such equipment are necessary. There must also be concerted efforts to ensure that resource conservation does not threaten those dependent on these resources for their livelihoods.

In all of these areas the world community must forge a global partnership to halt the current devastation of the Earth's natural resources. This partnership must move quickly and decisively to adopt means to reverse the destruction wherever feasible and institute efficient and sustainable resource use practices. The critical need is to adopt a precautionary approach to sustainable resource use. There must be aggressive long-term defensive strategies to protect the Earth's natural resources while ensuring their careful use. Only through a true global effort to protect our shared resources can a better quality of life for both present and future generations be assured.

Land Use Planning and Management

Land is a physical entity as well as a system of natural resources. Land resources include the soils, minerals, water, plants and animals in all their biological and genetic diversity. All of these various elements interact to provide essential actions that maintain the productive capacity of the environment, such as the recycling of wastes and materials, formation of soils, moderation of the water cycle and pollination of plants. These interactions form an important component of global cycles and processes and are closely linked to climate and other atmospheric phenomena. Land must be regarded primarily as a set of essential terrestrial ecosystems and only secondly as a source of resources.

This complex system provides much of the basic capital and resources on which development is built. It satisfies primary human requirements for food, fiber and fuel; supplies many basic materials for industry and manufacturing; and provides space for human habitation and activities.

Land also meets the needs of all other terrestrial species, be they wild or managed. Land resources are of vital importance to all human activities—from agriculture, forestry, water management and energy production to industry and construction, human settlements, communications infrastructure and waste disposal.

This finite resource cannot easily provide for rapidly increasing numbers of people and for a growing intensity of human activities. Intense conflicts over land use are on the rise: among different social and economic interests, between humans and the environment and between immediate and long-term needs. Current management practices tend to approach these needs in isolation from each other, with the result that important links and impacts are ignored. Pressures on certain land resources are leading to their deterioration and, eventually, permanent degradation. In the past, traditional social systems tended to take account of the land's complexity and diversity and evolved effective land management practices that conserved the resource base. However, these traditional systems have not been able to cope with the sheer scale of modern activities. If development is to be sustainable, these conflicts over the use of land and its resources must be resolved. More effective practices must be developed to promote the ecologically and economically efficient allocation of land resources. There must be new systems developed which have as their goal both the effective management of land resources and their socially-equitable use.

An integrated and coherent approach to the planning and management of land resources is essential. Such a system must be able to deal with the broad issues but leave sufficient flexibility for decentralized resource management. It must be able to handle diversity and change. The goal of such land management must be to satisfy the need for economic development and equity while protecting the environmental and resource base that makes sustainable development possible. Land resources are used in a variety of ways which interact and may compete with each other. An integrated approach to land use will allow planners to understand all of the purposes of land use.

Such an approach should take place on two levels. First, the environmental, economic and social factors of proposed land use should be taken into account. This will allow the impacts of the various uses on humans to be appreciated. How the land use affects humanity would be the focus of the first step of this approach. Second, the impact of human uses on the environment and natural resources should be examined in a comprehensive manner. The consequence of human use of the land resources on the air, water, soil, plants and animals should be looked at in an all-encompassing manner. How humanity affects the land would be the focus of the second step in this process.

An integrated approach to land use will provide a broader perspective from which to make informed choices regarding the safest and most efficient use of land resources. This will enable humanity to obtain the maximum sustainable use of the resources, while providing for the long-term protection of those resources. Many of the techniques, frameworks and processes of such an integrated approach are already in place. They must expanded, strengthened and used much more often at the crucial initial stages of land use planning and development. This section of *AGENDA 21* is concerned primarily with the actual framework for land use planning. The actual decisions regarding resource use and development are dealt with in the other relevant areas of this text.

Programs and Activities

Governments and local, national and international groups should give immediate priority to promoting the most efficient use of land and land resources. To that end, the following activities are proposed:

- Mechanisms must be created or enhanced which allow for the active involvement by all parties concerned in decision-making regarding land use, particularly communities and people at the local level.

- Whenever possible, policy-making should be delegated to the most localized level of public authority. Among other issues, the rights of women, the rights of indigenous people and private property rights should be taken into account.

- Goals should be set and policies formulated to address the environmental, social and economic factors involved in finding the best possible land and resource use. Out of this, policies should be enacted to encourage both the efficient use, protection and management of land resources and an improved distribution of population and activities according to the productivity of the land resource base.

- Economic mechanisms and incentives should be used to encourage the best possible land resource use.

- Regulatory and legal frameworks should be reviewed to identify improvements that are needed to support a land use system which encourages productive and environmentally sound management of the land. Current laws and regulations do not always allow a broad, comprehensive view of land management to be applied.

- The general framework for land use planning should be based on complete units, such as an entire ecosystem or watershed. Within such broad units, more specialized plans can be developed.

- Better and more efficient land use plans can be developed with an understanding of how the entire ecosystem may be affected by those plans. Actual management systems for land and resource use must be strengthened.

- Traditional methods of efficient land and resource use should be encouraged, such as terraced agriculture, pastoralism and Hema reserves (traditional Islamic land reserves).

- Improved planning and management systems require more appropriate tools for data collection and interpretation. Detailed land inventories must be undertaken to determine the actual capacities of local land areas.

- More accurate assessments and accounting of values, costs, benefits, risks and impacts of land use must be made.

- Low-cost, community managed systems for the collection of information must be developed and implemented. Such systems can provide vital information on the status and changes in land resources, including soils, forest cover, wildlife, climate and other elements.

- Far more research is needed regarding land resource use potential and the interactions between the various factors affecting land use. Pilot projects based on an integrated approach to land use must be developed and tested. The results of these projects must be distributed to local and community land use planning groups in order to enable them to make decisions based on the latest available information.

- The curriculum of technical, vocational and university training programs should be reviewed and redirected to emphasize interdisciplinary approaches to land use problems.

- Community and extension service training programs must be assisted in efforts to promote efficient land management techniques which have been successful elsewhere.

- The technologies and techniques that have been used successfully in developing sustainable uses of resources must be transferred to those areas where they are needed. Technicians and support workers must be trained to implement these techniques, with a focus on local participation.

- The need for an integrated approach to land use planning must be conveyed to both the public and decision-makers at all levels.

- Public awareness campaigns should be launched in order to educate people on the vital importance of resource management and inform them of the important roles that they can perform in such planning.

- The active participation of the public is essential for such land use planning to be effective. This participation must be strongly encouraged, particularly among groups that have often been excluded, such as women, youth, indigenous people and local-level individuals.

- All individuals who are involved with the planning and management of land resources must begin to adopt a comprehensive approach to land use. Both the environmental and economic consequences of land resource use must be taken into account at all steps in the decision-making process. In agriculture, energy production, manufacturing and other resource-based industries, a concern for the broad impact of resource use must become an integral part of the decision-making process. Leaders in the business community must begin to understand and appreciate the long-term consequences of their corporate decisions and actions. Governments must act forcefully to encourage such an approach in both industry and in governmental affairs at all levels—from the local to the international.

Financing

The annual cost estimates for the implementation of this portion of *AGENDA 21* is approximately $50 million from the international community in the form of grants.

Fresh Water Resources

Fresh water is a finite resource, indispensable for the sustenance of life on Earth and of vital importance to all human economic activity. Human development is not possible without the direct utilization of water. The use of fresh water resources for agriculture, industry, urban development, hydropower, inland fisheries, transportation, recreation and many other activities is essential. The control of deforestation and desertification rely on adequate sources of fresh water.

Fresh water is also of paramount importance for the proper functioning of the Earth's environment. Fresh water wetlands across the world are vital for the health and existence of many plant and animal species. The indispensable biodiversity of plant and animal life on Earth depends, in large part, on a clean and adequate source of fresh water.

Urbanization, industrial production and agricultural activities have reached the stage where the availability of fresh water is often the limiting factor. Poor land-use planning, including wide-scale deforestation and non-sustainable agriculture are also leading to increases in erosion and soil loss. The subsequent loss of soil nutrients leads to increased fertilizer use in an effort to sustain crop production levels. Such excess fertilizer use decreases coastal fishery yields and leads to the acidification of surface water. Rain with high acid levels due to air pollution also adds to increasing acid levels in surface and ground water. This leads to the death and depletion of fresh water animal and plant life, contributing to the loss of biodiversity. These forces, in turn, serve to degrade the quality and quantity of fresh water available for human use as well.

The construction of dams for both hydropower and irrigation, channelization of rivers and the over-extraction of water from aquifers also is placing a severe strain on the fresh water resources of our planet. The widespread use of bodies of water as open sewers for the discharge of both domestic and industrial waste contributes to the degradation of our precious water resources. These aspects of human development are leading to the salinization of rivers, lakes and soils around the world—with an accompanying loss of soil fertility and food production. Salt intrusion in coastal fresh water aquifers is causing the rapid loss of water supplies in some areas. Virtually everywhere in the world, serious water pollution is an urgent problem.

Fresh water, however indispensable, is also a carrier of disease and often poses a major health problem in many developing countries. An estimated 80 percent of all diseases and over one-third of deaths in developing countries are caused by disease-contaminated water. Diseases caused by microbiological pollution of water supplies, transmitted by water or related to inadequate sanitation and the absence of clean water, are widespread. This problem is intensified by the rise in water consumption due to economic growth and population increase. This results in greater volumes of sewage requiring treatment and disposal. In addition, the introduction of water-intensive industries and agricultural techniques is placing severe stress on water supplies in many locales.

Should climate changes occur as a result of global warming trends, it would affect low-lying fresh water resources and might affect the world's fresh water resources through the melting of the polar ice masses. This could threaten coastal fresh water supplies through sea level rises. Changes may also occur in the precipitation patterns of the world, leading to possible decreases of rain in many areas of the northern hemisphere, with accompanying decreases in soil moisture and river run-off. These possibilities could be disastrous for world food production. Even without global warming, natural variations in precipitation can be expected, with potentially devastating effects on local environments. In many areas of the world, floods and droughts have become more extreme and dramatic in recent years.

The global objective is to ensure and maintain adequate supplies of good quality water for the entire population of this planet. The vital ecological functions of fresh water must also be preserved and protected. Human activities must be adapted to the capacity limits of nature. This section of *AGENDA 21* examines four aspects of fresh water use: the management of water resources, water quality and sanitation, agricultural water use and the effects of climate change on water resources.

Water Management and Assessment

The extent to which water contributes to economic productivity and social well-being is not usually appreciated. All human social and economic activities rely heavily on the supply and quality of fresh water. As human populations and activities grow, many countries are rapidly reaching conditions of water scarcity. 70-80 percent of water demand worldwide is for agricultural irrigation, less than 20 percent is for industrial use and a mere 6 percent is for domestic consumption. In many regions, there is a widespread scarcity of fresh water resources. The progressive encroachment of human activities and the gradual pollution and destruction of finite water supplies requires that comprehensive water use plans be developed.

Sound water management should view water as an integral part of the ecosystem, a natural resource and a social and economic good. In order to satisfy water needs for human development, the availability and quality of water resources must be protected. Due consideration must also be afforded to the vital need for fresh water in the functioning of all aquatic ecosystems. To meet these needs, a comprehensive approach to water resources assessment and management is required.

Programs and Activities

- Technological, social, economic, environmental and human health considerations must be integrated into a dynamic approach to water resources management. The planning for the rational use and protection of water sources should stem from local community needs and priorities.

- The full participation of the public, especially water-user groups and indigenous people, must be encouraged. Water should be managed at the lowest appropriate level, involving district water committees and river basin authorities.

- This approach must include the identification and protection of potential sources of fresh water supply.

- There is an urgent need for the technology and training of personnel to assess the water resources of each country on Earth.

- Research world-wide must be enhanced to help decision-makers understand the long-term implications of loss of vegetation, land restoration, water consumption and other water-related issues.

- At the global level, all nations should aim for the protection of water quality and aquatic ecosystems. Countries should participate in international water quality monitoring and management programs.

- Control programs should also be pursued to reduce the prevalence of water-associated diseases. Water quality management programs require a certain minimum infrastructure and staff in order to implement technical solutions, enforce regulations and maintain the facilities.

- The effective protection of water resources and ecosystems from pollution requires the considerable upgrading of most countries' present capacities.
- Newer technology is also required for developing countries to meet the increasing need for water management. This technology must be made available and usable by technicians in the developing countries of the world.
- Rational water use schemes must also be supported by water conservation and waste minimization measures.
- The use of water tariffs and other economic incentives must also be developed and promoted.
- The various options for charging for water use must be explored, with a view to encourage more efficient and environmentally sound use of water resources.
- A prerequisite to the sustainable management of a scarce natural resource must be the acknowledgement of its true value. Planning considerations must incorporate the actual economic and environmental costs of water use.
- New and alternative sources of fresh water must be researched, including sea water desalinization, reuse of municipal sewage in agriculture, industrial water recycling and artificial groundwater recharging.
- The development of water-saving devices should be encouraged and promoted.
- More efficient methods of crop irrigation must be developed, tested and implemented.
- Innovative and applied research is essential to develop the technical means to conserve and protect the world's water supply. The diffusion of water resource technology throughout the world must be a priority.
- Community involvement in the decision-making and actual control of water resources is essential. Public participation must be encouraged.
- Effective water management skills must be developed by municipal authorities and agricultural and industrial users.

- Awareness of the need for water conservation and environmental protection of water supplies is vital. Educational programs must be instituted on all levels of society. The appropriate training of the necessary professionals, including agricultural extension workers, is also required to convey the appropriate message to water users in the field.

The effective management of the world's fresh water resources will require people around the world to gather and analyze water use information. The integration of this information into the decision-making processes must be viewed as essential in water management. The management of our finite sources of fresh water must begin to take into consideration the long-term consequences of human water consumption and pollution. The sustainable management of water supplies must become a priority for both local and national governments.

Financing

The costs which are estimated to be necessary to implement the programs in the area of water resource management are about $115 million annually for the period from 1993-2000. This entire total is proposed to be provided by international grants or aid. The funding necessary to establish all of the programs in the areas relating to water resource assessment are estimated to be approximately $355 million annually. Of this amount, about $145 million will be required from the international community.

Water Quality and Sanitation

Because of the interconnectedness of the global ecosystem and the pervasive influence of human activity, there are very few regions of the world that remain exempt from water quality problems. Extensive losses of fresh water supplies, prevalent contamination of surface and groundwater sources and widespread pollution have raised water quality to a global-level problem. Major problems have arisen from inadequately treated sewage, the uncontrolled discharge of industrial waste, the ill-considered placement of industrial plants and extensive deforestation. Uncontrolled and mismanaged agricultural cultivation and poor agricultural practices have lead to the leaching of nutrients and pesticides into groundwater. Aquatic ecosystems and water quality are also often adversely affected by dams, river diversions and irrigation schemes. The extent and severity of the contamination of groundwater aquifers has long been underestimated due to the relative inaccessibility of the aquifers. Recent evidence shows extensive contamination of nearly all global aquifers.

Safe drinking water supplies and waste sanitation are vital to protecting the environment, improving health and alleviating poverty. The consumption of contaminated water in the developing countries of the world accounts for an enormous amount of disease and death—over three-fourths of all disease and over one-third of all deaths. One in three people in the developing world utterly lacks safe drinking water and sewage disposal.

Many of these problems have arisen from development planning which entirely fails to take environmental concerns into consideration. The ecological and human health effects of this poorly managed development of water is a measurable consequence. There is a widespread lack of perception of the link between the careful use of water resources and the ecosystems that provide that water.

The main objectives proposed by this section of *AGENDA 21* are threefold: first, to maintain and protect the ecosystems of drainage basins worldwide; second, to provide safe drinking water supplies to all humanity and third, to strengthen and localize water management programs. All three of these major objectives are necessarily interconnected in many ways. Maintenance and protection of drainage basin ecosystems will lead to safe supplies of drinking water. In order to implement such protection and maintenance, effective local water management programs must be implemented. The entire issue of safe water supplies must be viewed as an integral part of improving global environmental quality, enhancing living standards and health and providing for the sustainable development of the Earth.

Programs and Activities

- The drive for safe water must include a global effort to identify all fresh water resources and analyze the effect of human activities on them. Once identified, realistic and comprehensive water quality standards must be put into place.

- Standards for the discharge of waste water and effluents must also be developed. Compliance with water quality standards must be monitored closely.
- Rehabilitation of degraded water sources must be a priority.
- Effective water pollution prevention must entail a major increase in the construction of domestic sewage treatment plants.
- Effective local and traditional methods of sanitation must be integrated with the latest technology.
- The focus must be on reducing pollution of fresh water sources. This can be accomplished by processes which reduce pollution at the source, by recycling and recovery of waste and by environmentally safe treatment and disposal of waste products.
- Landfills must be designed and managed with a view to reducing pollution of water resources.
- Facilities and technology for the treatment of industrial waste must also be developed and widely disseminated worldwide.
- Application of the "polluter pays" principle must be initiated for both on and off-site sanitation pollution.
- Technology to reduce the production of industrial waste should be encouraged.
- The development of innovative biotechnology sources for waste treatment and the production of biofertilizers must be advanced.
- As the world population increases and demand for food rises, special efforts must be taken to ensure that the production of food does not harm the fresh water resources of the Earth.
- The management of fresh water resources must also encompass consideration of inland fisheries, aquaculture, animal grazing and all agricultural activities. Pollution from all of these sources must be taken into account and methods to manage such pollution must be developed.
- Treatments of municipal waste water for safe reuse in agriculture and aquaculture must be developed and encouraged.
- Agricultural practices which do not degrade groundwater resources must be developed.

- The use of nitrogen fertilizers and other agrochemicals must be limited to rational and planned applications which do not pollute fresh water sources.

- Agrochemical use must be carefully regulated and monitored.

- Degraded agricultural lands should be rehabilitated as the availability of fresh water permits.

- Remaining wetlands must be conserved and protected and the trend to drain them for agricultural use should be halted.

- The integrated management of water resources and liquid and solid wastes is a prerequisite to providing a safe drinking-water supply and healthy sanitation. Deep changes in attitudes and behavior are necessary to effectively provide a safe water supply worldwide.

- This approach entails community management of services, backed by measures to strengthen local implementation of sanitation programs.

- The principle that decisions should be made at the lowest appropriate level should be applied to water supply management.

- Literacy and health and hygiene education must be dramatically increased.

- Local communities must be trained in appropriate water management techniques, including reducing waste, safe reuse of water and general sanitation.

- Technical cooperation among developing countries in this area is important, especially with regard to the exchange of information and experiences.

- Programs to train the personnel to manage and monitor water resources, treatment plants and waste discharge are needed.

- Adequate training programs for women in maintenance, management and sanitation must be included.

- In order to realistically meet the goals of safe water and sanitation worldwide by the year 2000, low-cost pollution control and waste treatment technology must be developed.

- The focus should be on technology which can be implemented, maintained and repaired locally in community-based programs. In order to maximize local involvement, these technologies must be developed with regard for traditional and indigenous practices.

The provision of safe drinking water and basic sanitation must be seen as an important and integral part of protecting the environment, alleviating the effects of poverty and raising living standards worldwide. Development planning must integrate an understanding of the essential need for safe water and sanitation into every aspect of decision-making.

Financing

The annual cost estimates to establish the *AGENDA 21* programs in the area of the protection of water resources are approximately $1 billion, including $340 million from international funding. To implement the programs relating to drinking water supplies and sanitation, the annual estimated expenditures will be $20 billion, with about $7.4 billion required from grants or aid from the industrialized world.

Agricultural and Rural Water Supplies

The sustainability of global food production increasingly depends on efficient water use. Irrigation, water control in rain-fed areas, livestock water supplies, inland fisheries and agro-forestry are all important aspects of agriculture which must be addressed in water supply programs. In order to protect and maintain the water sources necessary for these types of activities, water saving technology and management must be applied to all of the areas. The goals of this section of *AGENDA 21* are: (1) to provide safe water supplies for human, agricultural, fishery and livestock needs and (2) to provide for new irrigation development, improvement of existing irrigation schemes and reclamation of degraded irrigation lands.

The lack of water is a significant limiting factor to livestock production in many countries. The improper disposal of animal waste results in the pollution of precious human and animal water supplies across large areas. The current global livestock drinking water requirement is about 60 billion liters per day. Based on livestock growth estimates, this daily demand is predicted to increase annually by 400 million liters per day for the foreseeable future.

Inland fisheries, totally dependent on clean and sanitary water, are an important source of food and protein worldwide. The present level of production of freshwater fish is about 7 million tons and this production could more than double by the year 2000—to 16 million tons. Any increases in environmental stress and fresh water pollution could seriously jeopardize this vital rise in global food production.

Soil erosion, the mismanagement of water resources and intense competition for water have all influenced the extent of poverty, hunger and famine in developing countries. Soil erosion caused by overgrazing of livestock has lead to silt build-up in many lakes and rivers. In recent years, there has been great progress in implementing water control programs in rain-fed agricultural areas, which has lead to significant expansions of agricultural production. However, in areas dependent on irrigation, major problems have arisen—particularly the waterlogging and salinization of soils.

The amount of new areas to be developed into productive agricultural use by irrigation is estimated to be approximately 15.2 million hectares in the developing countries of the world by the year 2000. The development of irrigation schemes is generally done without any regard to the environmental impact of such water use. Within the watershed of river valleys, the social impact of reduced water caused by irrigation diversion is also seldom considered. Irrigation schemes have the potential to supply great increases in food production, but also contain the potential for the destruction of wetlands, water pollution, increased sedimentation, salinization of soils and loss of biodiversity.

Programs and Activities

- 12 million hectares of existing irrigation systems must be improved and upgraded. These current irrigation systems must be modified to increase their efficiency, productivity and environmental soundness.

- The development of new irrigation areas must by accompanied by environmental impact assessments and a careful appraisal of the type of technology anticipated. The use of relatively brackish water for irrigation must be researched and developed.

- Programs must be developed for the control of animal waste and the protection of both human and animal water supplies. Both the quality and quantity of water for livestock must be increased. For livestock in extensive grazing areas, this is critical in order to reduce the distance needed to travel for water and to prevent the overgrazing around limited water sources.

- The multiple use of water supplies should be encouraged through the promotion of joint agricultural/livestock/fishery systems.
- Water spreading schemes should be developed to increase the water retention in grassland areas, to stimulate forage production and to decrease run-off.
- A program for the water management of inland fisheries and aquaculture should work to conserve water quality and quantity for optimum production. It should also assist countries in managing inland fisheries through the promotion of sustainable management as well as the development of environmentally sound means to intensify aquaculture.
- Appropriate aquaculture techniques should be introduced in those countries which can safely sustain such production. The use of marginal quality water in aquaculture should be evaluated.
- International action on water for sustainable food production and rural development is necessary to assist developing countries in managing water resources on an integrated basis to meet present and future agricultural needs.
- There is an urgent need for countries to monitor their agricultural water sources and quality. Inventories of the type and extent of rural water use must be undertaken.
- Agricultural water management plans must be developed within a comprehensive set of policies for health, food production and environmental protection.
- Local community participation is essential. In view of the critical role women in many rural areas play in the practical day-to-day supply, management and use of water, women must be ensured of full involvement in all phases of water management.
- Appropriate low-cost and environmentally sound technologies must be developed which will allow local and community-based efforts in agricultural water use to succeed. The goal should be to promote increased efficiency and productivity in agricultural water use.
- The results of research into water-related farming and fishing topics must be translated into practical and usable advice and techniques. Much greater efforts must be taken to support the rapid adoption of such techniques at the field level.

- Adequate technical advice and support must accompany the transfer of any such technology. Community ownership and management of water supply and sanitation facilities should be encouraged wherever possible.
- Efforts in this area should explicitly focus on water use efficiency, recycled wastewater, small-scale irrigation schemes, waterlogging and salinity control and drainage in irrigated areas.
- Drinking water supply and sanitation is a necessity for the unserved rural poor to prevent disabling diseases and to maintain their productive agricultural capabilities.
- Basic hygiene education has to be extended and the participation of local communities encouraged, particularly women and water user groups.
- Farmers, fishermen/women and members of local communities must be trained in methods for the optimal and environmentally sound use of water resources.
- There must be functional and coherent institutional frameworks at the national level to promote water for sustainable agricultural development.
- In addition, an adequate legal framework of rules and regulations should be in place to encourage sound agricultural water use, drainage, water quality management and small-scale water development programs.
- To protect and maintain the world's agricultural production, the value of water resources must be fully taken into account in all levels of decision-making.

The level of food production on Earth is directly related to the careful management of fresh water resources. The finite volume of global fresh water requires a global shift to agricultural water use that relies on efficiency, conservation and environmental protection.

Financing

The estimate for the full funding necessary to implement all of the programs in the area of providing adequate fresh water supplies for agricultural and rural use is $13.2 billion, with approximately $4.5 billion being required from international grants or aid.

Climate Change

At present, there is scientific uncertainty regarding the prediction of climate change on a global level. Higher global temperatures and decreased precipitation would lead to decreased water supplies and increased water demand. Such changes might cause the deterioration in the quality of fresh water bodies, putting strains on the already fragile balance between water supply and demand in many countries. Even where precipitation might increase, there is no guarantee that it would occur at the time of year when it could be effectively used. Increased precipitation could cause widespread flooding. Any rise in the sea level caused by climate change will likely cause the intrusion of salt water into river estuaries, small island and coastal aquifers. This and the increased likelihood of flooding in coastal areas puts low-lying countries at great risk. Climate changes may also increase the frequency and severity of floods and droughts.

The potential impact of such climate change could pose an environmental threat of unknown magnitude and could even threaten human survival in certain areas, particularly islands, coastal and arid and semi-arid regions. Among the most important impacts of such potential climate change is the effect on water cycles and water resources.

Programs and Activities

- The very nature of this topic calls first and foremost for more information and a greater understanding of the threat being faced. The impact of climate change on fresh water resources and areas prone to drought and floods must be understood.

- Soil moisture, groundwater balance, sea level, temperature and precipitation changes and other climatological factors must be carefully monitored, particularly in those countries which are most likely to suffer the effects of climate change.

- Research must be undertaken to establish if there is a current link between ongoing climate change and the current increase in droughts and floods in certain areas.

- When the threat of impact is sufficiently confirmed, national plans of action must be available to counteract the effect of climate change on local areas.

- This will require innovative use of technology and engineering, including the installation of flood and drought warning systems. The construction of new water resource projects will also be required—dams, aqueducts, water wells, levees, banks, drainage channels, treatment plants and desalination works. These projects must be developed with a careful consideration of the environmental impact of these projects themselves on the local environment.

- Both the research and innovative development work necessary will require increased academic training in all related fields.

- International projects can provide climate projections and enumerate alternative strategies to cope with the impact of climate changes. Each country, however, must develop the scientific and engineering expertise needed to confront the challenges to be faced.

- Possible responses to the potential effects of changes in water resources must be made on the basis of the latest information. Perhaps the most critical requirement in this area is the pressing need for a mechanism by which the latest predictions regarding climate change can be reviewed and understood.

- In order for nations to make the necessary judgements and decisions, the latest scientific knowledge regarding the impact of climate change must be made available. Each country needs a body of dedicated individuals who are able to interpret the complex issues concerned for those leaders who are required to make broad policy decisions.

Financing

The total cost estimated to implement all of the actions associated with understanding the effect of climate change on fresh water resources amounts to approximately $100 million, with $40 million of that total coming from international sources.

Energy Resources

Energy is one of the most essential of the Earth's resources. Energy use is required to produce the heat, light and food that fuel human survival. The attainment of higher living standards is, in many respects, directly related to the ability to consume energy. The world is presently on a path of energy production and consumption which cannot be sustained. Most of the energy consumed on this planet comes from fossil fuels. 40 percent of world energy is derived from oil, 30 percent from coal or wood and 20 percent from natural gas. Nuclear, hydropower, solar and all other sources supply less than 10 percent of world energy. This overwhelming use of fossil fuel is a significant source of many atmospheric pollutants such as lead, sulphur dioxide and the greenhouse gas carbon dioxide. Acid rain, global warming and climate change are increasingly linked to the enormous increase in the use of fossil fuels in this century.

Because of a history of relatively cheap energy supplies, the current methods for utilizing energy have tended to be highly inefficient and wasteful. Energy development must be modified to place a higher value on protection of the environment. In order to both preserve the finite non-renewable resources and protect the atmosphere from the effects of fossil fuel use, efficiency in the use of energy must be greatly increased. In general, the consumption levels of all fossil fuels must be lowered and the increasing needs of humanity must be met with other energy sources, particularly safe and renewable sources of energy.

One of the most significant impacts of energy use is on the global atmosphere. A comprehensive consideration of world energy use is, therefore, included in the discussion on protection of the atmosphere in Chapter 4: The Protection of Our Global Commons.

Agriculture and Rural Development

Along with fresh water, clean air and energy, food is one of the most essential resources for human survival. Adequate food is an absolute requirement for human existence. Without sufficient food, human physical and mental development is dramatically impeded. Despite abundant agricultural resources, world food production is not currently able to meet the needs of a large portion of humanity. Hunger and malnutrition are endemic among developing countries. By the year 2025, approximately 83 percent of the expected global population of 8.5 billion will be living in developing countries. The capacity of available resources and technology to meet the enormous food demands of this growing population are by no means certain.

The fundamental challenge facing agriculture in developing countries today is to increase food production in a sustainable way and feed the expanding populations. Such an increase must come primarily through an intensified level of agricultural production on currently producing areas, as the potential for bringing new land under cultivation in many countries is very limited. If hunger is to be eventually eradicated in these countries, this intensification of agriculture must be both ecologically and economically sustainable far into the future. The goal is to ensure universal access to stable supplies of nutritionally adequate food which has been produced in an environmentally sound manner. The development of employment and markets for agricultural products is also important in the overall effort to alleviate poverty.

Agriculture is an important industry in the economies of most developing countries. In many, it is the backbone of the entire economic structure. Agricultural products often represent the major share of export earnings for developing countries. In order to reduce poverty in these countries, efficient agriculture will need to be able to create jobs both on and off the farm. Over the next 10 years, the agricultural portion of society will bear most of the responsibility for providing rural economies with sufficient growth to offer employment to the bulk of their population. Without this growth, the present rural-urban exodus is certain to accelerate, leading to unmanageable urban squalor and, in all likelihood, major social upheavals. The need for sustainable non-agricultural rural development is also a critical need in order to relieve the pressure on the world's urban areas.

Agricultural Policy and Food Security

To meet these enormous challenges, major adjustments are needed in national and international policies. In promoting sustainable agriculture and rural development, the commitment of national governments and the support of the international community is crucial. Economic conditions must be created which are supportive of sustainable agriculture and rural development. Emphasis must be given to reforming agricultural policies which relate to prices, subsidies, trade, land tenure and appropriate farm practices and technologies. In order to effectively promote sustainable agricultural and rural development, major investments in rural infrastructure will be required. The full cooperation and support of national governments and the international community in implementing the following action programs is crucial.

There is a general absence in most countries of a coherent national strategy on agriculture. In particular, the countries which are currently making the economic transition from centrally-planned to market-oriented economies need such a framework. It is necessary for decision-makers to understand the impact of all phases of economic activity on agriculture. An appreciation of the environmental impact of agriculture is also an integral part of any national farm policy.

Programs and Activities

- National governments should implement policies pertaining to land tenure, population trends, appropriate farm technologies and a more open trading system that would enhance rural households' access to food. Food security is the ultimate goal—stable access to adequate food supplies for all members of society.
- Long-term food production policies need to be developed in all countries to ensure such security.
- Foreign trade policies, prices, exchange rate policies, farm subsidies and agricultural product taxes are all instruments that can be used to develop a comprehensive agricultural strategy.
- Local participation is essential in implementing any agricultural strategy. There must be greater public awareness of the vital role of local community organizations, women's groups, indigenous people and small farmers in developing sustainable agriculture.
- Such local participation can act to ensure that rural populations have fair access to land, water and forest resources and to the necessary technologies, financing, marketing and distribution to adequately take advantage of such resources.
- In this regard, agricultural extension services must be developed and improved.
- Clear land titles and rights of cultivation must be assigned to rural populations.
- Protection of natural resources must be made a priority at the local level.
- Programs to develop more efficient subsistence agriculture must be adopted, as well as programs to cultivate and distribute more market-oriented crops.

- In order to meet future needs, agricultural production must be intensified. This must be done without increasing environmental stress or inducing market fluctuations.
- A primary method in increasing food production is by diversifying crops and increasing efficiency. Information on these issues must be developed and disseminated to farming households.
- Specific and easy-to-understand information on crop rotation, organic manuring, reducing the use of chemicals, agricultural waste recycling and other similar topics is vital to increase sustainable farm yields.
- Rural financial networks must be promoted to encourage local investment in agriculture.
- The rural infrastructure must be upgraded to allow better access to markets and to reduce food losses.
- Other rural employment opportunities must be developed. Cottage industry programs, environmentally sound wildlife use, aquaculture, local food processing, light manufacturing and recreation are all activities that can be developed to slow the rural exodus.
- Such alternative livelihoods for rural dwellers will also serve to relieve the pressure to farm more and more marginal areas. The development of rural employment must focus on small-scale community based job creation.
- From international levels to local-level programs, coherent strategies must be developed to confront the challenges to agriculture brought on by population increases. To increase food production and yet maintain the quality of the rural environment must be the ultimate goal of any agricultural policy.

Financing

The funding requirements necessary to implement the *AGENDA 21* programs in the area of farm policy and food security are $3 billion annually for the period from 1993-2000. Of this total, approximately $450 million will be required from international financial aid sources.

Agricultural Land Use Planning and Soil Erosion

Uncontrolled land use is one of the primary causes of destruction of land resources. Present land use often totally disregards the actual carrying capacities and limitation of the land. As the world's population surpasses 6 billion by the turn of the century, the need to increase food production will place enormous environmental pressure on already taxed natural resources, including land itself. The techniques for increasing food production and conserving soil are already available but are not widely applied. A systematic approach to land use must be adopted.

The problem of soil degradation is the most important environmental problem affecting many areas, both in developing and developed countries. Soil erosion is particularly acute in developing countries, while salinization, waterlogging, soil pollution and loss of fertility are increasing in all countries. Because of soil degradation, the agricultural production of huge areas of land is decreasing just as demand for more farm production is increasing. Populations are rapidly increasing and the demand for food, fibre and fuel is consequently spiralling upwards. To date, efforts to slow such soil degradation have had limited success. Land use planning and better land management can provide long-term solutions to this problem. However, there is an urgent need to halt soil loss and erosion immediately in the most critically vulnerable areas. Priority must be given to maintaining and improving the capacity of higher potential agricultural lands to support an expanding population. At the same time, conserving and rehabilitating lower potential land is essential.

Programs and Activities

- Land conservation and rehabilitation programs with strong political support and adequate funding are required. With the participation of local communities, effective conservation and rehabilitation measures to address this serious threat must be put into place before the year 2000.

- Economic incentives must be provided to local communities to maintain soil conservation programs.

- The physical, social and economic causes of soil degradation must be identified and removed.

- Land tenure systems, pricing structures and trading systems which encourage overexploitation of land must be altered.
- Agricultural markets must be used to encourage soil conservation.
- Programs must be developed to systematically identify sustainable land uses and production systems for each land and climate zone and to control inappropriate land use.
- In many developing countries where population growth exceeds agricultural production, the goal is to increase agricultural production substantially without destroying soil fertility.
- This will require the use of organic matter, fertilizer and other sources to enrich soil and increase farming efficiency and production.

Financing

Costs for implementing all of the programs relating to agricultural land use planning are estimated at $1.7 billion annually through the year 2000. Of this total, about $250 million is sought from international aid and grants. The funds necessary to establish the various programs for agricultural land conservation and rehabilitation are estimated to be approximately $5 billion per year, including about $800 million from the international community.

Genetic Resources

The enormous variety of the genetic makeup of the plants and animals of Earth provides much of the strength of our global ecosystem. Standardization of crops and livestock can seriously lessen the genetic resources available for future improvement of our agricultural base. Local plant and animal species have unique attributes for adaptation to climate, disease resistance and specific uses that are vital to ensuring the continued health of the Earth's agricultural system. Threats to the biological diversity of the Earth's plants and animals are growing. The introduction of exotic species, use of hybrid crops and other causes can lead to the extinction of species and loss of vital genetic resources.

There is an urgent need to safeguard the world's plant and animal genetic resources. Current efforts to conserve, develop and use genetic resources are underfunded and understaffed. In some cases, existing gene banks are totally inadequate and the loss of genetic diversity in the gene banks is as great as it is in the field.

Programs and Activities

- Decisive efforts must be taken to safeguard the world's genetic resources. This must include measures to conserve genetic resources in the field, as well as increased use of germ plasm and gene banks.
- Special emphasis must be on collecting and preserving minor crops and species, including tree species.
- As soon as possible, on a worldwide basis, the safe duplication and first regeneration of all existing collections of genetic resources should be undertaken.
- Research efforts into the sustainable use of plant genetic resources must be properly funded. Poorly known, but potentially useful plants must be identified. New plants with value as food crops should be promoted in order to diversify local agriculture.
- The sharing of the benefits and results of plant breeding must be encouraged. Particularly in developing countries, propagation and plant multiplication facilities should be developed.
- Community-based programs for plant breeding and seed production should be developed. Cost-effective methods for keeping duplicate sets of germ plasm collections should be developed.
- Similarly, actions on the conservation and sustainable use of animal genetic resources for agriculture are important. To increase the quantity and quality of animal products and conserve the existing diversity of animal breeds to meet future requirements, efforts to preserve animal genetic resources must be increased.
- Animal breeds that are at risk must be identified and protected. Programs to guarantee their survival and avoid the risk of their loss through cross-breeding must be developed.
- Indigenous breeds must be identified and semen/embryo collections developed. Cryogenic storage facilities must be prepared.
- The storage and analysis of animal genetic data should be handled at the global level. A world watch list of endangered breeds should be established.

- On a local basis, breeding farms and artificial insemination centers should be established.

Financing

The necessary financing for the establishment for all of the *AGENDA 21* proposals in the area of plant genetic resources is approximately $600 million annually, all of which is sought from international grants and aid. For the programs relating to animal genetic resources, the annual cost estimates are $200 million, including $100 million in international source financing.

Pest Control

World food demand is expected to increase by 50 percent by the year 2000 and double again in the next 50 years. Of world food production, between 25 percent and 50 percent of pre- and post-harvest losses are estimated to be caused by pests. Pests affecting animal health also cause heavy losses and, in many areas, prevent livestock development. Attempts at the chemical control of agricultural pests have dominated efforts, but pesticide overuse has had adverse effects on farm budgets, human health and the environment. Despite, or in some cases because of, chemical pest control, new pest problems continue to develop. Integrated pest management and control which minimizes the use of pesticides is the best option for the future. This management technique combines a variety of biological, cultural, chemical methods, and also uses plant resistance and appropriate farming practices. Placing the components of such a strategy within the economic reach of the farmer guarantees yields, reduces costs and is environmentally friendly. Integrated pest management should go hand in hand with appropriate pesticide management to allow for pesticide regulation and control, including trade. Such integrated pest management programs should also allow for the safe handling and disposal of pesticides, particularly those that are toxic.

Programs and Activities

- By the year 2000, mechanisms should be put into place to reduce the use and control the distribution of pesticides worldwide.

- Farmer networks and extension services must be improved to promote the use of integrated pest management.

- Research must continue into developing pesticides which are target-specific and which readily degrade into harmless component parts after use.

- Research into the environmental damage and human side-effects of pesticide use must also continue.

- Pesticide labeling must be improved to provide farmers with understandable information about safe handling, application and disposal.

- Information on the use of pesticides which have been banned or restricted must be widely available.

- Techniques for the use of traditional and non-chemical methods of pest control must be collected and made available.

- Biological and organic pesticides must be thoroughly tested and the results must be widely disseminated.

- Local farmer and women's groups must be trained in the use of alternative methods of controlling agricultural pests.

Financing

The annual cost estimates for implementing the *AGENDA 21* programs in the area of pest control are estimated to be approximately $1.9 billion, of which $285 million will be required from international sources.

Food Production

Particularly in developing countries, plant nutrient depletion is a serious problem which results in loss of soil fertility. In many developing countries, population growth rates exceed 3 percent per year and agricultural production has fallen behind food demand. In these countries, food production must be increased by at least 4 percent per year, using methods which do not destroy soil fertility. The high potential areas of each country should be the target for increased production. Trained labor, proper tools and technology, the use of plant nutrients and soil enrichment will all be essential.

In many areas, there are dramatic annual losses in agricultural productivity. In sub-Saharan Africa, plant nutrient losses from all sources currently exceed plant nutrient supplies by nearly four to one. The total net loss of plant nutrients in this area is estimated at 10 million tons per year. As a result, farmers are forced to cultivate more marginal land with increasingly fragile ecosystems. This, in turn, results in further soil degradation. An integrated approach to plant nutrition aims at ensuring a sustainable supply of plant nutrients to increase future yields without harming the environment or losing soil fertility.

Programs and Activities

- Strategies to enhance soil fertility must include policies to use organic and inorganic plant nutrients and mineral fertilizer.

- Processes to recycle organic and inorganic waste into the soil must be developed which do not harm the environment, inhibit plant growth or jeopardize human health.

- A comprehensive program to assess the available resources to restore soil fertility should be developed in each country.

- The use of local mineral deposits, recycling, waste products, discarded organic material and other fertilization techniques must be investigated and implemented.

- New technologies must be developed which can be used to enhance soil fertility and produce topsoil from locally available resources.

- Extension officers and researchers must be trained to translate scientific data into realistic approaches to this problem.

- Farmers, local farm groups and women's groups must be trained in plant nutrition management, with a special emphasis on the conservation and production of topsoil.

Financing

The costs of implementing all of the programs and activities in this area are estimated at approximately $3.2 billion annually, including about $475 million from international sources.

Rural Energy Supplies

The energy supplies in many countries are not sufficient for their development needs. The inadequate energy available is often overpriced and unstable. In the rural areas of developing countries where a large proportion of humanity lives, the chief sources of energy are fuelwood, crop residues and manure. The exploitation of these organic sources for energy decreases the availability of such sources for soil enrichment, thereby leading to the increased loss of soil fertility. The increasing harvesting of fuelwood to supply the energy needs of a growing population denudes wide areas of land and leads to soil erosion and silt build-up. The use of more energy in rural areas is a requirement to increase food production and allow depleted soils to be rehabilitated. An economically and environmentally sound mix of fossil fuel and renewable sources of energy must be developed for rural areas. The use of renewable forestry crops can be one method utilized to increase the energy supply to rural areas. Other methods for supplying energy to rural areas must be developed which do not cause further harm to the environment.

Programs and Activities

- By the year 2000, the goal is to encourage a transition to alternative new and renewable sources of energy in rural and agricultural areas.
- The emphasis should be on the development of self-reliant rural programs which favor the use of local renewable sources.
- Improved energy efficiency must also be a vital component of rural energy programs.
- Energy technology that can be directly applied to local agricultural production and post-harvest activities must be developed.
- Pilot programs and projects must be devised which field-test new and appropriate technology.
- Gasifiers, biomass, solar driers, wind-pumps and combustion systems that use locally-available and renewable resources for agricultural processing activities should be developed.
- The focus should be on the production and development of low-cost and easily-maintained technology that is environmentally sound.

Financing

Implementation of the various *AGENDA 21* programs in the area of rural energy use will cost an estimated $1.8 billion per year through the year 2000. Approximately $265 million of this total will be required from international financing sources on a grant or aid basis.

Ultraviolet Radiation

The increase of ultraviolet radiation due to the depletion of the ozone layer has been recorded in various parts of the world, in particular in the southern hemisphere. Action needs to be taken to evaluate the effects of ultraviolet radiation on plants and animals caused by the depletion of the stratospheric ozone layer and to take appropriate remedial measures. The objective in this area is to undertake research to determine the impact of the recorded increases in ultraviolet radiation on agriculture and plant and animal life. No financing estimates were prepared for this area of *AGENDA 21*. The depletion of the Earth's ozone layer is discussed further in Chapter 4: The Protection of Our Global Commons.

* * *

In all areas of *AGENDA 21* related to agriculture, the participation of local people and communities is crucial for the success of sustainable agriculture. The major development efforts must be to strengthen the capacity of rural institutions, extension services and local groups to take control over the safe and efficient use of the local natural resources. Decentralized decision-making also works to guarantee that rural people, particularly women, have fair access to land, water and other natural resources which are needed to produce food for the world. The ultimate goal of sustainable agriculture is to ensure that sufficient food can be produced to feed the population of the world indefinitely. To reach this goal, everyone involved in the production of food must understand the concept of sustainable agriculture. This entails a local grasp of long-term goals and objectives. From researchers to politicians, from farmers to consumers; there must be a thorough understanding of the impact of human activity on the ecology of Earth. Efforts at short-term economic gain which damage the environment in the long-term have a widespread effect, both economically and environmentally. This core concept must be fully understood for *AGENDA 21* to succeed.

Forests

Forested areas worldwide are under severe pressure from the intensifying impact of human activity. Wide areas across the globe are being deforested at an accelerating rate. Increasing attention is being given to the condition of the world's forests and to the vital role that they play in local economies and quality of life. While public concern has focused in recent years on the plight of tropical forests, it is now clearly accepted that all types of forests should be taken into consideration. Recent estimates indicate that annual deforestation rates of tropical forests amount to some 17 million hectares worldwide. Little is known, however, of the overall situation of other forests (boreal, sustral, sub-temperate and temperate) or of their exact quantity, quality and rates of change.

Deforestation is a result of many causes. Some of the causes are natural but most are a result of human development. Inappropriate land tenure systems, pressure to expand agricultural areas and increasing demand for forest products all contribute to deforestation. Lack of forest-fire control, unregulated commercial logging, overgrazing and browsing and the harmful effects of airborne pollutants all add to the problems that forests face. Central to all of these difficulties is a general lack of understanding and information on the value of forests.

The benefits to be derived from trees, forests and forest lands are wide and varied. Forests are not only a source of timber and firewood, but also play an important role in many vital areas. Soil conservation, the regulation of water cycles, the exchanges of gases and nutrients, including carbon dioxide and the maintenance of reservoirs of rich biodiversity are but some of their valuable roles. Many local populations have understood the multiple benefits to be obtained from forests, yet only recently has the fundamental value of forests emerged on a wider national scale. The realization that forests significantly affect the lives of both local and distant populations has helped place forest-related issues on the international agenda.

Maintaining and increasing the Earth's forest cover will contribute to improved human living conditions and the preservation of biodiversity, particularly through environmentally sound land management practices. While preserving primary forest areas is critical for biodiversity protection, planting new forests will significantly contribute to timber and firewood production and the protection of watersheds and soil. New forests can function as carbon sinks (for the absorption of excess carbon dioxide produced through the use of fossil fuels) and, in general, lessen the pressure of exploitation on the remaining primary forests.

Multiple Forest Uses

The first priority in the sustainable development of forests and wood-lands should be to address the multiple roles of trees, forests and forest lands. The sustainable production of forest goods in both developed and developing countries should be ensured.

Programs and Activities

- The scope and effectiveness of tree conservation programs and forest expansion activities should be enhanced.
- To this end, the technical and professional skills of those involved in forest development must be increased.
- Adequate government staffs for environmentally sound forest development must be trained and supported.
- Forest extension services must be expanded and developed in coordination with public education services to ensure a better awareness and appreciation of the multiple roles and values of forests.
- Official decision-making must be decentralized to take advantage of local knowledge in forest areas.
- The full participation of the public at every level of forest conservation and reforestation must be encouraged.
- Labor unions, rural cooperatives, private forest protection organizations, women's and youth groups must all be enlisted in the effort to protect and preserve the Earth's forests.
- The forestry industry must take an active role in developing trained staff with understanding of the environmental consequences of forest use.
- Research into the sustainable and multiple use of forests must be sufficiently funded.
- Collecting, compiling and distributing information on forest cover, endangered species, traditional forest usage, biomass and other forest resources must be a priority.

- There must be efforts to ensure wide public access to information regarding forests. Educational programs must be launched regarding forests and woodlands, specifically graduate and post-graduate degree programs and extension service training programs at the vocational and technical level.

Financing

Approximately $2.5 billion is estimated to be required to implement all of the program activities in the area of multiple-use of forests. $860 million of this total will be required from sources in the industrialized world in the form of grants or aid.

Protection and Reforestation

Fueled by increasing human demands, forests worldwide have been threatened by uncontrolled exploitation and conversion to other types of land use. The loss of forests leads directly to soil erosion, the loss of biological diversity, destruction of wildlife habitats, damage to watershed areas and the reduction of development options for forest lands. Urgent and consistent action is required to conserve and sustain the remaining forest resources and to expand forested areas and tree cover. Reforestation is an effective way of increasing public support and awareness in protecting and managing forest areas.

Programs and Activities

- Sustainable management of all forest ecosystems must include efforts to rehabilitate deforested areas to restore both their productivity and environmental contributions.
- Protected forest areas must be expanded worldwide. Nomination as World Heritage Sites is one appropriate method to accomplish this, particularly for primary old-growth forests.
- Forest conservation must include measures to utilize the biological resources of a forest in a sustainable manner.
- Conservation must also include efforts to preserve the biological diversity of forests and to maintain and preserve the traditional forest habitats of indigenous people.

- Revegetation of degraded farm lands, highlands and bare lands in order to prevent erosion should be a priority.

- Measures must be taken to upgrade and expand current human-planted forests in order to increase their contribution to human needs and relieve pressure on primary old-growth forests.

- Master plans for human-planted forests must include efforts to improve the rate of return and provide for increased yields. The use of native species must be given a greater emphasis in the development of planted forests.

- There must be plans to provide for increasing the protection of forests from many sources, including pollutants, fire, pests and diseases.

- Strong efforts must be made to reduce damaging human interference with forests, such as forest poaching, uncontrolled mining and the introduction of exotic plant and animal species.

- Decisive efforts must be made to halt destructive shifting cultivation habits (such as slash and burn farming) that are traditional in certain forest areas. The underlying social and economic causes of such cultivation patterns must be addressed.

- Urban reforestation must also be made a priority. The greening of urban areas and rural human settlements for aesthetic, social, recreational and actual production purposes must be increased.

- Increased research in all of these areas is required. Data on appropriate land use, reforestation and forest rehabilitation plans is necessary.

- Research into the genetic improvement of trees and the application of biotechnology to improve tolerance to environmental stress is required.

- Tree breeding facilities, seed procurement programs and germ plasm banks must be established and supported.

- Reforestation and planting demonstration areas should be developed. The support of the public and community-based groups is vital to the success of any reforestation and conservation efforts. Wide public participation must be encouraged on all levels.

- Detailed information on forest destruction is an integral component in any conservation planning efforts. Much more complete scientific information is needed on the influence of air pollutants and emissions on the health of forests.

- The greening of appropriate areas of the Earth is a task of global importance and impact. The international community must provide technical cooperation in the areas of reducing pollutants and fossil fuel emissions.

Financing

Cost estimates in *AGENDA 21* for the annual funding necessary for the protection and reforestation of the world's forested areas are approximately $10 billion per year through the year 2000. Of this total, about $3.7 billion is thought to be necessary from international grants.

Forest Resources

The vast potential of forests and forest lands as major resources for development has not yet been fully realized. The improved management of forests can increase the production of wood and non-wood forest products and increase the economic value of forests. By helping to generate additional employment and income, by adding value to the forest products through processing and by increasing the forest-related contribution to foreign exchange earnings, careful forest management can enhance the appreciation of the value of forests in many countries. Forest resources, being renewable, can be effectively managed in a sustainable manner that is compatible with environmental conservation. It is also possible to increase the value of forests through other non-damaging forest uses such as eco-tourism and the managed supply of genetic resources. Concerted action is needed on all fronts to increase people's perception of the value of forests and the benefits they provide to humanity. The survival of forests worldwide and their continued contribution to human welfare depends to a great extent on succeeding in this endeavor.

The objectives in this section of *AGENDA 21* are to improve the recognition of the social, economic and ecological values of trees and forests.

Programs and Activities

- To ensure that forests are maintained in a sustainable manner, efforts must be undertaken to incorporate the full value of trees and forests into national economic accounting systems.

- Efficient and sustainable uses of forests and forest-products must be developed. Forest-based processing industries, value-added secondary processing and trade in forest products must be increased and conducted in a sustainable manner.
- More efficient methods must be developed for using forests and trees as fuelwood and energy sources.
- The values of maintaining virgin and old-growth forests for eco-tourism must be incorporated into forest management plans.
- Methods to encourage investment in sustainable forest use must be developed.
- Environmentally sound practices of selective forest harvesting must be improved and implemented.
- Improvements in the use of equipment, storage and transportation of forest products must be made.
- Forest waste products must be utilized more fully and the value of wood and non-wood products improved.
- Non-wood forest products must be promoted and popularized. These can include medicinal plants, dyes, fibers, gums, resins, fodder, cultural products, rattan and bamboo.
- The efficiency of forest-based processing industries to add value to the forest products should be improved.
- Underutilized species should be promoted and new uses researched and developed.
- New markets for forest products must be promoted and improved worldwide.
- Small-scale forest-based enterprises should be encouraged and developed to support rural development and local entrepreneurship.
- The strengthening of existing systems and establishment of new ones for assessing and periodically evaluating forests and forest lands must be a priority. In many cases, even basic information on forests and forest use is unavailable.
- In many developing countries, there is a lack of structures and institutions to carry out these functions. There is a vital need to correct this situation to gain a better understanding of the role and importance of forests. Without clear data on the current status and uses of forests, it

will be impossible to realistically plan for their effective conservation and management.

- A continuing process of research and in-depth analysis is necessary to provide planners, economists, decision-makers and local communities with adequate information on forests.

- Forests play a critical role in global environment and development issues and warrant coordinated international efforts to develop strategies to protect and conserve them. International cooperation, particularly at the regional level, can address specific issues that national governments are sometimes not equipped to pursue.

- While a relatively small forest might not warrant a large national investment on the climatic function of forests, such a globally relevant activity might have great value internationally. International and regional cooperation is required to ensure the development of local participation and the local organizations responsible for forest conservation and sustainable management.

- Of particular importance is the need for the international community to support the negotiations on global principles on the management, conservation and sustainable development of all types of forests.

Financing

The total estimated costs to implement all of the international planning, trade and assessment of forest resources are approximately $750 million, of which $530 million will be sought from direct grants from international sources.

Deserts and Drought

Each year, enormous areas of the Earth's surface are transformed into deserts. Desertification takes place in arid, semi-arid and dry sub-humid areas and is caused by many factors, including climatic variations and human activities. It affects about 1 billion people and one quarter of the world's total land area. Desertification is most severe in the world's drylands, affecting 70 percent of all drylands globally, amounting to about 3.6 billion hectares. There are many consequences which arise from the process of desertification. Desertification causes the destruction of rangeland for livestock and currently affects 3.3 billion hectares of the total area of rangeland available globally. This encompasses 73 percent of the Earth's rangeland that has a low carrying capacity for humans and livestock. Desertification also intensifies the decline in soil fertility and soil structure. This ominous decline is taking place on about 47 percent of the dryland areas worldwide which constitute marginal rainfed cropland. Finally, desertification has increased the degradation of irrigated cropland worldwide. This affects approximately 30 percent of the Earth's dryland areas with a high population density and high agricultural potential. The decline in productivity and loss of crop and livestock production in these areas has resulted in widespread poverty, hunger and malnutrition. Desertification plays a key role in the famine which continues to afflict sub-Saharan Africa, the Sahel and Somalia.

The main priority in combating desertification should be the implementation of preventive measures for lands that are not yet affected or are only slightly affected. Severely degraded areas, however, should not be neglected. More information is necessary on the process of desertification and the status of the world's lands. Efforts must be increased to actively combat the process of desertification through soil conservation and reforestation programs. New sources of employment and food production must be developed for inhabitants of threatened areas. Drought relief programs must be strengthened and widened. The full participation of local populations and community groups is vital to the success of any programs to conquer the human consequences of desertification.

The global effort to reduce the effects of drought and desertification must be increased on all fronts. The environmental toll of drought is enormous, but it is the human price that is, perhaps, more tragic. As climate and weather patterns change worldwide, whether a result of natural trends or human activity, drought and desertification will continue to have a considerable effect on humanity. *AGENDA 21* has outlined the steps necessary to reduce the environmental and human impact of this phenomenon.

Information and Monitoring of Desertification

Access to up-to-date information regarding the status of desertification is essential for allowing decision-makers to formulate plans from a basis of knowledge. Monitoring the global effects of desertification and drought is a massive job which will require a joint effort between international agencies, national governments, private organizations and local groups.

Programs and Activities

- In combatting desertification and drought, national governments and the international community should aim to strengthen the knowledge base and develop information and monitoring systems for all areas which are prone to desertification and drought.
- Global assessments of the status and rate of desertification should take into account both the social and economic causes and the interaction of climate and weather patterns on drought.
- Adequate worldwide observation systems are required for the development of effective anti-desertification programs.
- A coordinated information observation system embracing global, regional, national and local levels is essential for understanding the dynamics of desertification and drought processes.
- Existing environmental monitoring systems, such as Earthwatch and the Sahara and Sahel Observatory, should be strengthened.

Financing

The estimated costs for information-gathering and monitoring desertification are approximately $350 million, including about $175 million from international sources.

Soil Conservation and Reforestation

Efforts to combat desertification must include intensified soil and water conservation, afforestation and reforestation activities. Increasing the vegetation cover on all lands which are periodically affected by drought will promote and stabilize water cycles in dryland areas. The greening of drylands will help to maintain the land quality and increase the productivity of the land. Conservation and reforestation efforts must become a major component in all efforts to address the problems of drought and desertification.

Programs and Activities

- For areas not yet affected or only slightly affected by desertification, the careful management of existing natural formations (including forests) must be pursued.

- The goal should be to attempt to sustain the current productivity levels of moderately desertified lands.

- Economically and environmentally sound methods of agriculture must be introduced and encouraged in all areas which are at risk.

- Improved management of forest resources must be undertaken, specifically by attempting to reduce the local use of wood for fuel consumption. This may be accomplished by programs which encourage more efficient utilization of wood and the development of other sources of energy, including alternative energy sources.

- Improved types of wood-burning stoves should be developed and distributed.

- Innovative technology or the use of adapted traditional techniques to reduce the pressure on forests and shrubs should be encouraged.

- Efforts must be made to ensure that the local land users, particularly women, are the main participants in programs to improve the use and productivity of the lands.

- In dryland areas which are severely desertified, including areas which are affected by sand dune movements, the efforts should be aimed at rehabilitation.

- Pastoral and forestry activities are the most effective means by which to reestablish a level of food productivity to lands which have been seriously degraded.

- Intense efforts must be made to increase the vegetation cover of damaged lands. Accelerated efforts must be undertaken to reforest such areas with fast-growing and drought-resistant species. Native species should be used whenever possible, including hardy legumes.

- Research and testing programs must be pursued to determine the proper balance of vegetation to reclaim desertified areas, keeping in mind the need to preserve the biodiversity of such regions.

- The creation of large-scale forest greenbelts should be considered to prevent the further spread of desert areas and to reclaim drought stricken lands.

- Efficient extension service facilities must be developed to train local farmers and livestock herders in the improved management of land and water resources in dryland areas.

Financing

The estimated costs of implementing the measures in this area are $6 billion, with international financing suppling 50 percent of this annual total.

Alternative Livelihoods

There is an urgent need to develop and strengthen programs to eradicate poverty and promote alternative livelihood opportunities in areas prone to desertification and drought. Current livelihood and resource use systems are losing ground. In most arid and semi-arid areas, the traditional livelihoods of agriculture and livestock herding cannot provide for adequate living standards in fragile areas experiencing drought and increasing population pressure. To a major extent, poverty has accelerated the rate of environmental destruction and desertification.

Programs and Activities

- Immediate action is needed to rehabilitate and improve subsistence agriculture and pastoral systems for the sustainable management of rangelands.
- A decentralized approach to land use must be developed. Local village communities and groups must be encouraged and enabled to take charge of the management of their land on a socially equitable and environmentally sound basis.
- Local groups must be given the authority to take the appropriate steps in promoting efficient long-term land use.
- The property rights of all rural dwellers, including women and children, must be protected. Special attention must be given to ensuring property rights and land access to nomadic and pastoral/herding communities.

- Agriculture and livestock production systems must be improved to achieve greater productivity while conserving the natural resource base in drought-prone areas.
- Village associations which are focused on economic activities must be created or strengthened.
- Market gardening activities should be expanded.
- Local efforts to process agricultural products should be encouraged.
- Herding and livestock processing associations which use environmentally sound and sustainable techniques should be promoted.
- An infrastructure must be developed in communities which involves the local people directly in increasing their production and marketing capacities.
- Efforts must be supported which are aimed at introducing and using innovative technologies for the generation of alternative income.
- Rural credit and banking systems must be established. The mobilization of rural savings for the benefit of the local community can be greatly increased.
- Revolving funds for credit to rural entrepreneurs can facilitate the establishment of cottage industries and small business ventures.
- The availability of credit can also foster the use of sound forestry and agricultural techniques which would otherwise be beyond the reach of local populations.
- Members of rural organizations must also be trained in management skills and technical areas such as agroforestry, small-scale irrigation and soil and water conservation.
- Nationally, governments must make efforts to inventory natural resources and determine the current characteristics of local and traditional land use.
- Contact with the local population is vital to develop this information base. Information and ideas must be shared and exchanged with other governments which face similar problems.
- The information collected must also be distributed to local groups for their use in making decisions and implementing programs to combat desertification. Local land-use research institutions must be established in this regard.

Financing

The total annual financing to implement all of the activities in this areas is included in the costs associated with the *AGENDA 21* programs for combatting poverty in Chapter 1 and the *AGENDA 21* programs for promoting sustainable agriculture earlier in this chapter.

Drought Relief

Drought, in differing degrees of frequency and severity, is a recurring problem throughout much of the developing world, particularly in Africa. An estimated 3 million people died in the mid-1980's as a direct result of drought in sub-Saharan Africa and many thousands are currently dying in Somalia. Apart from the toll on human lives, the economic costs of drought-related disasters are very high, due to lost production and the diversion of scarce development resources. In a number of developing countries, the natural resource base subject to desertification is the main resource upon which any future development must depend. The traditional human social systems that use these land resources make the problem much more complex and necessitate a land management approach which takes social, economic and environmental concerns into account. Developing comprehensive anti-desertification programs and integrating them into national planning is essential.

Programs and Activities

- Efforts should be made to develop comprehensive drought preparedness and relief schemes for drought-prone areas. Local self-help programs must be an integral part of any such plans.
- Early warning systems which forecast drought will make possible the effective implementation of drought preparedness schemes.
- Programs at local levels, such as alternative cropping strategies, soil and water conservation and the promotion of water harvesting techniques, could reduce the impacts of drought. These programs should be directed towards enhancing the capacity of land to cope with drought conditions while providing basic necessities.
- At the same time, programs must be developed to ensure that emergency relief is available in periods of acute scarcity.

- Contingency plans must also be designed and developed to cope with the mounting problem of environmental refugees.

- Strategies must be designed to deal with acute deficiencies in food supplies during periods of national shortages.

- Food storage contingency plans must be developed, along with plans to cope with increased pressure on port facilities from imports and plans to deal with the transportation and distribution of food imports.

- Contingency arrangements must be developed for food, water and fodder distribution in times of emergency.

- Budgetary mechanisms must be established for immediate access to resources for drought relief in times of emergency.

- In all countries affected by drought, major national anti-desertification awareness programs and training programs are necessary. These programs should be conducted through national mass media facilities, all educational networks and through newly-created or existing extension services. This must be done to ensure that people have access to knowledge of desertification and drought and to any national plans to combat desertification.

Financing

The cost of developing anti-desertification, drought-preparedness, environmental refugee and drought-relief programs is estimated at $1.2 billion annually, of which $1.1 billion will be required to be obtained from international financing sources.

Local-Level Program Support

Encouraging and promoting popular participation in desertification control programs is an integral element in ensuring the success of such programs. Environmental education for local groups which focuses on management of the effects of drought is also crucial.

Whether projects related to desertification and drought control succeed or fail has been shown to be directly related to the amount of popular involvement in the programs. It is necessary to go well beyond the theoretical ideal of popular involvement and focus on obtaining direct and actual active participation by the local populace. This popular participation must be rooted in the concept of partnership and the sharing of responsibilities by all parties.

Programs and Activities

- Public awareness of the problems of drought and desertification must be increased. Environmental education components should be included in all primary and secondary school curriculums.

- Training programs to generally increase the level of education among the populations in drought-stricken areas must be implemented.

- Local media, schools and community groups should all be used as resources to educate the public on issues relating to drought and desertification.

- The participation of private organizations must also be encouraged on all levels.

- More extension service officers must be appointed to assist in the efforts to combat desertification. Members of local rural organizations must be trained to support these officers.

- Governments at all levels must adopt policies to allow a more decentralized structure for decision-making.

- Local residents must be given a responsible role in the actual planning and execution of drought relief projects. Efforts by local communities to combat desertification must be supported.

- Rural banking systems and credit facilities must be established to allow local populations to finance locally initiated projects and to promote rural savings.

- Governments should take steps to stimulate both public and private investment.

- Marketing outlets for products from drought-prone areas should be developed.

- The development of technological know-how must be accelerated. Appropriate and environmentally sound technology must be made available to local populations. The use of indigenous technology should also be encouraged and supported where it has proved successful.

- Applied research results on soil and water issues, the introduction of appropriate plant and animal species and sustainable agricultural techniques must be made understandable and available.

Financing

The estimated costs required to implement all of the *AGENDA 21* programs in the area of local programs related to desertification and drought is approximately $1 billion annually with 50 percent of this total coming from international sources.

Mountain Ecosystems

Globally, mountain ecosystems are an important source of biological diversity, water and mineral resources. Forestry, agriculture and recreation also constitute important economic activities in many mountain areas. As a major ecosystem of our planet, mountain environments are essential to the survival of humanity. Unfortunately, mountain ecosystems are rapidly changing. The ability of mountain ecosystems to continue contributing to human development is diminishing due to a variety of natural and human factors. Mountain areas are susceptible to accelerated soil erosion, landslides and the rapid loss of habitat and genetic diversity. About 10 percent of the Earth's population live in mountain areas with higher slopes, while some 40 percent occupy the adjacent medium and lower-watershed regions which draw on mountain resources, particularly water. In many mountain areas, natural resource degradation is causing widespread poverty among local inhabitants. The proper management of the Earth's mountain resources and social and economic development of mountain residents deserves immediate action.

Mountain habitats encompass a rich variety of ecosystems. A single mountain slope may include tropical, subtropical and temperate climates, each representing microcosms of habitat diversity. The conservation and sustainable development of mountain resources require, as a priority, strengthening knowledge about the ecology and sustainable development of mountain ecosystems. The promotion of alternative livelihood opportunities and integrated watershed development programs are necessary.

Scientific Information

Mountain areas are highly vulnerable to human and natural ecological imbalance. Of all the areas on Earth, mountains are the most sensitive to climatic changes in the atmosphere. In order to make informed decisions, it is vital that decision-makers have access to specific information on the ecology, natural resource potential and economic activities in mountain ecosystems.

Programs and Activities

- There is a general lack of knowledge of mountain ecosystems. The creation of a global mountain area database is vital to launching programs that contribute to the sustainable use of mountain areas.

- Surveys should be undertaken on the soils, forests and water use in mountain areas. Detailed information on crop, plant and animal resources in mountain ecosystems is essential.

- Existing national and local institutions should be strengthened to generate an ecological knowledge base on mountain ecosystems. These institutions must identify hazardous areas that are most vulnerable to erosion, floods, earthquakes, snow avalanches and landslides.

- Identification of mountain areas which are threatened by air pollution from neighboring industrial and urban areas is also necessary.

- The effective gathering of knowledge will require the establishment of extensive meteorological, hydrological and physical monitoring systems.

- Scientific research and technological development programs should be strengthened. Meteorology, hydrology, forestry, soil sciences and plant science programs should be developed and fostered.

- Higher education in these areas should be supported through fellowships and research grants for environmental studies in mountains and hill areas. Candidates from indigenous mountain populations should be given priority in obtaining such grants.

- In order to help rural mountain populations better understand the ecological issues relating to their mountain ecosystems, extensive environmental education programs should be developed for farmers and women.

- Training and extension programs in environmentally appropriate technologies suitable to mountain areas should be developed.
- Incentives should be provided to local people to promote the use and transfer of environmentally friendly technologies.
- Improved farming and conservation practices should be encouraged at the local level.
- Mountain areas contain many of the world's endangered plant and animal species. The highest priority should be given to gathering information on those plant and animal species which are under the threat of extinction.
- Forest and wildlife reserves in species-rich areas should be developed. Some of the most important plant and animal resources on Earth are found in mountainous areas. The genetic resources of these species must be safeguarded through the use of protected areas and the improvement of traditional farming and animal husbandry techniques.
- In order to diversify mountain economies, environmentally sound tourism should be encouraged.

Financing

The annual cost estimates for establishing all of the proposed programs relating to gathering scientific information on mountain areas is approximately $50 million, all of which will be required from international funding sources on a grant or aid basis.

Alternative Livelihoods and Watershed Conditions

Nearly half of the world's population is affected in various ways by mountain ecology. Mountain water is a vital resource for these people. Mountain areas make vital contributions to agricultural production in many areas on Earth. In recent years there has been serious ecological deterioration in mountain watershed areas. This decline is largely due to poor land management practices and the cultivation of marginal lands due to expanding populations. In the hillside areas of the Andean countries of South America, large portions of the farming population are faced with rapid deterioration of the land. Similarly, the mountain and upland areas of the Himalayas, Southeast Asia and Central Africa are threatened by cultivation of marginal lands. The resulting soil erosion

111

can have a devastating impact on vast numbers of rural people who depend on rainfed agriculture in the mountain and hillside areas. There is widespread poverty, unemployment, poor health and bad sanitation in many of these fragile areas. The objectives in this area are to prevent soil erosion, increase biomass production and maintain the ecological balance in mountain habitats.

Programs and Activities

- A priority must be to promote alternative income generating activities such as sustainable tourism, fisheries and environmentally sound mining.
- Promoting environmentally sound watershed development through the effective participation of local people is a key to preventing further ecological imbalance.
- A comprehensive approach is needed for conserving, upgrading and using the natural resource base of land, water, plant, animal and human resources.
- The promotion of alternative livelihood opportunities is also central to sustainable mountain development and to improving the living standards of the large rural populations in mountain areas.
- Local infrastructure and social services must be improved to protect the livelihoods of local communities.
- In addition, international technical assistance will be required to help mitigate the effects of natural disasters in mountain areas. This assistance can entail hazard prevention measures, identification of high-risk areas, early warning systems, disaster forecasting, evacuation plans and emergency supplies.
- Local awareness must be raised regarding disaster prevention and disaster relief.
- Local initiatives should be supported with extension services in the areas of animal husbandry, forestry, horticulture and rural development. Popular participation in the management of local resources should be the goal.
- Governments must develop mechanisms which will act to preserve threatened areas and establish national parks in order to protect wildlife and conserve biological diversity.

- Cottage and local agricultural processing industries should be established, such as the cultivation and processing of medicinal and aromatic plants.

- Farmers and local populations should be provided with incentives to undertake conservation measures and use environmentally-friendly techniques and technologies.

- Data must be collected and used regarding the extent of alternative livelihoods. Information on annual tree crops, livestock, poultry, bee-keeping, fisheries, village industries, markets and transportation systems must be gathered. This vital local information must then be integrated into the decision-making process on every level.

- Conservation technologies to control erosion must be promoted which are low-cost, simple and easily adopted by local people.

- These technologies should include information on moisture management, improved cropping, fodder production and planted forestry.

- The use of such techniques must be supported by involving local men and women, researchers and extension agents in carrying out experiments and trials under local conditions.

- Mini and micro-hydro projects should be developed to provide energy to support local cottage industries.

- There must be a special emphasis on developing pilot projects that combine environmental protection with development in a manner that incorporates the best of traditional environmental management practices.

The protection of the fragile mountain ecosystems of Earth must be undertaken with a commitment to provide sustainable livelihoods for mountain dwellers. To accomplish this without further ecological damage will require an immediate international effort.

Financing

The annual cost estimates for implementing all of the *AGENDA 21* programs relating to alternative livelihoods and watershed development in mountain areas is $13 billion, with about $1.9 billion coming from international aid.

Biological Diversity

Biological diversity (or "biodiversity") is the term applied to the variety of the genes, species and ecosystems found on our planet. It embraces all life forms—from plant and animal life to microorganisms—and the water, land and air in which they live and interact. This richness—the Earth's living wealth—provides an abundant and essential supply of indispensable goods and services for humanity. Biological resources feed and clothe us and provide housing, medicines and spiritual nourishment.

Although only about 1.4 million species have been described, it has been estimated that there are at least 5 million and perhaps as many as 100 million species on Earth. Most of these species are found in the natural ecosystems of forests, savannas, pastures and rangeland, deserts, tundra, rivers, lakes and seas. Farmer's fields and gardens are also of great importance as repositories of biodiversity. Gene banks, botanical gardens, zoos and other germplasm repositories make small but significant contributions.

Conservation

Despite mounting efforts over the past 20 years, the loss of the world's vital biodiversity has continued. The current decline in the Earth's biodiversity is largely the result of human activities. Humanity has systematically destroyed animal habitats, over-harvested lands, inappropriately introduced foreign plants and animals throughout the world and polluted every region on Earth. Although the full consequences of this loss of biodiversity are unknown, there are compelling scientific and ethical, as well as economic, reasons for conserving the many life forms on Earth. Biological resources constitute a capital asset with great potential for yielding sustainable benefits. New ways are constantly being found in which the Earth's rich store of biodiversity can contribute to sustainable development; for example, through new foods, pharmaceuticals and many other products. Efforts must be intensified to conserve the worlds's biodiversity while a comprehensive survey is conducted of all of the potential uses of plant and animal genetic material.

Programs and Activities

- Urgent and decisive action is needed to conserve and maintain genes, species and ecosystems, with a view to the sustainable management and use of biological resources.

- Capacities for the assessment, study and systematic observation of biodiversity need to be reinforced at all levels.

- Immediate national action and international cooperation are required for the protection of ecosystems and for the conservation of biological and genetic resources.

- The participation and support of local communities is essential to the success of such an approach.

- Recent advances in biotechnology have pointed to the potential use of the genetic material contained in plants, animals and micro-organisms for agricultural, forestry, health and environmental purposes. Mechanisms should be developed for the improvement and sustainable use of biotechnology and its safe transfer. The issues of biotechnology are developed in the next section of this chapter.

- The objectives of the *AGENDA 21* program for the conservation of biological diversity include pressing for adoption of the Convention on Biological Diversity with the widest possible global participation.

- The development of comprehensive national strategies for the conservation of biological diversity must be made a priority.

- Measures for sharing the benefits derived from the development and use of biological and genetic resources should be enacted. National studies and the production of regular world reports on biodiversity are also important.

- The recognition and fostering of traditional methods and the knowledge of indigenous people and their communities is vital.

- Steps must be undertaken to ensure the opportunity for local individuals and groups to share in the economic and commercial benefits derived from the use of such traditional methods and knowledge.

- Broader international and regional cooperation are critical to furthering scientific and economic understanding of the importance of biodiversity.

115

- Arrangements must be developed to ensure that the countries providing genetic resources are able to equitably share in the benefits derived from the commercial use of those resources.

- Ensuring the rights of the country of origin of genetic resources is particularly important in circumstances in which the resources are the basis of biotechnological development.

- The conservation of biological diversity must be integrated into environmental and developmental programs at all levels.

- Special priority must be given to the preservation of land and aquatic genetic resources which may be valuable sources of food.

- Surveys must be undertaken to identify the various components of biological diversity.

- Economic values must be ascribed to specific genetic and biological resources in order to protect them and ensure their prudent use. The potential economic implications of conserving biological diversity must be evaluated.

- Effective economic and social incentives must be provided to encourage the conservation of biological diversity and the sustainable use of biological resources.

- Sustainable methods of agriculture, forestry, range and wildlife management must be developed and introduced which maintain or increase biodiversity.

- Actions must be taken immediately to record, protect and promote the wider application of the knowledge and practices of indigenous and local communities which protect biodiversity.

- Efforts must be taken to ensure that the benefits arising from the use of such traditional techniques and methods are shared fairly with the local communities.

- Long-term research projects must be undertaken into the importance of biodiversity and the role of ecosystems in producing goods and services which support sustainable human development.

- The biology and reproductive capacities of land and water species must be studied in detail, including native, cultivated and cultured species.

- The rehabilitation and restoration of damaged areas must be promoted in order to attempt the recovery of threatened and endangered species.
- Protected land and aquatic areas should be reinforced. Freshwater wetlands, coastal estuaries, coral reefs, mangrove swamps and other particularly vulnerable areas should be provided special protection.
- Actions should be taken to preserve primitive cultivated species and their wild relatives. Viable populations of such species should be maintained in their surroundings, preferably in the country of their origin.
- Governments should set up programs for the exchange of information on the conservation of biological diversity and the sustainable use of biological resources.
- With the close participation of local and indigenous communities, surveys of the current status of biologic and genetic resources should be undertaken.
- The potential economic benefits and social implications of the sustained use of biologic resources must be understood.
- Human activities with significant impacts on biodiversity must be identified and actions taken to limit such impacts.
- Proposed projects in ecologically sensitive areas should undertake environmental impact assessments. Information regarding such environmental assessments must be made widely available and public participation in the decision-making processes encouraged.
- Special attention should be given to transferring appropriate technology to developing countries.
- Biodiversity research and management facilities, such as herbaria, museums, gene banks and laboratories, must be developed and supported in these countries.
- Special emphasis must be accorded the development of technologies that make efficient use of genetic resources yet cause no significant damage to the environment.
- International and national attention needs to be focused on the critical importance of conserving the Earth's biodiversity.
- The sustainable use of the world's biological resources must be integrated into the policy-making and decision-making levels in all

governments, business enterprises and lending institutions. These topics must also be included in educational programs in all countries. The protection of the rich biological diversity of this planet is vital to the continued health and welfare of humanity.

Financing

The estimated average annual total cost of implementing all of the *AGENDA 21* programs relating to conserving biodiversity is $3.5 billion. About $1.75 billion is required from international grants or aid.

Biotechnology

Biotechnology is a set of techniques for bringing about specific man-made changes in the genetic material in plants, animals and microbes. The goal of modern biotechnology is to develop useful products and technology from these plant, animal and microbe sources. In recent years, there has been much hope that biotechnology can alleviate many of the problems related to humanity's impact on the Earth. By itself, biotechnology cannot resolve all the fundamental problems of environment and development. Expectations for the potential of biotechnology need to be tempered by realism. Nevertheless, the safe use of biotechnological processes promises to make a significant contribution to sustainable development. Modern biotechnology offers the hope of better health care, enhanced food security through sustainable agricultural practices, improved supplies of safe drinking water, more efficient industrial development processes, support for sustainable methods of reforestation and the detoxification of hazardous wastes. Biotechnology also offers new opportunities for global partnerships. Those countries that are rich in biological and genetic resources but are lacking the necessary expertise and investments to apply biotechnology can enter valuable partnerships with those countries that have developed the technological expertise to transform the biological resources.

The process of biotechnology brings with it the promise of increasing the availability of food, feed and renewable raw materials for humanity. Improving human health is also a central focus of this new technology. Enhancing the protection of the environment is another area in which the development of biotechnology may offer considerable hope. Developing and engendering public trust and confidence in the process of biotechnology is also a vital component of success in this area. Internationally agreed-upon principles need to be applied to ensure the environmentally sound management of biotechnology. Biotechnology can be a useful tool in the quest to improve the quality of human life and protect the Earth's environment. The development and implementation of biotechnological products must be done very carefully and with an acute concern for human safety and the protection of the environment.

Food, Feed and Raw Materials

The first area of the *AGENDA 21* program on biotechnology focuses upon the need for increasing the availability of food, feed and renewable raw materials. To meet the accelerating demands of a growing world-wide population, the challenge is to not only increase food production, but also to improve food distribution significantly. In the future, efforts to meet these challenges will be through the successful and environmentally safe application of biotechnology in agriculture. Most of the investment in biotechnology has been in the industrialized world. Since much of the increased food productivity will need to take place in the developing countries, significant new investments in biotechnology will be required in the developing world.

Programs and Activities

- The objective is to apply biotechnology to increase to the optimum possible yield of major crops, livestock and aquaculture species. This will be done by combining the resources of modern biotechnology with conventional plant and animal improvement techniques.

- More diverse use of plant and animal genetic material resources, both hybrid and natural, will be required.

- To insure the sustainable use of forests, the yield of forest products will also be similarly increased.

- To reduce the need for volume increases of food, feed and raw materials, the nutritional value of the crops, animals and microorganisms can be improved.

- In order to eliminate over-dependence on agricultural chemicals, integrated pest, disease and crop management techniques will be increased through the application of biotechnology.

- Biotechnology should be used to evaluate the agricultural potential of marginal lands.

- Applications of biotechnology in forestry should be expanded, particularly in developing countries, both to increase yields and to improve reforestation techniques.

- Efforts to increase the efficiency of nitrogen fixation and mineral absorption in higher plants will also be a major focus of biotechnology research.

- All aspects of the use of biotechnology in the field of agriculture must be done with particular attention to maintaining environmental integrity.

- Governments, academic and scientific institutions should work together to improve plant and animal breeding programs. The aim should be to improve food productivity and the nutritional quality and shelf-life of food and animal feed products.

- Efforts should include attempts to limit pre- and post-harvest crop losses. The development of plant strains which have increased resistance to pests, stress and diseases should be sought.

- The use of underutilized crops should be promoted, particularly those with possible future importance to human nutrition and to the supply of industrial raw materials.

- The safe international exchange of plant, animal and microbial germ plasm should be a goal, including the search for better methods of rapid propagation.

- Improved diagnostic techniques and vaccines need to be developed to prevent the spread of disease and to allow the rapid assessment of toxins in products for human use or livestock feed.

- More productive strains of fast-growing trees, especially for fuel-wood use, need to be developed. Methods to increase the propagation of these species need to be developed to aid in their wider dissemination and use.

- The use of biotechnology to improve the yields of fish, algae and other aquatic species should be evaluated.

- Existing research centers should be strengthened and encouraged to pursue the development of environmentally safe products that are economically and socially feasible.

- Processes need to be developed to increase the availability of the materials developed through biotechnology for use in food, feed and raw material production.
- Potential food production technologies must be compared and the possible effects on international trade in agricultural commodities assessed.
- The implications of withdrawing subsidies that promote the use of agricultural chemicals should also be considered.
- Data banks regarding the health and environmental impact of organisms should be developed. Developing countries must be assisted in accelerating the acquisition of technologies that can promote their food security.
- Creating awareness of the benefits and risks of biotechnology is essential. Training of competent professionals in basic and applied sciences at all levels is one of the most necessary components for the success of biotechnology programs.
- Intensive training programs must be developed for specific projects within developing countries. The availability of comprehensively trained personnel capable of using advanced technology is crucial in the field of biotechnology. Close collaboration should be encouraged between scientists, extension workers and actual users of biotechnology.

Financing

The estimated annual funding required to implement all of the *AGENDA 21* programs in the area of biotechnology research into food, animal feed and raw materials is $5 billion. This total is expected to include about $50 million in concessional grants and aid from the international community.

Human Health

The second program area in the biotechnology section focuses on improving human health. The improvement of human health is one of the most important objectives of development. Increasing levels of environmental degradation, along with poor and inadequate development, continue to take a heavy toll on human health. The world suffers from an accelerating deterioration of environmental quality, particularly air, water and soil pollution from toxic chemicals, hazardous wastes and radiation. Malnutrition, poverty, poor human settlements, lack of clean water and inadequate sanitation add to the problems of communicable and non-communicable diseases. As a consequence, the health and well-being of the populations in many regions of the world are exposed to increasing pressures.

New and improved medicines and other pharmaceutical products have an increasingly important contribution to make in tackling the causes of poor health. The priority objectives of this section are to contribute to an overall health program to help combat the major communicable diseases, as well as to promote good general health among people of all ages. Additional goals are to develop and improve programs for the treatment and protection from major noncommunicable diseases, to develop appropriate safety procedures and to enhance research capacities.

Programs and Activities

Governments, academic and scientific institutions, and the pharmaceutical industry are urged to cooperate in developing the necessary biotechnology to confront global health problems.

- Programs should be developed for identifying those populations in the world most in need of improvement in general health and protection from disease.

- Screening and evaluation procedures for drugs and medical technologies must be established. These procedures should be aimed at barring those that are unsafe and ensuring those that are related to reproductive health are safe and effective.

- Measures should be introduced to improve and evaluate drinking water quality, including the diagnosis of water-borne pathogens and pollutants.

- New and improved vaccines against the major communicable diseases should be developed and made widely available. Such vaccines should be safe, effective and offer protection with the minimum number of doses. Intense efforts should be directed at vaccines to combat the major common diseases which afflict children.

- Biodegradable delivery systems for vaccines which eliminate the need for multiple doses and reduce the costs of immunization should be developed.
- Effective and environmentally sound biological methods to control disease-transmitting carriers, such as mosquitos, must be developed.
- Using modern biotechnological tools, improved diagnostic systems, new drugs, improved treatments and better delivery systems should be sought.
- More effective uses for medicinal plants should be developed and improved.
- New processes must be developed to increase the availability and use of materials derived from biotechnology for use in improving human health.
- Research must be increased into the social, environmental and financial costs and benefits of different technologies for providing basic and reproductive health care.
- A priority must be to develop public education programs directed at both decision-makers and the general public which encourage an awareness of both the benefits and risks of modern biotechnology.
- There must be greater support for the development of national programs for protection from major communicable diseases, common childhood diseases and disease-transmitting carriers.
- Training programs must be developed, particularly in developing countries. Such programs should develop expertise at three levels: for scientists in basic and product-oriented research; for health personnel in the safe use of new products; and for technical workers who will actually deliver the products to people in the field.

Financing

The estimated costs for implementing these programs are about $14 billion annually for the period from 1993 to the year 2000. Approximately $130 million of this total should be supplied by grants or aid from the industrialized countries of the international community.

Environmental Protection

The third biotechnology program area is aimed at enhancing the protection of the environment. Poor land and waste management and the increasing use of chemicals, energy and other resources by an expanding global population have all led to major environmental problems. Despite increasing efforts to prevent waste accumulation and promote recycling, the quantity of waste generated continues to grow. Biotechnology is one of many tools which can help in the efforts to rehabilitate degraded ecosystems and landscapes. Through the development of new techniques for reforestation and afforestation, germplasm conservation and cultivation of new plant varieties suitable for fragile environments, biotechnological advances can significantly enhance the rehabilitation of damaged land and water resources. Biotechnology can also contribute to the study of the effects on ecosystems of organisms which are introduced by humanity. The objective of this program is to prevent, halt and eventually reverse the effects of environmental degradation through the safe use of biotechnology. This will entail the adoption of production processes which make optimal use of natural resources. Success in this area will also require the active promotion of the use of biotechnologies for the rehabilitation of land and water, waste treatment, soil conservation, reforestation and afforestation. The application of biotechnologies and their products for upgrading damaged land and water must always be made with a view to obtaining long-term ecological security.

Programs and Activities

- Alternatives and improvements to production processes which are environmentally damaging must be developed. It is essential that these new processes be as environmentally sound as is possible.

- Industrial applications which minimize the use of synthetic chemicals should be developed. Such applications should maximize the use of environmentally sound products, including natural products.

- Processes must be developed to reduce waste generation and make use of biodegradable material. Processes must also be developed to recover energy and provide renewable energy sources, animal feed and raw materials from the recycling of organic waste and biomass.

- Efficient and inexpensive methods to remove pollutants from the environment must be developed. Such removal methods should also include processes for the clean-up of accidental oil spills.

- In order to increase reforestation efforts and increase sustainable yields from forests, processes should be developed to increase the availability of planting material, particularly stress-tolerant varieties.

- Efforts should be made to promote the judicious use of pest management based on biological control agents and to promote the use of bio-fertilizers.

- Easily-applicable technologies should be developed for the treatment of sewage and organic waste.

- New biotechnologies should be developed and promoted for the tapping of mineral resources in an environmentally-sustainable manner.

- Mechanisms must be developed for the rapid production and distribution of biotechnologies which have high environmental importance. This is particularly important for those types of technology which may have limited commercial potential.

- Close cooperative measures must be undertaken between countries to ensure that useful and environmentally safe biotechnology is available for transfer to those countries where the need is greatest.

- Universities and technical institutes must increase the availability of training programs for all levels of technical and support personnel. This training should include the exchange of support personnel between countries.

- There is also an urgent need to increase the level of understanding among decision-makers regarding the benefits and dangers of biotechnology.

Financing

Implementing the various programs related to the use of biotechnology for environmental protection purposes is estimated to require approximately $1 billion annually for the period from 1993-2000. Of this total, about $10 million will be necessary from international funding sources on a grant or direct aid basis.

Safety and International Cooperation

Integral to the application of biotechnology is a program area for enhancing safety and developing international mechanisms for cooperation. There is an urgent need for the further development of internationally agreed-upon principles on risk assessment and management of all aspects of biotechnology. These international safety principles can build upon those developed at national levels. Only when adequate and unambiguous safety procedures are in place will the world community be able to derive the maximum benefits from biotechnology. With readily-understandable safety principles in place, humanity will be in a much better position to accept the potential benefits and risks of biotechnology. The objective is to ensure safety in the development, application and transfer of biotechnology. Human health and environmental considerations are paramount. The widest possible public participation in developing and implementing safety standards is necessary.

Programs and Activities

- All existing safety procedures relating to biotechnology need to be compiled. These current safety procedures should be made widely available and evaluated by the scientific community.

- These existing safety procedures must then be further developed into a framework of internationally-agreed upon safety principles for the development and use of biotechnology.

- These international safety procedures must be made widely available. Training programs must be undertaken regarding the application of the proposed technical guidelines.

- An information exchange should be developed for providing assistance in the safe handling and management of biotechnology. Information relating to the conditions for release of biotechnological organisms must be accessible.

- There must also be procedures set up for providing immediate assistance in the case of any biotechnological emergencies.

Financing

The average annual total cost of implementing these aspects of biotechnology is approximately $2 million, all from international sources.

Applications of Biotechnology

The final *AGENDA 21* biotechnology program in this area is aimed at establishing mechanisms for the environmentally sound application of biotechnology. A major international effort will be required to apply the results of rapid advances in biotechnology, particularly in the developing countries of the world. These efforts need to be coupled with efforts to enhance training capacity, technical know-how, research and development facilities, industrial capacity and expertise regarding the protection of intellectual property rights.

Programs and Activities

- The objective is to provide the necessary support for research and product development and to raise public awareness of the benefits and risks of biotechnology.

- In addition, the aim must be to help create a favorable climate for investments, industrial development and the distribution and marketing of biotechnological products.

- Efforts must also be aimed at encouraging the international exchange of scientists, yet discourage "brain drain" of key scientists from the developing world.

- Additionally, efforts must be made to foster the traditional methods and knowledge of indigenous people and their local communities and enable them to participate in any benefits arising from developments in biotechnology.

- Increased training at all university levels must be encouraged. Graduate, post-graduate and post-doctoral studies in biotechnology must be increased, as well as the training of technicians and support staff.

- In addition, training must be offered in design, engineering, marketing and consultant services to support the application of biotechnology.

- Training programs for lecturers to train scientists throughout the world will also need to be developed.

- Biotechnology research and development is undertaken both in highly sophisticated conditions and at the practical level. Efforts will be needed to ensure that research, extension and application facilities are available on a widespread basis.

Financing

The total estimated costs for implementing all of the activities proposed in *AGENDA 21* relating to the application of biotechnology are approximately $5 million annually in funds from the international community.

* * *

All of the preceding program areas of *AGENDA 21* focus on the natural resources of the Earth. There is an urgent need to reverse the destruction of renewable resources and to implement strategies for the sustainable use of land, fresh water and biological and genetic resources. The central thrust of these Agenda 21 action programs is to incorporate a comprehensive understanding of natural resources into economic development. The multi-interest uses of these resources for agriculture, forestry, industry, fisheries, recreation and other activities must be developed with a concern for the protection of the environment. The core challenge here is to raise productivity and incomes, especially of the poor, without irreversibly degrading and depleting the fragile environments of Earth. Such development must be done in a manner that raises productivity and meets rising human demands while ensuring the sustainable management of the Earth resources. The world's fresh water resources must be carefully protected and sustained. The gift of agriculture must be honed to achieve a balance with the environment upon which it depends. The Earth's most fragile ecosystems—its deserts, mountains and forests—must be provided with special protection. The rich biodiversity of our planet must be conserved and managed in a manner that will sustain the human benefits of such diversity well into the future. Biotechnology can assist humankind in these efforts, but prudent conservation practices and the development of sustainable techniques must remain the central approach to these problems.

Chapter 4

The Protection of Our Global Commons

The development of human society has historically been based on a close relationship with the local environment. The focus of most current environmental protection efforts is also on the local environment. Although world trade enables virtually all regions of the Earth to have access to the products and resources of the entire planet, it is only in recent years that humanity has begun to grasp the importance of the portions of the Earth that are shared by all—the global commons. The sustainable management of the world's common global resources—its atmosphere and oceans—is of vital interest to the future of humanity. Environmental changes to the atmosphere or oceans can fundamentally affect the habitability of the entire planet. The ways in which human activities affect these essential global resources are diverse and complex, yet the severity of human influence on the atmosphere and oceans is beyond question.

Early in 1992, two events highlighted the growing problems of human impact on these global common areas. Depletion of ozone over the northern latitudes was found to be creating a hole in the atmosphere similar to the one discovered earlier over Antarctica. At the same time, the largest city in the world was partially shut down by air pollution that reached extremely hazardous levels. Climate change is perhaps the most intractable threat to human well-being and the survival of many species on Earth.

Though its full consequences are uncertain, atmospheric pollution, and particularly the threat of greenhouse warming, is today a major concern to the international community. This is due to both its potential impact upon human welfare and its profound implications for policy making, particularly energy policy. There is a growing scientific consensus that the emission of greenhouse gases by modern human society is causing fundamental changes in the Earth's climate. The industrialized countries of Earth are responsible for most greenhouse gas emissions, yet it is the developing countries which are most likely to experience the worst impacts of climate change. Even a small rise in the Earth's sea level could have disastrous consequences on humanity, particularly on islands and in low-lying coastal areas. Increased financial and technical support to developing countries will be needed to enable them to respond to climate change and to allow them to take less polluting paths in their development.

The pollution of the world's oceans and the over-exploitation of its living marine resources are devastating their enormous productive potential. These activities are also immediately threatening the human populations which are dependent on the sea for their sustenance and livelihoods. Overfishing and the degradation of marine habitats throughout the world are depleting a major global food resource. Steps must be taken to maintain fish populations at sustainable levels. National licensing programs should be used to allocate access to fish resources more equitably among commercial and recreational fishers. Developing countries need assistance to promote deep-sea fishing to reduce the use of coastal fisheries.

These global problems present a formidable challenge for all humanity. The nations of the world must be united in cooperation and commitment if efforts to solve these problems are to succeed. The causes of these problems, many of them indirect, are highly interwoven into modern production processes and contemporary consumption patterns. Solving these problems will require the world community to act outside of the normal time scales of political and economic decision-making. Many of the necessary decisions will need to be based on evidence that, while compelling, is incomplete. In some important cases, the evidence itself is controversial. Even developing a basic understanding of these complex problems will require considerable monitoring and increased information-gathering on both global and local levels. The sustainable management of the common resources of Earth will inevitably affect human lifestyles and welfare everywhere. The global dimension and threats of ozone depletion, climate change, air pollution, marine pollution and depletion of marine life resources require a commitment and partnership between all nations to curtail harmful activities and to ensure the equitable and sustainable use of these shared resources.

The Atmosphere

The Earth's protecting atmosphere is beset today by three major interrelated problems. Increasing greenhouse gas concentrations threaten to provoke abnormal and drastic climate change. The combustion of fuels is causing extensive local and international air pollution. Finally, emissions of halocarbons are gradually destroying the Earth's protective ozone layer.

Greenhouse gases include carbon dioxide, methane, nitrous oxide, halocarbons and atmospheric water vapor. All of these gases except halocarbons are naturally occurring. However, the rapid increase of human activities has changed the net emission rates of these gases to the point that their overpresence in the atmosphere is beginning to cause serious environmental impacts. Greenhouse gases are emitted through energy conversion, as well as through industrial and agricultural activities. Consequently, any strategy to address climate change must address a number of segments of human society simultaneously.

Fueled by the increase in human activity, greenhouse gases are building up in the atmosphere of the Earth. At the same time, the forests and soils that provide natural sinks for carbon dioxide, the most important greenhouse gas, are being threatened by air pollution, land clearing and other harmful man-made processes. These forest and soil resources help to absorb excess levels of carbon dioxide in the Earth's atmosphere. So, as certain human activities are causing an increase in the levels of greenhouse gases, other human actions are destroying important segments of the Earth's natural abilities to counteract this dangerous buildup.

Local and international air pollution originates from the combustion of fossil and, to a lesser extent, biomass fuels. Air quality in many urban areas has deteriorated and resulted in an increased incidence of respiratory diseases and other health ailments. In some industrialized countries, international air pollution has caused severe acidification of forests, lakes and soils. In the developing countries, indoor air pollution produced by the traditional burning of low-quality biomass fuels (such as dung or wet wood) and fossil fuels (such as low-quality coal) has harmed the health of women and children in particular. Unsustainable energy supply and consumption patterns lie at the core of the air pollution problem. Consequently, promoting sustainable energy development is a major priority for solving global air pollution problems.

In order to improve atmospheric problems associated with fossil fuel use, concerted action is required in a number of economic areas, including energy, industrial manufacturing, transportation, agriculture, forestry and other land-use industries. The energy industry is the largest contributor to these problems, but it also has the largest potential for improvement. The world community should rapidly begin to make an energy transition to patterns of energy production and consumption that rely more on environmentally sound energy systems. Such new energy systems must place a high value on efficiency of energy production and consumption. Worldwide, countries need to promote energy efficiency measures in the use of conventional fossil fuels, particularly in the use of oil and coal. The nations of the world must also increase the percentage of their energy supply mix which is devoted to new and environmentally sound energy systems, particularly renewable energy sources.

To confront the enormous problems posed by damage to the Earth's atmosphere will require a global approach. There are 8 program areas in *AGENDA 21* relating to protection of the atmosphere. These areas deal with the need for more scientific information, the promotion of sustainable development, energy efficiency, transportation, industry, land and resource use, ozone depletion and air pollution.

Scientific Knowledge

Although there exists a substantial body of knowledge about the atmosphere, concerns about climate change, air pollution and ozone depletion have created new demands for information. There is an urgent need to address the uncertainties in this area and provide a scientific basis for decision-making. Expanded research will be required to better understand the physical, chemical and biological properties of climate and how these properties affect local and global ecosystems and human health. By intensifying scientific and technological research, particularly on climate change, vital information will be accessible. Making the results of such research immediately available world-wide will be a priority. This will allow the world's leaders to be better able to implement the necessary programs to confront the problems of atmospheric change. Comprehensive observing systems to detect both the current state and trends in the atmosphere and in ecosystems will also be required. Further research on the effects of these changes and possible global responses are also an essential requirement.

The basic objective of this program area is to improve human understanding of the processes that influence and are influenced by the Earth's atmosphere. These include physical, chemical, geological, biological, oceanic and hydrological processes. It is also necessary to improve human understanding of the economic and social consequences of atmospheric changes.

Programs and Activities

- Governments should promote research related to the natural processes affecting and being affected by the atmosphere. More research is also necessary into the critical links between development and atmospheric changes. Atmospheric impacts on human health, ecosystems, economic activities and society must be fully understood

- Systematic observation stations and early detection systems should be developed to monitor changes and fluctuations in the atmosphere. Methods should also be implemented to predict such changes and fluctuations and to assess the resulting environmental, social and economic impacts of climate change.

- Research is necessary to identify threshold levels of atmospheric pollutants, as well as levels of greenhouse gas concentrations that can cause dangerous interference with the climate system and the environment as a whole. It is also essential to establish the rates of change in the levels of greenhouse gases and pollutants that may overwhelm the ability of global ecosystems to adapt naturally.

- Finally, governments should cooperate in the exchange of scientific data and information and the training of experts and technical staff in the fields of research, data assembly, assessment and observation, particularly in developing countries.

Financing

The estimated annual costs associated with implementing all of the programs for increasing scientific knowledge about the atmosphere are $640 million, all of which is expected to be provided by grants and aid from the international community.

Energy Efficiency and Development

Energy use is essential to economic and social development and the improved quality of human life. Much of the world's energy, however, is currently produced and consumed in ways that cannot be sustained, particularly if the overall quantities of fuel consumed were to increase substantially. Even at current levels, there is a critical need to control the emissions of greenhouse gases and other substances which harm the Earth's atmosphere. Increasingly, energy production, transmission, distribution and consumption will need to be based on efficiency. There must also be a growing reliance on environmentally sound energy systems, particularly new and renewable sources of energy. New and renewable energy sources are solar thermal, solar photovoltaic, wind, hydro, biomass, geothermal, ocean, animal and human power. All energy sources will need to be used in ways that respect the atmosphere, human health and the environment as a whole.

Increasing the use of environmentally sound energy will require much effort. Funding for research and development of these options will need to be increased considerably. Countries must act to remove any market barriers to the development and use of environmentally sound energy. More efficient energy use patterns and an increased supply of environmentally sound energy can be achieved in different manners by various countries, in accordance with their economic, political and technical circumstances. However, any set of measures will have to feature a mixture of economic instruments that will provide incentives for energy suppliers and consumers to make environmentally sound choices. From an industrial standpoint, methods must be developed to incorporate the environmental costs of industrial production into the price of the final products. These true costs must include the cost of treating and disposing of industrial wastes. The decision-making processes in the energy and manufacturing industries must include a consideration of these environmental costs.

The basic and ultimate objective of this area is to reduce adverse effects on the atmosphere from energy use by promoting policies which increase the use of environmentally safe and sound energy systems, particularly new and renewable ones. Less polluting and more efficient energy systems are the goal. This objective must reflect the need for adequate energy supplies and increasing energy consumption in developing countries. In achieving this goal, the situations of countries that are highly dependent on income generated from the production, processing, export or consumption of fossil fuels must also be taken into consideration. Countries that may have serious difficulties in switching to alternative energy sources must also be considered. Countries which are highly vulnerable to the adverse effects of climate change must be given special attention.

The following *AGENDA 21* program areas all relate to global energy use: energy efficiency, transportation, industrial development and land-use and resource development. The financing requirements for all four of these energy program areas are combined and listed after the programs and activities relating to land-use and resource development.

Programs and Activities

- There must be a global effort in identifying and developing economically viable and environmentally sound energy sources. These efforts must be directed at increasing the energy supplies in developing countries.

- Environmental impact assessments should be employed at the national level to promote integrated energy, environmental and economic policy decisions.

- Research, development, transfer and use of improved energy-efficient technologies should be promoted. Special attention should be given to the rehabilitation and modernization of current power systems, particularly in developing countries.

- Research and development must also be increased into environmentally sound energy systems, including new and renewable energy systems. The transfer and use of these systems must be encouraged.

- Current energy supply mixes should be reviewed to determine how the contribution of environmentally sound energy systems could be increased in an economically efficient manner. Measures should be developed to overcome any barriers to their development and use.

- New and more efficient systems for the distribution of environmentally sound renewable energy sources should be sought.

- National administrative, social and economic policies should be put into effect which promote energy efficiency. Energy efficiency and emission standards aimed at the development and use of technologies that minimize adverse impacts on the environment should be developed.

- Education and awareness-raising programs must be instituted at the local and national levels regarding energy efficiency and environmentally sound energy use.

- Labelling programs for products should be established in order to provide decision-makers and consumers with information on opportunities for energy efficiency.

Transportation

Transportation is crucial for any modern economy. The transportation industry consumes a particularly large portion of energy and, in the process, produces large amounts of greenhouse gases as well as other air pollutants. The energy efficiency of virtually all transportation systems can and must be increased considerably. At the same time, innovative technical measures can considerably reduce emissions. These can include new engine designs, alternative fuels and add-on pollution abatement devices. Especially in urban areas, a shift in transportation from inefficient polluting modes to more efficient and cleaner modes should be encouraged. Rail and mass transit systems should be encouraged.

These technical solutions, however, only address a minor dimension of the transportation issue. The design of urban, suburban and industrial developments, including the location of dwellings and workplaces, must begin to take into account fundamental environmental considerations, such as atmospheric pollution, noise and congestion. The basic objective is to develop and promote cost-effective policies or programs to limit, reduce or control harmful atmospheric emissions and other adverse environmental effects of the transportation industry.

Programs and Activities

- There must be a much greater effort to develop and promote cost effective, more efficient, less polluting and safer transport systems; particularly rural and urban mass transit systems.

- Environmentally sound road networks must also be planned and developed, particularly in developing countries.

- Developing countries must be afforded access to safe, efficient and less polluting transportation technologies. The transfer of such technologies on reasonable terms must also be increased and promoted.

- Appropriate training programs for personnel to implement and support such technology must also be developed.

- Efforts at collecting, analyzing and exchanging information on the relationship between the environment and transportation must be increased.

- National policies which encourage the use of transportation that minimizes adverse impacts on the atmosphere should be developed.

- Comprehensive transportation strategies must be integrated into all urban planning, with a view to reducing the environmental impacts of all modes of transportation.

Industrial Development

Industry is essential for the production of goods and services and is a major source of employment and income. Industrial development is essential for economic growth. At the same time, industry is a major resource and materials user and industrial activities result in extensive emissions into the atmosphere and the environment as a whole. Protection of the atmosphere can be enhanced by increasing resource and material efficiency in industry, by installing or improving pollution abatement technologies and by replacing chlorofluorocarbons (CFCs) and other ozone-depleting substances with appropriate substitutes. The reduction in industrial wastes and by-products will also reduce industrial pressure on the environment. The goals of this area are to encourage industrial development in ways that minimize adverse impacts on the atmosphere. These objectives may be met by increasing industrial efficiency in the production and consumption of all resources and materials and by developing new environmentally sound technologies.

Programs and Activities

- National policies and programs should be developed which use various administrative, social and economic measures in order to minimize industrial pollution and adverse impacts on the atmosphere.

- Industry must be encouraged to develop technologies, products and processes which are safe, less polluting, and make more efficient use of all resources and materials, including energy. There must be much greater cooperation in the transfer of such industrial technologies to developing countries.

- To foster sustainable industrial development, environmental impact assessments of all industrial development must be developed and applied.

- In order to encourage industry to understand the economic and environmental benefits of using resources more efficiently and producing less wastes, the efficient use of materials and resources must be promoted.

- Industry must be encouraged to take the full life cycles of products into account in their planning and decision-making processes.

- With a view to limiting industrial pollution, governments must support the promotion of less polluting and more efficient technologies and processes in industries.

Land-Use and Resource Development

Global land and resource-use practices both affect and are affected by changes in the atmosphere. Many current resource and land-use practices are decreasing greenhouse gas absorption and, at the same time, increasing atmospheric emissions. Atmospheric changes can have important impacts on forests, biodiversity and freshwater and marine ecosystems, as well as on economic activities, such as agriculture. The loss of biological diversity may reduce the global resilience to climatic variations and air pollution damage.

Together with animal and human energy, in the rural areas of most developing countries the main source of energy is biomass. At the household level, biomass fuels (wood, crop residues and manure) account for over one-third of the energy supplies in the developing world. These fuels are primarily used for cooking. The pollution and health consequences of this cooking method, often in confined indoor spaces, are very serious in many countries. Apart from improving the efficiencies of biomass cooking stoves, the transition to more efficient commercial energy sources for cooking in developing countries should be an integral part of long-term household energy strategies.

Rural energy policies and technology should promote a mix of fossil and renewable energy sources that is sustainable and ensures sustainable agriculture and rural development. In rural areas, the energy transition from wood fuels to more diversified sources of energy must ensure that communities have a stable and affordable energy supply to succeed the informal wood-based energy markets.

The objectives of this program area are to promote resource and land-use practices that contribute to reducing atmospheric pollution and enhancing the sinks and reservoirs for greenhouse gases. Such practices must also have as a goal the conservation and sustainable use of natural resources.

Programs and Activities

- National policies must be developed which use social and economic measures to promote and encourage environmentally sound land-use practices.

- At the same time, policies and programs should be implemented that discourage inappropriate and polluting land-use practices and promote the sustainable use of land and marine resources.

- Efforts must be undertaken to promote the development and use of resources and land that will be more resilient to atmospheric changes and fluctuations.

- Cooperation must be increased in the conservation and management of the global reservoirs for greenhouse gases, including the forests and the oceans.

Financing

The cost estimates for implementing all of the *AGENDA 21* program areas related to energy, including the programs on energy efficiency, transportation, industrial development and resource/land-use are in the range of $20 billion. All of this funding is necessary from international sources on grant or aid terms.

Ozone Depletion

The problem of ozone depletion is one of major proportions for the global environment. In recent years, there has been definitive scientific evidence that the global ozone layer is being depleted by human activity. Analysis of recent scientific data has confirmed the continuing depletion of the Earth's stratospheric ozone layer by reactive chlorine and bromine from man-made CFCs, halons and related substances. This depletion is largely caused by halocarbon emissions from industrial sources. The result of this ozone depletion is that increased amounts of ultraviolet radiation are reaching the Earth's surface. The most serious confirmed effects of this increased radiation are on human health in the form of increased skin cancers and eye diseases. Increased ultraviolet radiation is thought to have major, but as yet not fully determined, effects on micro-organisms living in the surface layers of the ocean, which may in turn affect the entire oceanic food chain. Some of the proposed replacements for ozone-depleting substances are themselves also potent greenhouse gases.

In 1985, the world community recognized the problem of ozone depletion and enacted the Vienna Convention for the Protection of the Ozone Layer. This agreement was significantly strengthened in 1987 with the Montreal Protocol on Substances that Deplete the Ozone Layer, and again in 1990 in London with amendments to the Montreal agreement. While implementation of the 1987 Montreal Protocol (as amended in London in 1990) will limit halocarbon emissions, there are current indications that more radical cutbacks are in order. Despite these important international actions to protect the Earth's ozone layer, the total atmospheric content of ozone-depleting substances has continued to rise.

A number of actions are being proposed which, if implemented, will contribute to preventing stratospheric ozone depletion.

The main objectives of this program area are to realize the objectives defined in the Montreal Protocol and its 1990 London amendments for limiting the production and use of substances that deplete the ozone layer. Technologies and natural products that reduce demand for these substances should be encouraged. Nations must also act cooperatively to develop strategies aimed at mitigating the adverse effects of ultraviolet radiation which is reaching the Earth's surface as a consequence of depletion of the stratospheric ozone layer.

Programs and Activities

- All governments must ratify, accept or approve the Montreal Protocol and its 1990 amendments and pay their contributions towards the Vienna and Montreal trust funds.

- Immediate efforts must be taken to make substitutes for CFCs and other ozone-depleting substances available around the world. Transfer of the necessary technologies to avoid CFC use must be made rapidly to developing countries in order to enable them to comply with the obligations of the Montreal Protocol.

- The Global Ozone Observing System must be expanded, especially in the tropical belt in the southern hemisphere.

- There must be continuous assessment of scientific information regarding the health and environmental effects of stratospheric ozone depletion. The technological and economic implications of eliminating CFC use must also be carefully considered.

- Based on the results of research on the effects of the additional ultraviolet radiation reaching the Earth's surface, governments must consider taking appropriate remedial measures in the fields of human health, agriculture and marine environment.

- Efforts must be taken throughout industry to replace CFCs and other ozone-depleting substances, recognizing that a CFC replacement's suitability should be evaluated holistically and not simply based on its contribution to solving one atmospheric or environmental problem.

Financing

The estimated average total annual costs (1993-2000) of implementing the activities in this area are in the range of $160-590 million. This total will be will be required from the international community on grant or aid terms.

Air Pollution

There is a global scientific consensus that increased concentrations of greenhouse gases will lead to an overall global warming. An anticipated doubling of carbon dioxide concentration between now and 2025-2050 is projected to raise the global mean temperature 1.5-5 degrees centigrade and surface ocean layer temperatures by 2-2.5 degrees centigrade. The impacts of such a rise would be felt everywhere, particularly the polar regions. Such a global warming would raise sea levels 0.3-0.5 meters by 2050 and about 1 meter by 2100. The impacts on low-lying coastal areas and island nations could be devastating. The effects on ecosystems are not certain, but local climatic patterns, including precipitation, wind and temperature patterns would almost certainly change. Such climate changes would significantly and unpredictably affect the Earth's agriculture, forests, natural vegetation and wildlife.

International air pollution has also been shown to cause adverse health effects on humans. Tree and forest loss and the acidification of water bodies are also the direct result of air pollution. The geographical distribution of pollution monitoring networks is uneven, with the developing countries severely underrepresented. The lack of reliable emissions data outside Europe and North America is a major constraint to measuring international air pollution. There is also insufficient information on the environmental and health effects of air pollution.

The international community is now developing a framework convention on climate change in order to tackle this problem in a comprehensive and equitable manner. In the negotiations on the convention, commitments on greenhouse gas reductions, on maintaining carbon sinks and on financing the required transition in developing countries are being discussed. Stabilizing and reducing global greenhouse gas concentrations to tolerable levels is also being discussed. The need to adopt more sustainable production and consumption patterns is also a part of negotiations to confront the challenges of climate change and air pollution.

In order to mitigate the human production of carbon dioxide, it is important to create new natural reservoirs for carbon dioxide and enhance existing ones, particularly through increasing forestry and soil management activities. Reducing the rates of deforestation may be a first step, followed by increased reforestation efforts. Use of wood fuel to replace fossil fuels is another way to reduce carbon dioxide emissions. Other techniques, such as increasing the carbon content of soils, can provide temporary carbon sinks or reservoirs. Countries whose agricultural practices produce high methane emissions should adopt cropping and fertilizing systems to reduce such emissions.

The overall objective in the area of global air pollution is to develop methods to better assess and monitor the extent and effects of global atmospheric pollution. Efforts must then be directed at reducing international air pollution at its sources and mitigating the effects of any necessary pollution.

Programs and Activities

- Regional agreements regarding international air pollution control must be established. There must also be much greater cooperation, particularly with developing countries, in the areas of observation and assessment of air pollution. In this context, greater emphasis should be put on understanding the extent, causes, health and social and economic impacts of ultraviolet radiation, acidification of the environment and photo-oxidant damage to forests and other vegetation.

- Early warning systems and emergency response mechanisms for international air pollution which results from industrial accidents, natural disasters and the deliberate or accidental destruction of natural resources should be established.

- Programs should be implemented to identify specific actions to reduce atmospheric emissions and to address their environmental, economic, social and health effects.

- Existing legal instruments have created institutional structures which address many of these programs and objectives. Efforts must be made

to ensure compliance with the existing international agreements relating to international air pollution.

- Education and awareness-raising programs need to be introduced and
strengthened at the local, national and international levels concerning
the protection of the atmosphere.

Financing

AGENDA 21 has provided no cost estimates for the implementation of
the programs in the area of international air pollution. The costs related
to this area will be provided in other areas of *AGENDA 21*.

The Oceans

At an earlier point in history, the oceans were regarded as infinitely
vast. The ocean's living resources were considered unlimited. The capacity of the oceans to absorb and recycle the waste of human society was
considered endless. Current trends in marine pollution and fishing have
shown that this is no longer the case. The world's oceans are in trouble—
serious and potentially catastrophic trouble.

The world's oceans and seas—the marine environment—comprise an
essential component of the global life support system. The Earth's oceans
and seas cover 70 percent of the planet's surface and play a dominant
and decisive role in the Earth's biological, geological and chemical processes. Global energy, climate and weather, the hydrological and carbon
cycles, and atmospheric and physical processes are all critically influenced by oceanic processes. Yet our understanding of these processes
lags far behind our knowledge of the Earth's land and atmospheric processes. The long-term sustainable management of the world's resources
must be based both on a sound understanding of how the ocean shapes
global conditions and on a proper evaluation of the potential benefits of
marine resources.

Degradation of the marine environment results from a wide range of
activities on land, often due to an excess of economic and industrial
growth. Human populations and their land use, agriculture, forestry,
fisheries, urban development, tourism and industry all influence the marine environment. Of the land-based sources of marine pollution, some
30 percent arrives via industrial and urban runoff and through rivers. 20

percent of marine pollution is deposited via the atmosphere, while municipal wastes contribute about 50 percent. Contaminants which pose the greatest threat to the marine environment include sewage, agricultural run-off, pesticides and fertilizers, synthetic organic compounds, sediments, litter and plastics, metals, radionuclides, oil/hydrocarbons, and polycyclic aromatic hydrocarbons. Marine pollution is also caused by shipping and sea-based activities. Approximately 600,000 tons of oil enter the oceans each year, as a result of normal shipping operations, accidents and illegal discharges.

Coastal and island settlements are threatened by human activities such as fishing, shipping, tourism, urban waste and pollution These fragile areas are impacted by all types of human development—industry, agriculture and forestry. Half of the world's population lives less than six kilometers from the sea. By the year 2020, three-fourths of humanity may reside in this coastal zone, which today includes many poor, densely crowded settlements. The well-being of the inhabitants of these areas is closely related to the condition of fragile coastal environments. Environmentally destructive practices in coastal regions must be curbed and damaged areas must be restored.

Ocean management policy must be integrated horizontally, across all disciplines, departments and specialized agencies, as well as public and private organizations. Ocean management must also be conducted vertically, through national, regional and global levels of governance. International law, as reflected in the United Nations Convention on the Law of the Sea, offers the most appropriate and comprehensive framework as a legal instrument for the management of the world's oceans. This international agreement effectively integrates the protection of the environment from pollution, whether land-based, oceanic or atmospheric, with the economic development of living and non-living ocean resources. The Law of the Sea establishes an important balance between the rights of nations and their obligations, including those relating to conservation of the marine environment and its resources.

The programs proposed in this section of *AGENDA 21* encompass several areas of oceanic protection: coastal areas, marine environmental protection; the conservation of marine living resources; scientific uncertainties regarding the marine environment and climate change; international cooperation and protection of island nations.

Coastal Areas

The coastal areas on Earth are one of the most important regions in terms of human development. More than 60 percent of the people on Earth live within 60 kilometers of an ocean or sea shoreline. This percentage could rise to three-quarters by the year 2020. Two-thirds of the world's cities with populations of 2.5 million or more are near tidal estuaries. Many of the world's poor are crowded into the coastal areas. The resources in these fragile coastal environs are vital for many local communities and indigenous people. Coastal zones, the interface between land and sea, are not simply transition areas. They contain highly diverse ecosystems and some of the world's most biologically productive habitats. Human uses of coastal space are many and include settlement, food production, derivation of energy, minerals and other raw materials, tourism, recreation and transportation. Currently, coastal zone boundaries are defined by various political, administrative and ecological considerations.

Coastal zones, in a sense, act as the "sink" of the continents. Their degradation and pollution have both local and distant inland sources. Inland sources of pollution which impact upon coastal areas include poor land-use practices, over-fertilization, pest control, poor watershed management and the clearing of forests on steep lands. Local sources of pollution stem from the general increase in industrial output and the rapid expansion of human settlements, ports and recreational areas. Despite major efforts, the current approach to coastal development does not provide an effective framework for achieving sustainability and resolving conflicts over resource use. Without effective action, the vital coastal environment is being rapidly degraded and eroded in many parts of the industrialized and developing world.

The current patterns of coastal area management reflect historical conditions which are no longer valid. For example, in the past, coastal populations were low and their fishing technologies less advanced, so the supply of ocean and coastal resources was sufficient. Today, however, expanding populations have greatly increased the demand placed on coastal fisheries. Current policies regarding the uses of coastal environments are creating conflicts among users, as well as significant resource depletion and environmental degradation. Coastal management plans must recognize the need for strategies that prevent environmental damage and promote economic growth while ensuring the equitable allocation of user-rights. This requires a comprehensive management approach that fully evaluates the coastal resource base and its opportunities and constraints.

Programs and Activities

- To effectively develop and protect the world's coastal areas, a key priority must be to prepare guidelines and adopt comprehensive local, national and regional coastal zone management plans. This is particularly important with regard to the fragile inter-related ecosystems such as those found in low-lying countries and enclosed and semi-enclosed seas. Existing and projected uses of coastal areas should be identified.

- National resource and environmental accounting systems must be implemented which reflect changes in value resulting from the uses of coastal areas, including pollution, marine erosion, loss of resources and habitat destruction.

- Appropriate policies and legal frameworks for land-use should be formulated. These policies should regulate all phases of the management and use of coastal areas and promote environmentally sound technology and sustainable practices.

- Environmental impact assessments should be mandatory for all coastal development.

- Contingency plans should be prepared to deal with potential natural disasters, including potential sea-level rise due to climate changes.

- Contingency plans must also be developed to deal with increasing levels of pollution, including potential future oil spills.

- The human settlements in the coastal areas must be improved. Better housing must be developed; drinking water supplies must be protected; and immediate efforts must be taken to upgrade the disposal of sewage and solid and industrial waste. The problems of human coastal settlements are more fully dealt with in Chapter 5: The Management of Human Settlements.

- Efforts must be undertaken to restore damaged wildlife habitats. Coastal nations should undertake measures to maintain the biological diversity and productivity of marine species within their jurisdictions.

- These measures should include surveys of marine life, inventories of endangered species, examinations of critical coastal habitats and the establishment and management of protected natural areas.
- Coastal nations should cooperate with each other in the development of coastal observation systems. Scientific research in all of these vital areas should be supported.
- Equally as important, the results of the research must be disseminated to all decision-makers and concerned members of the public in an understandable format.
- Mechanisms should be established to ensure the active participation of academic institutions, private industry, women, youth, indigenous people and local groups in all aspects of government planning.
- At all planning and decision-making levels, concerned individuals, groups and organizations must be given access to all relevant information. For comprehensive coastal management plans to succeed, public participation in the planning process is vital.
- Education and training must be increased with an aim to provide a core of professionals with a working knowledge of comprehensive coastal management.
- Scientists, technologists and managers (including community-based managers) must be trained. Indigenous people, fisherfolk, women and youth in coastal areas should be encouraged to participate in training and education programs.
- Environmentally sound management techniques and environmental protection concerns should be incorporated into any coastal management curricula.
- All coastal nations should establish mechanisms which allow for the consultation of all relevant groups in the planning and management of coastal areas. Such mechanisms should allow for input from the academic and business community, as well as from local groups and indigenous people.

Financing

The costs of implementing these programs for the protection and sound development of coastal areas are estimated to be $6 billion annually with about $50 million coming from the international community in the form of grants.

Marine Protection and Management

Degradation of the marine environment can result from a wide range of sources. Land-based sources contribute 70 per cent of marine pollution, while maritime transportation and dumping-at-sea activities contribute 10 per cent each. A wide range of activities on land contribute to the contamination of the marine environment. Human settlements, land use, construction of coastal infrastructure, agriculture, forestry, urban development, tourism and industry can affect the marine environment. Coastal erosion and siltation cause significant problems. Many of the substances which pollute the marine environment but which originate from land-based sources are of particular concern since they are often toxic, persistent and have a tendency to accumulate in the food chain. There is currently no global scheme to address marine pollution from land-based sources.

Marine pollution is also caused by shipping and sea-based activities. Approximately 600,000 tons of oil enter the oceans each year as a result of normal shipping operations, accidents and illegal discharges. Discharges from offshore oil and gas activities are currently regulated internationally and the nature and extent of environmental impacts from these activities generally account for a very small proportion of marine pollution.

Protecting the marine environment requires an approach that anticipates problems rather than merely reacts to difficulties. Such an approach should involve the use of environmental impact assessments, application of specific criteria for classifying hazardous substances and a comprehensive approach towards addressing damaging impacts from air, land and water pollution. Systematic data on the marine environment will be needed to apply comprehensive management approaches and predict the effects of global climate change on fisheries. In order to determine the role of the oceans in driving global systems, mechanisms that collect, analyze and disseminate ocean information from research and monitoring activities need to be restructured and reinforced considerably. This will also enable scientists to predict natural and man-induced changes in marine and coastal ecosystems. A coordinated approach which integrates all relevant environmental and developmental aspects of ocean resources is essential.

Programs and Activities

- All activities related to the oceans must generally apply preventive and anticipatory approaches in order to avoid pollution of the marine environment, as well as to reduce the risk of long-term or irreversible adverse effects upon it.

- There must be prior environmental impact assessments made of activities that may have significant adverse impacts upon the marine environment.

- Economic incentives to apply clean technologies should be developed. "Polluter pays" principles and other economic methods to value environmental costs should also be applied to those activities that contribute to marine pollution.

- The living standards of coastal populations, particularly in developing countries, must be improved in order to contribute to reducing the degradation of the coastal and marine environment.

- National governments need to comply with and consider updating, strengthening and extending the Montreal Guidelines for the Protection of the Marine Environment from Land-Based Sources.

- New means must be developed for providing international guidance on technologies to deal with the major types of pollution of the marine environment from land-based sources.

- Sewage treatment concerns must be considered whenever coastal development plans are formulated or reviewed.

- Sewage treatment facilities must be located and built so as to maintain an acceptable level of environmental quality and to avoid exposing shell fisheries, water intakes and bathing areas to pathogens. Environmental impact assessments should be performed for all new sewage treatment installations.

- Environmentally sound treatment of domestic and industrial effluents must be developed and implemented. This must include promoting the primary treatment of all municipal sewage discharged into rivers, estuaries and the sea. The development and application of effluent recycling technologies is also a requirement.

- The development and application of low-cost and low-maintenance sewage installation and treatment technologies for developing countries must be a priority.

- An international funding mechanism should be created for the application of appropriate sewage treatment technologies and building sewage treatment facilities.

- Regulatory and monitoring programs must be established to control effluent discharge, using minimum sewage effluent guidelines and water quality criteria.

- The emission or discharge of organohalogen compounds that threaten to accumulate to dangerous levels in the marine environment must be totally eliminated.

- The emission or discharge of other synthetic organic compounds that threaten to accumulate to dangerous levels in the marine environment must be reduced.

- Controls over the inputs of nitrogen and phosphorus that enter coastal waters must be established, especially in areas where problems, such as eutrophication, immediately threaten the marine environment or its resources.

- Industrialized countries must cooperate with developing countries, through financial and technological support, to control and reduce the discharge of substances and wastes that are toxic, persistent or liable to accumulate in marine food chains. To this end, environmentally sound land-based waste disposal alternatives to sea dumping should be established.

- Environmentally sound land-use techniques to reduce run-off must be developed and implemented.

- The use of environmentally less harmful pesticides and fertilizers and alternative methods for pest control must be promoted. Those agricultural chemicals which have been found to be environmentally unsound should be prohibited.

- At the national level, new initiatives for controlling the input of land-source pollutants must be undertaken. Such initiatives will require broad changes in sewage and waste management, agricultural practices, mining, construction and transportation.

- The control and prevention of coastal erosion and siltation due to land-use and construction techniques and practices must be a priority.

- Watershed management practices which prevent, control and reduce degradation of the marine environment should be promoted.

- Greater efforts should be taken in monitoring marine pollution from ships, especially from illegal discharges. Aerial surveillance should be increased in this regard.

- There must be increased actions to assess the state of pollution caused by ships, particularly in sensitive, rare or fragile ecosystem areas, such as coral reefs and mangroves.

- Rules regarding the discharge of ballast water to prevent the spread of non-indigenous organisms should be developed and implemented.

- In order to reduce the risks of marine accidents, navigational safety should be promoted by adequate charting of coasts and ship-routing.

- The need for stricter international regulations to further reduce the risk of accidents and pollution from cargo ships (including bulk carriers) should be investigated. A complete consideration of a code on the carriage of irradiated nuclear fuel in flasks on board ships must be undertaken.

- Appropriate measures for reducing air pollution from ships and the development of international rules governing the transportation of hazardous substances carried by ships should be developed.

- Appropriate steps to stop ocean dumping and the open ocean incineration of hazardous substances should be taken.

- Existing regulatory measures regarding discharges, emissions and safety on offshore oil and gas platforms should be assessed.

- Major port facilities for the collection of oily and chemical residues and garbage from ships should be established. Similar smaller scale facilities in marinas and fishing harbors should also be promoted.

- Assessments must be made of the state of marine pollution in areas of congested shipping, such as heavily-used international straits, with a view to ensuring compliance with international regulations, particularly those related to illegal discharges from ships.

- All nations should take measures to reduce water pollution caused by organotin compounds used in marine anti-fouling paints.

- The use of persistent organohalogens that are liable to accumulate in the marine environment must be studied to identify those that cannot be adequately controlled and should be prohibited.

- Assistance should be provided to industries world-wide in identifying and adopting clean production or cost-effective pollution control technologies.

- Contingency plans on the national and international level for oil and chemical spills must be developed. Oil/chemical-spill response centers should be established or strengthened. Such plans should also include the training of spill-response personnel. Such training programs should be developed in cooperation with the oil and chemical industries.

- Appropriate oil- and chemical-spill control materials should be identified. These should include low-cost locally available materials and techniques which are suitable for pollution emergencies in developing countries.

- Building on existing facilities, systematic observation systems to measure marine environmental quality should be established. The information compiled should be regularly exchanged.

- A clearing-house on marine pollution control information and technologies should be established. This should include a global database providing information on the sources, types, amounts and effects of pollutants reaching the marine environment.

- Training for critical personnel required for the adequate protection of the marine environment must be provided on all levels. Marine environmental protection topics should be introduced into the curriculum of all marine studies programs.

- Efforts should be undertaken to provide secure financing for new and existing international centers of professional maritime education.

- Research facilities should be strengthened or developed in developing countries for the systematic observation of marine pollution and to support environmental impact assessment. Such facilities should be managed and staffed by local experts.

- In carrying out all of these activities, particular attention needs to be given to developing countries that would bear an unequal burden because of their lack of facilities, expertise or technical capacities.

Financing

The estimated average total annual costs (1993-2000) of implementing the activities of this program are about $200 million from the international community on grant or concessional terms.

Marine Living Resources

There is a wide spectrum of different types of life forms in the Earth's oceans. About 20,000 species of freshwater and saltwater living resources have been identified while many more species remain to be discovered. Of the roughly 9,000 species that are harvested, only 22 species support significant fisheries. Fishing yields have increased nearly fivefold over the past four decades. The commercial harvest of fishes, crustaceans and mollusks in 1990 amounted to 98 million metric tons, which is equivalent to the estimated sustainable annual yield from conventional fisheries. Over 80 percent of the commercial harvest is marine catch, mainly from the coastal and continental shelf seas which are within national jurisdictions. High seas fisheries represent only about 5 percent of the total world landings.

The cultivation and harvesting of captive and raised fish today yields approximately 5 million metric tons per year and this total is expected to double by the end of this century. In addition, small-scale local fisheries yield approximately 24 million metric tons annually. Socially, such small-scale local fisheries are the most important since they contribute significantly to fisheries employment and are critical in providing balanced food nutrition, particularly in coastal developing countries.

Marine living resources provide an important source of protein in many countries and their use is often of major importance to local communities and indigenous people. Such resources provide food and livelihoods to millions of people and, if sustainably utilized, offer great potential to meet nutritional and social needs, particularly in developing countries. At present, fisheries account for some 16 percent of the total animal protein consumption in the world. This contribution is about the same as for beef and pork. The diversity of fish species is important, in that it provides consumers with a wider choice in taste preference and promotes biodiversity by decentralizing fishing efforts. About a quarter of the world's marine production is processed into meal for livestock.

The rise in marine catches over the last two decades has largely been the result of discoveries of new resources, the introduction of new fishing technologies and the implementation of the Law of the Sea. However, management of high seas fisheries, including the enforcement of effective conservation measures, is inadequate in many areas. Many marine resources are currently over-harvested.

Many countries face mounting problems including local overfishing, unauthorized incursions by foreign vessels, environmental degradation, increased fluctuations in fish stocks, excessive fleet sizes, insufficiently selective gear, increasing competition between small-scale fishing and industrial fishing and conflicts between fishing and other types of activities. Coastal nations and developing countries must be enabled to obtain the full social and economic benefits from the sustainable utilization of marine living resources within their national jurisdiction. This is particularly critical in developing countries whose economies are overwhelmingly dependent on the exploitation of the marine living resources within their exclusive jurisdiction.

The problems relating to marine living resources extend well beyond fisheries. Coral reefs and other coastal habitats such as mangroves and estuaries are among the most highly diverse and productive of the Earth's ecosystems. They often serve important ecological functions, provide coastal protection and are critical resources for food, energy, tourism and economic development. In many parts of the world, such marine and coastal systems are under stress or are threatened from a variety of sources, both human and natural. Estuaries, near-shore environments and enclosed and semi-enclosed seas have been particularly degraded.

The sustainable use and conservation of marine living resources is of significant social, economic and nutritional importance to humanity. Marine living resources can make a substantial contribution to national food security. The use of marine species for human food should be increased by promoting direct consumption, avoiding wastage and improving techniques of harvest, handling and transportation. As the world's population increases to over 6.3 billion by the year 2000, it will be necessary to maximize food production from all sources, especially in light of existing pressures on agricultural land resources. To this end, it is necessary to maintain or restore populations of marine species at levels that can produce the maximum sustainable yield.

To realize the full potential of sustainable yield of marine resources requires improved knowledge and identification of marine living resource stocks, particularly of under-utilized and non-utilized stocks and species. The use of new technologies, better handling and processing facilities to avoid wastage, and improved quality and training of skilled personnel to manage and conserve marine living resources is also a priority requirement.

The emphasis in protecting the sustainability of the Earth's living marine resources should be on multi-species management and other approaches that take into account the relationships among species. These issues are important to preserve the vital biological diversity and ecological integrity of marine ecosystems by protecting critical habitats and endangered species. A central focus should be the provisions of the United Nations Convention on the Law of the Sea on marine living resources. This international agreement sets forth the rights and obligations of nations regarding the conservation and utilization of these vital resources.

The program and activity areas of this section will be divided into two sections: high-seas marine resources and marine resources which are under national jurisdiction.

High-Seas Marine Resources
Programs and Activities

- It is necessary for government and industry to promote the development and use of selective fishing gear and practices that minimize waste in the catch of target species.

- Measures must be taken to ensure that fishing activities by vessels flying their flags on the high seas take place in a manner that minimizes the incidental catch of non-target species.

- All nations should act to prohibit, limit or regulate the exploitation of marine mammals on the high seas more strictly. They should cooperate with a view to the conservation of marine mammals. In the case of whales and dolphins, all nations should work through the appropriate international organizations for their conservation, management and study.

- All nations should act to ensure that high-seas fisheries are managed in accordance with the provisions of the Law of the Sea. In particular, nations should give full effect to those provisions regarding fish stocks whose ranges lie both within and beyond national jurisdictions and those fish populations that are comprised of highly migratory species.
- New international agreements for the effective management and conservation of fishery stocks must be negotiated, particularly regarding fish stocks which straddle jurisdictions and highly migratory stocks.
- Effective action must be taken to monitor and control fishing activities by vessels flying their flags on the high seas to ensure compliance with all conservation and management rules, including full, detailed, accurate and timely reporting of catches and fishing efforts.
- Strong action must be taken to deter reflagging of vessels by their nationals as a means of avoiding compliance with conservation and management rules for fishing activities on the high seas.
- Dynamiting, poisoning, large-scale open-sea drift-net fishing and other comparable destructive fishing practices must be prohibited.
- Measures should be implemented to increase the availability of marine living resources as human food by reducing wastage, post-harvest losses and discards, and improving techniques of processing, distribution and transportation.
- There must be global cooperation in the collection and regular exchange of data necessary for the conservation and sustainable use of the marine living resources of the high seas.
- Cooperative databases on high-seas marine living resources and fisheries should be developed and made widely available.
- Analytical and predictive tools, such as stock assessment and bio-economic models should be developed and shared.
- Immediate efforts should be undertaken to assess high-seas resource potentials and develop profiles of all stocks (target and non-target).
- Data on the marine environmental situation should be gathered and analyzed, including the impacts of regional and global changes brought about by natural causes and by human activities.
- Efforts should be undertaken to develop technical and research programs to improve understanding of the life cycles and migrations of

species found on the high seas, including identifying critical areas and life stages.

- Training programs in high-seas fishing techniques and in high-seas resource assessment should be established, including efforts to develop personnel to deal with high-seas resource management, conservation and related environmental issues.

- Programs should be developed and enhanced to provide for the training of observers and inspectors to be placed on fishing vessels.

- All nations should cooperate to develop or upgrade systems for the surveillance, monitoring and control of high-seas fishing.

- In order that they may participate effectively in the conservation and sustainable utilization of high-seas marine living resources, developing countries will need special support to enhance their capacities in the areas of data and information, scientific and technological means, and human resource development.

Financing

The average total annual costs of implementing the activities of this program are estimated to be about $12 million, all of which will be necessary from the international community.

National Jurisdiction Marine Resources Programs and Activities

- All nations should commit themselves to the conservation and sustainable use of marine living resources under their national jurisdiction. To this end, it is necessary to develop and increase the potential of marine living resources to meet human nutritional needs, as well as social, economic and development goals. The harvesting of marine living resources should be developed to eliminate malnutrition and to achieve food self-sufficiency in developing countries.

- The traditional knowledge and interests of local communities, small-scale fisheries and indigenous people must be of paramount importance in the development of management programs.

- Special efforts must be taken to maintain or restore populations of marine species at levels that can produce the maximum sustainable yield according to all relevant environmental and economic factors.

- Governments and the fishing industry must cooperate in the development and use of selective fishing gear and practices that minimize waste in the catch of target species and minimize the catch of non-target species.

- Efforts must be taken to protect and restore endangered marine species and preserve rare or fragile ecosystems, as well as habitats and other ecologically sensitive areas.

- All nations should act to ensure that marine living resources under national jurisdiction are conserved and managed in accordance with the provisions of the United Nations Convention on the Law of the Sea.

- Coastal nations must develop inventories to assess the potential of marine living resources, including under-utilized or non-utilized stocks and species.

- To meet human nutritional and other development needs, national strategies for the sustainable use of marine living resources should be implemented, taking into account the special needs and interests of small-scale fisheries, local communities and indigenous people.

- Particularly in developing countries, mechanisms to develop mariculture, aquaculture and small-scale oceanic fisheries should be developed. This should be undertaken only after assessments show that marine living resources are potentially available and that the introduction of new species will result in no environmental harm.

- Both national governments and the fishing industry should take measures to increase the availability of marine living resources as human food by reducing wastage, post-harvest losses and discards, and improving techniques of processing, distribution and transportation of seafood.

- The use of environmentally sound technology should be developed and promoted, including assessment of the environmental impact of major new fishery practices.

- Coastal nations should explore the scope for expanding recreational and tourist activities based on marine living resources, including those for providing alternative sources of income. Such activities should be compatible with conservation and sustainable development policies and plans.

- Coastal nations should support the sustainability of small-scale fisheries by integrating small-scale fisheries development in marine and coastal planning. The representation of fisherfolk, small-scale fisherworkers, women, local communities and indigenous people should be encouraged in such planning.

- Systems should be developed for the acquisition and recording of traditional knowledge concerning marine living resources and the marine environment. Methods by which to incorporate such knowledge into management systems should be developed.

- In the negotiation and implementation of international agreements on the development or conservation of marine living resources, the interests of local communities and indigenous people must be taken into account, particularly their right to subsistence.

- All nations should prohibit dynamiting, poisoning and other comparable destructive fishing practices.

- Marine ecosystems with high levels of biodiversity and productivity and other critical habitat areas should be identified. Limitations on fishing and other use in these areas should be developed, for example through designation as protected areas. Priority should be accorded to coral reef ecosystems; estuaries; temperate and tropical wetlands, including mangroves; seagrass beds and other spawning and nursery areas.

- The collection and regular exchange of up-to-date data necessary for the conservation and sustainable use of the marine living resources under national jurisdiction must be enhanced.

- Comprehensive monitoring and assessment programs should be developed in order to obtain vital information on marine biodiversity, marine living resources and critical habitats. Such programs should take into account all changes in the environment which are brought about by natural causes and human activities.

- Efforts should be undertaken to develop financial and technical cooperation to enhance the capacities of developing countries in small-scale and oceanic fisheries, as well as in small-scale coastal aquaculture and mariculture.

- In order to promote access to markets, improve consumer confidence and maximize economic returns, measures should be taken to promote seafood quality, including national quality assurance systems for seafood.

- All nations should cooperate for the conservation, management and study of whales and dolphins.

- Methods should be developed to provide for the transfer of environmentally sound technologies to develop fisheries, aquaculture and mariculture, particularly to developing countries.

- Special attention should be accorded to mechanisms for transferring current information and improved fishing and aquaculture technologies to fishing communities at the local level.

- Sustainable aquaculture strategies should be established, including environmental management in support of rural fish-farming communities.

- Technical and financial assistance should be provided to organize, maintain, exchange and improve traditional knowledge of marine living resources and fishing techniques, and upgrade local knowledge on marine ecosystems.

- Much more study and scientific assessment is needed into the use of traditional fisheries management systems.

- Support should be provided to local fishing communities, in particular those that rely on fishing for subsistence.

- Increased scientific research should be undertaken on marine areas of particular importance for marine living resources, such as areas of high diversity, high productivity and migratory stopover points.

- Developing countries should be encouraged to expand multidisciplinary education, training and research on marine living resources, particularly in the social and economic sciences.

- Training opportunities should be created to support small-scale and subsistence fisheries and to encourage equitable participation of local communities, small-scale fisherworkers, women and indigenous people.

- Topics relating to the importance of marine living resources should be introduced into educational curricula at all levels.

- Special efforts will be needed to enhance the capacities of developing countries in the areas of data and information, scientific and technological means and human resource development in order to enable them to participate effectively in the conservation and sustainable use of marine living resources.

Financing

Implementing the activities of this program will cost an estimated $6 billion. This total cost includes about $60 million from the international community on grant or aid terms.

Increasing Scientific Understanding

The marine environment is vulnerable and sensitive to climate and atmospheric changes. Rational use and development of coastal areas and marine resources, as well as conservation of the marine environment, requires the ability to determine the present state of these systems and to predict future conditions. A relatively high level of scientific uncertainty exists regarding the extent and effects of human activity on the marine environment. This uncertainty has thwarted effective management of marine resources and limited the capacity to make useful predictions and assessments regarding oceanic environmental change.

There are many uncertainties about climate change and, in particular, sea-level rise. Small increases in sea-level have the potential to cause significant damage to small islands and low-lying coasts. Strategies to respond to these growing problems must be based on sound data. A long-term cooperative research commitment is needed to provide the data required for global climate models and to reduce scientific uncertainty. Meanwhile, measures should be undertaken to diminish the risks and effects of climate change, particularly on small islands and on low-lying and coastal areas of the world.

Increased ultraviolet radiation derived from ozone depletion has been reported in some areas of the world. An assessment of its effects on the marine environment is needed to reduce uncertainty and to provide a basis for action.

Systematic collection of data on the marine environment is needed to apply comprehensive management approaches and to predict the effects of global climate change on living marine resources and the marine environment. A much greater global research and observation effort is necessary in order to determine the role of the oceans and seas in driving global systems and to predict natural and human-induced changes in marine environments. The current mechanisms to collect, analyze and disseminate information from research and observation activities need to be restructured and reinforced considerably.

Programs and Activities

- At all levels, efforts should be undertaken to promote scientific research on and systematic observation of the marine environment, including interactions with atmospheric phenomena, such as ozone depletion.

- There must be provisions for the exchange of data and information resulting from such scientific research and observation and from traditional ecological knowledge. This must be done on a regular basis in order to ensure its availability to policy makers and the public.

- International cooperation is necessary for the development of standard procedures, measuring techniques, data storage and management capabilities for scientific research and observation of the marine environment.

- Efforts must be undertaken to provide improved forecasts of marine conditions for the safety of inhabitants of coastal areas and for the efficiency of maritime operations.

- Special measures to cope with and adapt to potential climate change and sea-level rise should be adopted. These measures should include the development of methods to assess the vulnerability of coastal areas, particularly low-lying coastal areas and small islands.

- Ongoing and planned programs of systematic observation of the marine environment should be coordinated, with a view to integrating activities and establishing priorities for oceans and seas.

- A research program to determine the marine biological effects of increased levels of ultraviolet rays due to the depletion of the ozone layer should be established.

- Recognizing the important role that oceans and seas play in moderating potential climate change, research should be carried out regarding the role of oceans as a carbon sink.

- There must be greater international cooperation in analyzing, assessing and predicting global climate and environmental change. To this end, the collection, analysis and distribution of data and information from the oceans and seas must be a priority.

- Technical assistance for marine research and observation must be provided to developing coastal and island nations .

- In recognition of the value of Antarctica as an area for the conduct of scientific research essential to understanding the global environment, nations carrying out such research activities in Antarctica should continue to ensure that data and information resulting from such research is freely available to the international community. Access of the international scientific community to such data and information should be increased, including through the encouragement of periodic seminars and symposia.

- There should be a global review of existing regional and global databases on the marine environment. Mechanisms to develop compatible techniques and formats for the presentation, storage and communication of information should be developed.

- Immediate efforts must begin for the systematic observation of coastal habitats and sea-level changes, inventories of marine pollution sources and reviews of fisheries statistics. One aim should be predicting the effects of climate-related emergencies on existing coastal physical, social and economic infrastructures.

- Based on the results of research on the effects of the additional ultraviolet radiation reaching the Earth's surface, nations should consider taking appropriate remedial measures in the fields of human health, agriculture and the marine environment.

- Industrialized countries should provide the financing for the further development and implementation of the Global Ocean Observing System.

- At every level, the global scientific community should share expensive and sophisticated equipment, develop quality assurance procedures and develop human resources jointly. Special attention should be given to the transfer of scientific and technological knowledge, particularly to developing countries.

• National scientific and technological oceanographic commissions should be developed or strengthened to coordinate marine science activities and work closely with international organizations.

Financing

Approximately $750 million is estimated to be required to implement all of the activities in this program area, including about $480 million from the international community in the form of grants or aid.

International Cooperation

The role of international cooperation is vital to support and supplement national efforts in the management and protection of the marine environment. Through *AGENDA 21*, all nations have agreed that environmental policies should deal with the root causes of environmental degradation. This will prevent environmental measures from causing unnecessary restrictions to international trade. Trade policy measures for environmental purposes should not constitute a means of arbitrary or unjustifiable discrimination or a disguised restriction on international trade.

Unilateral actions to deal with environmental challenges outside the jurisdiction of the importing country should be avoided. Environmental measures addressing international environmental problems should, as far as possible, be based on an international consensus. Domestic measures targeted to achieve certain environmental objectives may need trade measures to render them effective. Should trade policy measures be found necessary for the enforcement of environmental policies, certain principles and rules should apply.

These should include the principle of non-discrimination and the principle that the trade measure chosen should be the least trade-restrictive necessary to achieve the objectives. There should also be an obligation to ensure that the use of trade measures related to the environment are open and above-board and to provide adequate notification of national regulations. Consideration should be given to the special conditions of developing countries as they move towards internationally agreed-upon environmental objectives. No other specific program activities are delineated.

Financing

It is estimated that the average total annual cost of implementing this program will be about $50 million from the international community.

Islands

Small island developing nations and islands which support small communities are special cases for both environmental and developmental reasons. They are ecologically fragile and vulnerable. Their small size, limited resources, geographic dispersion and isolation from markets place them at a disadvantage economically. These factors also prevent them from taking advantage of economies of scale. For small island developing nations, the ocean and coastal environment is of strategic importance and constitutes a valuable development resource.

The relative geographic isolation of many small island nations has resulted in a comparatively large number of unique species of flora and fauna. Small island habitats contain a very high share of global biodiversity. They also have rich and diverse human cultures that have developed special adaptations to island environments. Because of their isolation, many of these cultures have a deep knowledge of the sound management of limited island resources.

Concentrated in limited land areas, small islands have all of the environmental problems and challenges of continental coastal zones. They are extremely vulnerable to global warming and any sea-level rise. Several small low-lying island nations face an intensifying threat of the loss of their entire national territory. Most tropical island nations are already now experiencing the increasing frequency of cyclones, storms and hurricanes associated with climate change. These natural disasters are causing major set-backs to their economic development. The economic development of many small island nations depends on the marine resources in waters under their national jurisdiction and on the high seas.

The small scale of many island nations places inherent limits on their total development potential. The total capacity of small islands will always be limited. Existing development on small islands must be restructured to efficiently meet the needs for sustainable development. New environmentally sound technologies should be used to increase the capacity of very small populations to meet their own needs. At the same time, adequate assistance from the international community must be directed at strengthening the full range of human resources needed to implement sustainable development plans on islands.

Programs and Activities

- In view of their limited capacity and financial means, it is very important for small island nations to adopt and implement sustainable development plans. These development plans should include strategies for meeting essential human needs, maintaining biodiversity and increasing the quality of life for island peoples.

- Medium and long-term plans for sustainable development should be developed that anticipate multiple uses of limited local resources.

- Such plans should also identify various types of development which would be compatible with the limits of these resources. This will involve adapting coastal area management techniques to the special characteristics of islands.

- Inventories of natural resources, critical habitats and species should be undertaken. Measures to protect endangered species and maintain biodiversity should be enacted.

- Actions to cope with environmental change and to mitigate impacts and reduce the threats posed to marine and coastal resources should be adopted.

- Since the small populations of many island nations cannot support specialized professionals in all of the necessary areas, education programs must be directed toward training managers, scientists and planners who are versatile in many areas.

- The overall carrying capacity of small island nations should be estimated under different development scenarios. The vulnerability of small islands to global change and potential sea-level rise should be assessed. Contingency plans to cope with potential climate change and sea-level rise should be developed.

- Additional information on the geographic, environmental, cultural and economic characteristics of islands should be compiled to assist in the planning process. Existing island databases should be expanded and geographic information systems developed to suit the special characteristics of islands.

- New technologies that can increase the output and range of capability of the limited human resources on small islands should be employed to increase the capacity of very small populations to meet their needs.

- Efforts must also be taken to identify technologies that should be excluded because of their threats to essential island ecosystems

- The development and application of traditional knowledge to improve the capacity of countries to implement sustainable development should be fostered.

- Small island developing nations should develop and strengthen inter-island and regional cooperation and information exchange, including periodic meetings on the sustainable development of small island nations. The first global conference on the sustainable development of small island developing nations should be held in 1993.

- Centers for the development of scientific information and advice on technical means and technologies should be established or strengthened.

Financing

The estimated cost of implementing all of the activities in *AGENDA 21* which relate to small islands is $130 million annually. Approximately $50 million of this total should be provided from international funding sources.

* * *

The protecting layer of the atmosphere is essential for the existence of all life on Earth. The enormous increase in the emissions of gases from human activity, particularly carbon dioxide from the use of fossil fuels, is creating a global greenhouse effect. The depletion of the ozone layer from halocarbons is now a scientific certainty. There is, however, no certainty as to what the long-term effects of such massive changes in the global environment will be. Potentially at least, the effects could be disastrous to much of humanity.

As we begin to understand more about the interconnectedness of the global environment, we can begin to appreciate the enormous role that the Earth's oceans play in providing the conditions that can sustain human life. With this increased understanding comes an appreciation of the extent of damage that human activities have already wreaked upon the oceans and the marine life within them.

Because of their unique status as areas under no country's jurisdiction, the Earth's common areas have lacked protection from the increasing activities of humanity. As human impact on these global common areas increases and the threat of irreversible environmental damage grows, the global community must begin to seriously cooperate in the protection and preservation of these vital areas. Immediate and decisive action is necessary to reverse the damage that humanity has caused to the mutual air and water resources of the Earth. Together the nations of the world must act to carefully manage these critical shared areas.

Chapter 5

The Management of Human Settlements

Shortly after the turn of the century, half of the world's population will be living in cities. This urbanization of society into human settlements is an expected outcome of the development of civilization. It opens new opportunities to society and allows for the efficient provision of basic services to urban inhabitants. Urbanization also consolidates the means of production, leading to greater industrial efficiency. Generating some 60 percent of the global Gross National Product, cities are a major force behind national economic growth. In developing countries, cities are enlarging by 60 million inhabitants annually, a pattern that will lead to a net doubling of urban populations in the next 25 years. This rapid and precipitous growth is putting enormous pressure on urban-area infrastructures—infrastructures which are already under severe stress and are unable to meet the current needs of existing inhabitants. Overcrowding, inadequate housing, insufficient access to clean water and sanitation, growing amounts of uncollected waste and deteriorating air quality are already serious problems in these cities. These urban difficulties may worsen substantially if effective and timely action is not taken to solve the problems of human settlements.

At present, urban human settlements absorb two-thirds of the total annual population increases in the developing world. At this rate, close to 2 billion people will populate the urban areas of developing countries by the year 2000. Of these, some 600 million will have been added to urban areas during the present decade alone. Another 2 billion people are expected to be added to the urban population of developing countries between 2000 and 2025. This rapid concentration of people into urban settlements presents complex planning and management problems in the areas of shelter, health, energy, transportation, water supplies and waste management. There is a dramatic need to develop policies that can connect public, private, academic and social institutions to provide solutions to these growing problems.

As enormous amounts of new inhabitants populate urban areas, safe and healthy shelter needs to be provided at an increasing rate. Comprehensive strategies must be adopted which can provide adequate quantities of satisfactory housing for all urban dwellers. The United Nations Global Strategy for Shelter to the Year 2000 is an effective plan to follow in meeting these needs.

Health considerations should be incorporated into all aspects of urban development policy. Factors which influence urban health include noise pollution, radiation and waste from factories and power plants. New technologies and a greater level of infrastructure are needed to monitor air and water quality. Anti-pollution laws need to be enacted and enforced. Indoor smoke from wood fires and coal stoves is a major health hazard for millions of urban dwellers in developing countries. Economic incentives and education campaigns are important to induce people to switch to healthier methods of heating their homes and cooking.

Rapid urban population growth is also endangering water supplies and quality. Access to safe water must be provided to all urban residents. The treatment and safe disposal of an increasing proportion of solid wastes, including sewage, needs priority attention. In the industrialized countries, this attention must involve avoiding the discharge of sludge into rivers and at sea. In the developing countries, less than 10 percent of urban waste receives any treatment whatsoever and only a small fraction of that treatment meets any quality standards. All countries need to establish disposal standards based on the local capacity of the environment to safely assimilate the waste produced. New approaches have to be developed for the collection, storage and disposal of urban waste products.

171

From the governmental to the individual level, a coordinated approach is necessary to ensure the provision of essential infrastructure and services, such as housing, transportation, clean water, municipal waste management, health services and employment. Policy management in these areas must be planned for not only the present inhabitants but also those expected to arrive in the coming decades. Only through such a comprehensive approach can governments effectively address the complex problems of sustainable urban development and realize the full economic and social potential that cities have to offer.

Cities are major catalysts of economic growth. In industrialized countries, the consumption patterns of cities are severely stressing the global ecosystem. On the other hand, urban settlements in the developing world need more raw materials, energy, and economic development simply to overcome basic economic and social problems. Economic activities tend to concentrate in the urban centers where today one-third of the total population generates some 60 percent of the global Gross National Product. Better urban management can improve living conditions, protect natural resources, support sustainable rural development and accelerate national growth. With proper management, cities can provide health, education and social services not only to their own residents but also to many more people who cannot find adequate services in smaller settlements and sparsely populated rural areas.

Human settlement conditions in many parts of the world, particularly the developing countries, are deteriorating. As the physical environment in and around growing cities declines, those affected most are the poor. Urban poor make up over one-third of the urban population in developing countries and their numbers are rapidly growing. For most city dwellers in the developing countries, living conditions are worsening as a result of the inability of city or national governments to provide satisfactory services for drinking water, sanitation, solid waste disposal, transportation and energy for cooking and heating. For the urban poor, the environmental priorities remain improved housing and the provision of basic health care, water and sanitation services at affordable costs.

A major reason for urban deterioration is the low level of government investment in the basic infrastructure of many cities. This lack of investment is directly attributable to the overall lack of resources in these countries. In the low-income countries for which recent data is available, an average of only 5.6 percent of central government expenditures went to housing, services, social security and welfare. In developing countries, Sri Lanka, which has embarked on a vigorous housing program, achieved a high of 15.1 percent. In industrialized countries, during the same year, the percentage of central government spending on the same items ranged from a minimum of 29.3 percent to a maximum of 49.4 percent, with an average expenditure of 39 percent.

Expenditures by international aid and finance organizations are equally low. Only 1 percent of the United Nations total grant-financed expenditures in 1988 went to human settlements. In 1991, loans from the World Bank and the International Development Association for urban development and water supply and sewerage amounted to only about 5.5 percent of their total lending.

On the other hand, available information indicates that international technical cooperation activities in urban settlements generate considerable public and private investment. For example, in 1988, every dollar invested by the United Nations Development Programme in technical cooperation activities on human settlements generated a follow-up investment of $122, the highest level of all U.N. Development Programme investments. This is the foundation of the "enabling approach" advocated in *AGENDA 21* for human settlements. External international assistance will help to generate the internal national resources needed to improve the living and working environments of all people by the year 2000 and beyond. At the same time, the environmental implications of urban development must be recognized and addressed by all countries. A high priority must being given to the needs of the urban and rural poor, the unemployed and the growing number of people in urban areas without any source of income.

The overall objective in the area of human settlements is to improve the social, economic and environmental quality of human settlements and the living and working environments of all people, in particular the urban and rural poor. Such improvement should be based on technical cooperation activities, partnerships among public, private and community organizations and participation in the decision-making process from community groups and special interest groups such as women, indigenous people, the elderly and the disabled. These approaches form the core principles of national settlement strategies.

In developing strategies to confront the problems of human settlements, nations will need to set priorities among the eight program areas in this chapter. The program areas included in this chapter are: adequate shelter, settlement management, land-use planning and management, urban infrastructure (water, sanitation, drainage, hazardous and solid waste management), energy and transportation, disaster-prone areas, construction industry and human resources.

Adequate Shelter

Access to safe and healthy shelter is essential to every person's physical, psychological, social and economic well-being. Providing adequate human shelter should be a fundamental part of national and international action. The right to adequate housing as a basic human right is enshrined in the Universal Declaration of Human Rights. Despite this, it is estimated that at the present time at least 1 billion people do not have access to safe and healthy shelter. If appropriate action is not taken, this number will increase dramatically by the end of the century.

A major world-wide program to address this problem is the Global Strategy for Shelter to the Year 2000, adopted by the General Assembly of the United Nations in December of 1988. Despite its widespread endorsement, the Strategy needs a much greater level of political and financial support to reach its goal of providing adequate shelter for all humanity by the year 2000. The objective in this area is to achieve adequate shelter for rapidly growing populations, particularly the urban and rural poor, through an approach to shelter development and improvement which is environmentally sound.

Programs and Activities

- As a first step towards the goal of providing adequate shelter for all, all countries should take immediate measures to provide shelter to their homeless poor.
- The international community and financial institutions should undertake actions to support the efforts of the developing countries to provide shelter to the poor.

- All countries should adopt or strengthen national shelter strategies with targets based on the principles and recommendations contained in the Global Strategy for Shelter to the Year 2000.

- All people should be protected by law against unfair eviction from their homes or land.

- All countries should support the shelter efforts of the urban and rural poor, the unemployed and homeless. This can be accomplished by adopting or adapting existing codes and regulations to facilitate their access to land, financing and low-cost building materials.

- Programs need to be instituted to actively promote the regularization and upgrading of informal settlements and urban slums.

- All countries should support and develop environmentally compatible shelter strategies through partnerships between the private, public, and community organizations.

- All countries, especially developing ones, should formulate and implement programs to reduce rural to urban emigration by improving rural living conditions.

- All countries should develop and implement resettlement programs which address the specific problems of displaced populations.

- All countries should document and monitor the implementation of their national shelter strategies by using internationally-accepted monitoring guidelines from the United Nations and the World Bank.

- Industrialized countries and funding agencies should provide specific assistance to developing countries in providing training for government officials, professionals, and individuals in community and private organizations. Greater efforts should also be made to strengthen local capacities for the development of appropriate technologies.

Financing

The estimated average total annual costs of implementing the activities of this program are about $75 billion, including about $10 billion from the international community on grant or concessional terms.

Settlement Management

By the turn of the century, the majority of the world's population will be living in cities. While urban settlements, particularly in developing countries, are showing many of the symptoms of the global environment and development crisis, they are also a highly-productive realm of human society. If properly managed, urban areas can develop the capacity to sustain their productivity, improve the living conditions of their residents and manage natural resources in a sustainable way.

Some metropolitan areas extend over the boundaries of several political and administrative entities (counties and municipalities) even though they constitute a continuous urban system. In many cases, this political heterogeneity hinders the implementation of comprehensive environmental management programs. A shared management approach will alleviate some of the problems that such urban areas are confronted with.

The objective in this area is to ensure the sustainable management of all urban settlements, particularly in developing countries. The goal of urban management is to enhance the ability of metropolitan areas to improve the basic living conditions of residents, especially the poor, unemployed and homeless.

Programs and Activities

- One existing framework for strengthening urban management is in the United Nations Development Programme/World Bank/United Nations Center for Human Settlements—Urban Management Programme. This joint program is a concerted global effort to assist developing countries in addressing urban management issues. Its coverage should be extended to all interested countries by the year 2000.

- All countries need to adopt and apply urban management guidelines in the areas of land management, urban environmental management, infrastructure management and municipal finance and administration.

- Efforts to reduce urban poverty must be accelerated. Action to generate employment for the urban poor, particularly women, should be increased.

- Urban employment can be increased through the provision, improvement and maintenance of urban infrastructure and services.

- Support should be provided for informal economic activities which can provide jobs: such as repairs, recycling, services and small commerce.

- Specific assistance must be provided to the poorest of the urban poor through the creation of a social infrastructure in order to reduce hunger and homelessness.

- Support and encouragement should be given to the development of community-based organizations, private voluntary organizations and other forms of non-governmental entities which can contribute to the reduction of poverty and improvements in the quality of life for low-income families.

- Innovative city planning strategies should be adopted which address environmental and social issues by reducing subsidies on and recovering the full costs of services (water supply, sanitation, waste collection, roads and telecommunications) which are provided to higher income neighborhoods. The infusion of income from recovering the full service costs from high-income areas should be used for improving the level of infrastructure and services in poorer urban areas.

- Efforts should be undertaken to develop local strategies for the improvement of the quality of life and the environment in urban areas. This drive should integrate land-use planning, public and private investment and the availability of human and material resources in an overall effort to generate employment which is environmentally sound and protective of human health.

- With the active participation of the business community, all countries should undertake pilot projects in selected cities for the collection and analysis of urban data. These projects should include environmental impact assessments.

- In order to relieve pressure on large urban areas of developing countries, strategies should be implemented for the development of intermediate-size cities.

- Urban planning and management approaches which are specifically suited to the needs and characteristics of growing intermediate-sized cities should be applied.

- Such medium-sized cities can create employment opportunities for unemployed labor in the rural areas and help to support rural-based economic activities.

- Sound urban management of such smaller metropolitan areas is essential to ensure that "urban sprawl" does not expand environmental degradation over an ever wider land area and increase pressures to convert open space and agricultural buffer lands for development. For this purpose, all countries should conduct detailed environmental impact assessments of urban growth.

- Activities aimed at facilitating the transition from rural to urban lifestyles should be developed. Such activities should include the development of small-scale economic activities, particularly the production of food.

- Individual cities must institutionalize an approach to sustainable urban development which is based on a continuous dialogue between everyone involved in urban development. Public, private and community-based groups must be encouraged to participate together in solving urban problems.

- Local communities must be involved in the identification of public services needs, the enhancement of public amenities and the protection and rehabilitation of older buildings, historic precincts and other cultural artifacts.

- Community groups, private organizations and individuals should assume the authority and responsibility for managing and enhancing their immediate environment through participatory tools, techniques and approaches which embrace the concept of environmental care.

- "Green works" programs should be activated to create self-sustaining human development activities and both formal and informal employment opportunities for low-income urban residents.

- Local governing bodies must be equipped to deal more effectively with the broad range of developmental and environmental challenges associated with rapid and sound urban growth.

- Cities should participate in international "sustainable city networks" to exchange experiences and mobilize national and international technical and financial support.

- Environmentally sound and culturally sensitive tourism programs should be formulated. This can be a strategy for decentralizing urban development and for reducing economic discrepancies between regions.

- Developing countries should focus on training and developing urban managers, technicians and administrators to successfully manage environmentally sound urban development and growth. Such personnel should be equipped with the skills necessary to analyze and adapt innovative experiences of other cities. For this purpose, the full range of training methods—from formal education to the use of the mass media—should be utilized, as well as the "learning by doing" option.

- Developing countries should also encourage training and research through joint efforts by donors, private organizations and private business. Such research and development should be in areas such as the reduction of waste, water quality, saving of energy, safe production of chemicals and less polluting transportation.

Financing

The total annual cost for funding all of the program activities in this areas is estimated to be about $100 billion. This total includes approximately $15 billion from the international community.

Land-Use Planning

Land resources are the basis for human settlements and provide soil, energy, water and opportunity for all human activity. When expanding urban slums take hold on peripheral, unsuitable land, they threaten the social and economic fabric of urban life. In rapidly growing urban areas, access to land is rendered increasingly difficult by the conflicting demands of industry, housing, commerce, agriculture, land ownership structures and the need for open spaces. In addition, the rising costs of urban land prevent the poor from gaining access to suitable land. In rural areas, the exploitation of marginal lands and the encroachment on forests and ecologically fragile areas by commercial interests and landless rural populations results in environmental degradation, as well as in diminishing returns for impoverished rural settlers.

179

The objective in this area is to provide for the land requirements of human settlements through environmentally sound planning in order to ensure access to land for all households.

Programs and Activities

- All countries should undertake a comprehensive national inventory of their land resources in order to establish a system in which land will be classified according to its most appropriate uses. In such systems, environmentally fragile or disaster-prone areas should be identified for special protection measures.

- All countries should also develop national land-management plans to guide development. National legislation should be adopted to implement public policies for environmentally sound urban development, land use, housing and urban expansion.

- Efficient and accessible land markets should be created by improving land registry systems and streamlining procedures in land transactions.

- Fiscal incentives and land-use control measures should be used to promote more rational and environmentally sound use of limited land resources.

- Partnerships among public, private and community groups in managing land resources should be encouraged.

- Appropriate forms of land tenure which provide security for all land-users should be established. Efforts should be directed particularly at increasing the land security of indigenous people, women, local communities, low-income urban dwellers and the rural poor.

- Efforts to promote access to land by the urban and rural poor should be accelerated. These should include credit programs for the purchase of land, and for building or improving safe and healthy shelters.

- Improved land management practices must be developed which deal comprehensively with competing land requirements for agriculture, industry, transportation, urban development, green spaces, preserves and other vital needs.

- A very high priority must be to promote understanding among policy makers of the adverse consequences of unplanned settlements in environmentally vulnerable areas.

- At the international level, action should be taken to promote the transfer of experiences on land-management practices to and among developing countries.

- All countries, particularly developing countries, should be given access to modern techniques of land-management, such as geographical information systems, satellite photography/imagery and other remote-sensing technologies.

- Environmentally focused training in sustainable land-use planning and management should be undertaken in all countries. Developing countries should being given assistance through international support and funding agencies in order to strengthen educational research and training institutions to provide formal training of land management technicians and professionals.

- In order to familiarize land management professionals and staff with up-to-date land-resource management technologies, periodic in-service refresher courses should be provided.

- Land management agencies should be equipped with modern equipment, such as computer hardware and software and survey equipment.

- The international exchange of information and experience in land management should be promoted through the establishment of professional associations in land management sciences and related activities, such as workshops and seminars.

Financing

The average total annual cost of implementing the activities of this program area is estimated to be about $3 billion for the years from 1993 to 2000. Approximately $300 million of this annual total is expected to be provided from international sources.

Urban Environmental Infrastructure

The sustainability of urban development is defined by many factors. Some of the most important of these factors relate to health, air quality, the availability of safe water supplies and provisions for sanitation and waste management. The concentration of people in urban areas can cause severe problems when local infrastructures are overloaded. In this section, the term "infrastructure" is used to denote those facilities of human settlements which provide water, waste disposal and sanitation services—the environmental infrastructure.

As a direct result of population density, urbanization offers unique opportunities for the supply of infrastructure services. Because of the numbers of inhabitants being served, access to services can be provided in manners which are economically and environmentally sound. In most developing countries, however, the inadequacy and lack of water and sanitation infrastructure is responsible for widespread ill-health and a large number of preventable deaths each year. Because the need for such services is growing faster than many governments' ability to respond, without immediate attention, conditions are expected to worsen in the near future.

Providing environmentally sound infrastructure facilities in human settlements, in particular for the urban and rural poor, is an investment which can result in an improvement in the quality of life, an increase in productivity, an enhancement in overall health levels and a reduction in the burden of investments needed for the alleviation of poverty.

Today, some 2.4 billion people in the world live in urban areas. In the industrialized world, most of the urban population are served with water piped into their homes as well as with municipal sanitation services. In contrast, 1.5 billion people in developing countries do not have safe water and over 2 billion lack safe sanitation. By the year 2025, the world's urban population is expected to reach over 5 billion. It is crucial that a high priority be given to providing for the environmentally sound management of water and sanitation services.

Rapid urban population growth and industrialization are putting severe strains on water resources for human consumption and industrial use. A high proportion of large urban areas are located around estuaries and in coastal zones. This has lead to the over-exploitation and municipal and industrial pollution of these water sources. Better management of urban water resources is essential for the alleviation of poverty and the improvement of the health and quality of life of the urban population. This must include the elimination of unsustainable water consumption patterns. In developing countries, specific measures such as low-cost water supply, sanitation and waste management programs need to be targeted at the large numbers of urban poor.

The overall priority is to identify and implement strategies to ensure the continued supply of affordable water for present and future needs and to reverse current trends of water degradation and depletion. In particular, activities should aim to ensure that, by the year 2000, each resident of Earth has access to at least 40 liters per day of safe water and that 75 percent are provided with on-site or community facilities for sanitation. It is also essential that the solid waste generated in urban areas be collected and recycled or disposed of in an environmentally safe manner.

Urban water resources should be protected through the introduction of a variety of techniques, including: sanitary waste disposal facilities based on ecologically sound, low-cost and upgradable technologies; urban storm water runoff and drainage programs; the promotion of recycling and reuse of wastewater and solid wastes; and the control of industrial pollution sources. Before investments are made in new systems, however, the operation and maintenance problems of current systems should be corrected.

The true costs of adequate water supplies are not always met through existing water systems. In certain instances, the failure of water supply facilities to adequately reflect the true cost of water has fostered the highly inefficient use of water. Water tariffs may need to be introduced to recover the actual cost of water, especially in industrial production usage. Economic and regulatory mechanisms must be backed by adequate monitoring and surveillance. In order to encourage its rational use and protect its quality, the public should also be made aware of water's social and economic value. The specific actions needed to satisfy these priorities are dealt with more fully in the section on Fresh Water Resources in Chapter 3: Efficient Use of the Earth's Natural Resources.

By the end of the century, over 1 billion people will be without sufficient solid waste disposal services. Municipal solid wastes include domestic refuse and non-hazardous wastes such as commercial and institutional wastes, street sweepings and construction debris. Inadequate waste disposal can lead not only to the serious, long-term pollution of land, air and water resources but also to wide-spread bacterial and parasitic infections. The health impacts are particularly severe on the urban poor. At present, as many as 5 million people—4 million under of the age of 5—die each year from waste-related diseases. The waste problem is particularly severe in the rapidly growing informal urban settlements of the developing world. In these areas, population densities and health risks are high and public awareness of the hazards of uncontrolled disposal is low. Consequently, the need for municipal waste disposal services is the greatest in these urban slums. The health and environmental effects of inadequate solid waste disposal are felt far beyond the unserved settlements themselves in the form of water, land and air contamination over a wide area. Extending and improving waste collection, processing and disposal services is vital to control mounting health problems and prevent further damage to the environment.

By the year 2025, with over 5.5 billion people expected to live in urban areas, waste generation is likely to increase some five-fold. As more and more non-organic materials and industrial wastes are discharged into municipal waste facilities, this increase is likely to be accompanied by a decrease in the biodegradability of many waste products. The best chance for reversing these trends is to address their root causes by attempting to change the patterns of production and consumption which generate waste. A strategy which focuses on waste prevention, waste minimization and waste reuse should become the foundation of all future solid waste management programs. Issues relating to solid waste disposal are addressed in more detail in Chapter 6: Chemicals and the Management of Waste.

Rapid urbanization, especially in developing countries, has outstripped society's capacity to meet basic human needs, leaving enormous portions of humanity with inadequate incomes, diets, housing, services or health care. The financial resources and the administrative capacity of municipal authorities often cannot meet the increasing environmental health service needs in urban areas. Environmental pollution in most urban areas is directly associated with increasing levels of disease and death. In many urban locations, the general environment is so badly polluted that the health of hundreds of millions of people is adversely affected. Many countries currently experience high levels of pollution in urban areas from industrial activities, energy production and use and transportation systems, most of which where developed with little or no regard for environmental protection. Overcrowding and inadequate housing also contribute to the urban health problems of respiratory disease, tuberculosis and meningitis. While there have been notable improvements in urban health care in most industrialized countries, this has not generally happened in developing countries. The deterioration of environmental conditions in many urban fringe areas continues unabated.

Inevitably, urban development has short and long-term environmental health implications. The dilemma is to minimize the conflicts between the economic development necessary for the immediate improvement of human health, and the environmental protection necessary for the long-term maintenance of human health. The central *AGENDA 21* activities relating to the improvement in human health are contained in Chapter 2: The Quality of Life on Earth.

This particular section of *AGENDA 21*, although based on the need for improved safe water, adequate sanitation and better health care in urban areas, is devoted to specific activities for the provision of adequate water and sanitation infrastructure facilities in all settlements by the year 2025.

Programs and Activities

- All countries should assess the environmental suitability of their water and sanitation infrastructure in human settlements. To that end, it will be necessary to develop national goals for the management of waste. It will also be necessary to develop national programs to implement environmentally sound technology to ensure that the environment, human health and the quality of life are protected.

- Programs should be designed to promote a comprehensive approach to the planning, development, maintenance and management of environmental infrastructure (water supply, sanitation, drainage and solid waste management).

- There must be increased coordination among various agencies which have authority over portions of infrastructure management.

- The activities of all agencies engaged in providing water, drainage and sanitation services should reflect a metropolitan-area approach.

- Collaboration between private industry and community groups should also be strengthened.

- Steps should be taken to strengthen the capacity of local authorities to enter into partnerships with local communities and private business to provide water supplies and sanitation facilities.

- A prerequisite for progress in enhancing access to water and sanitation services is the establishment of an institutional framework which ensures that the needs of presently unserved populations are reflected in urban development planning.

- External funding agencies should ensure that this approach is applied specifically to environmental infrastructure improvements in informal settlements and slums.

- Developing countries should be assisted at national and local levels in adopting a comprehensive approach to the provision of water, energy, sanitation, drainage and solid waste management services.

- All countries should adopt policies regarding water supplies and waste disposal that minimize or avoid environmental damage.

- Relevant decisions in the development of water supply and sanitation services should always be preceded by environmental impact assessments which take into full account the costs of any ecological consequences.

- Development of water and sanitation services should proceed in accordance with indigenous practices and take steps to adopt technologies which are appropriate to local conditions.

- Policies must be aimed at recovering the actual cost of infrastructure services, while at the same time recognizing the need to find suitable approaches (including subsidies) to extend basic services to all households, particularly low-income households.

- Legal and regulatory measures should be taken, including cross-subsidy arrangements, to extend the benefits of adequate and affordable water and sanitation services to unserved population groups, especially the poor.

- All countries should undertake training and popular participation programs aimed at raising awareness of the benefits of safe water and sanitation facilities, especially among indigenous people, women, low-income groups and the poor.

- Efforts should be undertaken to develop a core of professionals with adequate skills in the planning and maintenance of efficient, environmentally sound and socially acceptable water and sanitation systems.

Financing

The costs of implementing most of the activities of this program are included in cost estimates which are contained in other chapters, specifically in the areas of human health in Chapter 2, fresh water resources in Chapter 3 and solid waste disposal in Chapter 6. An additional average of $50 million for technical assistance from the international community will be required on an annual basis.

Energy and Transportation

At a global level, most energy for human use is derived from fossil fuels. Currently, most of the commercial and non-commercial energy produced today is used in urban human settlements. A substantial percentage of it is used for household heating and cooking. Transportation accounts for nearly 30 percent of global commercial energy consumption and 60 percent of the total global consumption of liquid petroleum. In developing countries, rapid motorization and the lack of resources for investment in urban transportation planning, traffic management and infrastructure have combined to create growing health, noise, congestion and productivity problems. All of these problems have a severe impact on urban populations, particularly low-income groups. Developing countries are faced with the challenge of increasing their energy production to accelerate development, meet transportation needs and raise the living standards of their populations while, at the same time, reducing energy production costs and energy-related pollution. Increasing the efficiency of energy use to reduce its polluting effects and promoting the use of renewable energies must be a priority in any action taken to protect the urban environment.

Major efforts must be made to promote sustainable energy and transportation systems through the development and use of environmentally sound commercial energy sources. This will involve commercializing and making socially acceptable such renewable energy sources as hydro- and wind-generated power, solar energy and biomass fuel. The biomass energy needs of lower income groups in urban and rural areas must also be supported with reforestation and national forest regeneration programs. Developing countries should work to provide adequate transportation while reducing energy demand by adopting urban transportation programs which favor mass-occupancy public transport and encourage non-motorized transportation by providing safe cycle and footways.

Industrialized countries, as the largest consumers of energy, are faced with the need for comprehensive energy planning and management. Many metropolitan areas are suffering from pervasive air quality problems related to ozone, particulate matter and carbon monoxide. The causes of this urban pollution have much to do with technological inefficiencies in energy use and with increased fuel consumption generated by high population and industrial concentration. The rapid expansion in the number of motor vehicles is also a major contributing factor. Industrialized countries must also take major steps to develop and promote renewable and alternate sources of energy.

There are two main objectives in this portion of *AGENDA 21*. The first is to extend energy-efficient technology and alternative and renewable sources of energy to human settlements world-wide. The second major objective is to reduce the negative impacts of energy production and use on human health and on the environment, particularly in urban areas. Many of the principal activities which are relevant to this program area are included in Chapter 4: The Protection of Our Global Commons in the sections on Energy Efficiency and Development and Transportation. The activities in the following section supplement these main energy and transportation actions.

Programs and Activities

- A comprehensive approach to human settlements development should include the promotion of sustainable energy development in all countries.

- In particular, national action programs should be developed to promote and support reforestation and national forest regeneration in order to provide for the biomass energy needs of the low-income groups in urban and rural areas, particularly women and children.

- National action programs to promote the development of energy efficient and renewable energy technologies should be implemented. In particular, energy technology based on the use of solar, hydro, wind and biomass sources should be supported.

- There should be increased support for the wide dissemination and commercialization of renewable energy technologies through various measures, including fiscal and technology transfers.

- Information and training programs should be directed at manufacturers and users in order to promote energy saving techniques and energy efficient appliances.

- Access to research and development results regarding the latest methods to increase energy efficiency levels must be make widely available.

- Promoting efficient and environmentally sound urban transportation systems in all countries should be a priority.

- Land-use and transportation planning efforts should encourage development patterns which reduce transportation demand.

- Urban transportation programs which favor high-occupancy public transportation should be adopted.

- The use of non-motorized modes of transportation should be encouraged by providing safe cycleways and footways in urban and suburban centers.

- Particular attention should be devoted to effective traffic management, the efficient operation of public transportation and the proper maintenance of transportation infrastructures.

- In order to enhance the skills of energy service and transportation professionals, all countries should provide on-the-job and other training of government officials, planners, traffic engineers and managers.

- Major efforts must be made to raise public awareness about the environmental impacts of transportation and travel behavior through mass media campaigns.

- There should be extensive support for private and community initiatives which promote the use of non-motorized transportation, shared driving and improved traffic safety measures.

Financing

The costs of implementing all of the activities in this area of *AGENDA 21* are included in the cost estimates for energy and transportation in Chapter 4: The Protection of Our Global Commons.

Disaster-Prone Areas

In many parts of the world, the toll of natural and man-made disasters has been unacceptably high. Natural disasters impact on human settlements in a variety of ways. Disasters can cause many injuries and the tragic loss of human life. Disasters disrupt economic activities and urban productivity, particularly for highly susceptible low-income groups. Disasters cause wide-spread environmental damage, such as the loss of fertile agricultural land and the contamination of water resources. Finally, disasters can lead to the forced major resettlement of populations. Over the past two decades, disasters have caused an estimated 3 million deaths and affected 800 million people worldwide. Global economic losses have been estimated by the Office of the United Nations Disaster Relief Coordinator to be in the range of $30-50 billion per year. In recognition of the damage and suffering caused by disasters, the General Assembly of the United Nations has proclaimed the 1990's as the International Decade for Natural Disaster Reduction.

In addition to the need to reduce the impact of natural disasters on humanity, there is an urgent need to address the prevention and reduction of man-made disasters and those disasters which are caused by industries, unsafe nuclear power generation and toxic wastes. The objective in this program area is to enable all countries, in particular those that are disaster-prone, to mitigate the negative impact of natural and man-made disasters on human settlements, national economies and the environment.

A wide range of actions is proposed. Three distinct areas of activity are foreseen under this program area: the development of a "culture of safety", pre-disaster planning and post-disaster reconstruction.

Programs and Activities

To promote a "culture of safety" in all countries, especially those that are disaster-prone, the following activities should be carried out:

- All countries should complete national and local studies on the nature and occurrence of natural disasters and their impact on people and economic activities. Studies are also needed on the effects of inadequate construction and land use in hazard-prone areas and the social and economic advantages of adequate pre-disaster planning.

- Countries prone to disaster must act to implement nationwide and local awareness campaigns through all available media, translating the above knowledge into information which is easily comprehensible to the general public and to the populations which are directly exposed to hazards.

- Global, regional, national and local early warning systems to alert populations of impending disasters should be developed.

- Major efforts should be taken to identify industrially-based environmental disaster areas at the national and international levels.

- In order to rehabilitate environmental disaster areas, efforts should be taken to restructure economic activities and promote new job opportunities in environmentally sound industries.

- Rehabilitation of environmental disaster areas will also require developing and enforcing strict environmental control standards.

In order to develop pre-disaster planning strategies, all countries should undertake the following activities:

- Every country should complete multi-hazard research into the risk and vulnerability of human settlements and settlement infrastructure, including water and sewage, communication and transportation networks. The multi-hazard aspect must be emphasized in such research; as one type of risk reduction may increase vulnerability to another. For example, an earthquake-resistant house made of wood will be more vulnerable to wind storms.

- Methods for determining risk and vulnerability within specific human settlements should be developed and incorporated into urban and rural planning and management.

- Inappropriate new development and settlements must be redirected to areas that are not prone to hazards.

- Guidelines on location, design and operation of potentially hazardous industries and activities should be prepared and distributed.

- Legal and economic tools should be developed to encourage disaster-sensitive development. Such tools should ensure that limitations placed on development options are not punitive to land-owners. Alternative means of compensation may need to be incorporated into such tools in order to effectively restrict inappropriate development.

- Information on disaster-resistant building materials and construction technologies for buildings and public works should be developed and distributed.

- Training programs for contractors and builders should be conducted on disaster-resistant construction methods. Some programs should be directed particularly to small enterprises which build the great majority of housing and other small buildings in the developing countries. Other construction training programs should be directed specifically to rural populations which build their own houses.

- Training programs for emergency site managers, private organizations and community groups should be developed and conducted. Such training should cover all aspects of disaster mitigation, including urban search and rescue, emergency communications, early warning techniques and pre-disaster planning.

- Procedures to enable local communities to receive information about local hazardous installations or situations should be developed. Local communities should be encouraged to participate in early warning and disaster plans.

- Plans for the reconstruction of settlements, especially the reconstruction of community life-lines, should be prepared and disseminated.

The international community is a major partner in post-disaster reconstruction and rehabilitation. In order to ensure that the countries involved derive the greatest benefits from the funds allocated, the following activities should be undertaken:

- Research on past experiences relating to the social and economic aspects of post-disaster reconstruction should be carried out.

- Strategies and guidelines for post-disaster reconstruction should be developed, with particular focus on the allocation of scarce reconstruction resources and on the opportunities which post-disaster reconstruction provides to introduce sustainable settlement patterns.

- International guidelines for post-disaster reconstruction should be developed and distributed.

- The efforts of national governments to initiate contingency planning for post-disaster reconstruction and rehabilitation should be supported. Participation of local communities in such planning should be encouraged.

- Scientists and engineers specializing in this field should collaborate with urban and regional planners in order to provide the basic knowledge and means to mitigate losses due to disasters.

Financing

The average total annual cost of implementing the activities of this program is estimated to be about $50 million, all of which is required from the international community on grant or aid terms.

The Construction Industry

The activities of the construction industry are vital to the achievement of the national goals of providing shelter, infrastructure and employment. However, construction activities can be a major source of environmental damage through the degradation of fragile ecological zones, depletion of natural resources, chemical pollution and the use of building materials which are harmful to human health. Construction activities also often consume excessive energy and increase air pollution.

The objectives in this area of *AGENDA 21* are two-fold. First, policies and technologies should be developed in order to enable the construction industry to meet development goals while avoiding harmful side-effects on human health and on the biosphere. Second, the employment-generation capacity of the construction industry should be enhanced. Governments should work in close collaboration with private industry in achieving these objectives.

Programs and Activities

- Local indigenous building materials industries should be strengthened and developed, based as much as possible on the use of locally available natural resources. The use of such resources must be conducted in a manner which is environmentally sound.

- Programs to enhance the use of local materials by the construction industry should be expanded. These programs should include technical support and incentive schemes for increasing the capabilities of small-scale and independent workers to make use of these materials in traditional construction techniques.

193

- Standards and regulations should be developed which promote the increased use of energy-efficient designs and technologies. Such standards should also promote the sustainable use of natural resources in economically and environmentally appropriate ways.

- Land-use policies and regulations should be developed which are specifically directed at protecting ecologically-sensitive zones from physical disruption by construction activities.

- Labor-intensive construction and maintenance technologies should be promoted and used whenever possible. This will generate employment in the construction industry for the underemployed labor force found in most large cities while at the same time promoting the development of construction skills.

- Policies should be developed to foster self-help housing builders and the informal portion of the construction industry.

- Such policies should include efforts to increase the affordability of building materials for the urban and rural poor. Methods may include measures to provide credit to the poor and the bulk procurement of building materials for sale to small-scale builders and local communities.

- The free exchange of information on the whole range of environmental and health aspects of construction should be encouraged. This should include the development and distribution of databases on the adverse environmental and health effects of building materials.

- Legislation and financial incentives should be introduced to promote the recycling of energy-intensive materials in the construction industry and to promote the conservation of waste energy in building-materials production methods.

- The use of economic instruments, such as product charges, should be developed to discourage the use of construction materials and products which create pollution during their life-cycle.

- The exchange and transfer of construction technology should be promoted, particularly as related to the use of non-renewable resources.

- The technical and managerial capacities of small entrepreneurs and the vocational skills of workers and supervisors in the building materials industry should be enhanced using a variety of training methods and programs.

- Countries should also be assisted in developing programs to encourage the use of clean technologies and to increase builder awareness of available environmentally sound technologies.
- By pursuing an innovative procurement policy, local authorities should play a pioneering role in promoting the increased use of environmentally sound building materials and construction technologies.

Financing

The cost of implementing the activities in this program area is estimated to be about $40 billion per year for the years 1993 through 2000. This total will include about $4 billion from the international community.

Human Resources

Most countries, particularly developing countries, face shortcomings in the availability of specialized expertise in the areas of housing, settlement management, land management, infrastructure, construction, energy, transportation and disaster planning and reconstruction. In addition, most countries also must contend with an environment which is incapable of integrating the resources and activities of government, private industry and community organizations. There is also a lack of specialized training and research institutions, and an insufficient capacity for technical training and assistance for low-income communities, both urban and rural.

The objective in this program area is to improve the development of human resources in all countries by enhancing the personal capacity of all people involved in human settlement development, particularly indigenous people and women. Specific human resource development activities have been built into each of the previous program areas of this chapter. More generally, however, additional steps should be taken to reinforce those activities.

Programs and Activities

- Public institutions should be provided with technical assistance and international cooperation in order to achieve substantial improvements in the efficiency of governmental activities by the year 2000.

- An environment which is supportive of the partnership between the government, private industry and community groups should be created and encouraged.

- Training and technical assistance should be provided for training technicians, professionals and administrators, as well as appointed, elected and professional members of local governments. Such training must make a special effort to strengthen their capacity to address the social, economic and environmental aspects of human settlement development.

- The activities of women, youth, community groups and private organizations in human settlement development should be facilitated and encouraged.

- Direct assistance for human settlement development at the community level should be provided by promoting programs for raising the awareness and potential of women and youth in human settlement activities.

- The inclusion of integrated environmental management into general local government activities must be encouraged and supported.

- International public and private organizations should support the above activities by providing updated training materials and widely disseminating the results of successful human resource programs and projects.

Financing

It has been estimated that the average total annual cost of implementing the activities of this program area will be about $65 million through the year 2000. All of this amount will be necessary from the international community on grant or concessional terms.

* * *

In all of the *AGENDA 21* program activities related to human settlements, the main objective is to enhance the overall social, economic and environmental quality of human life. In order to accomplish these lofty goals, governments, private industry and local and community-based organizations will have to develop unprecedented partnerships for change. Although the estimated costs to implement all of the activities in this area are high—over $218 billion per year—the economic and environmental benefits of improving human habitats are enormous. By working to provide every person on Earth with a safe, secure and environmentally sound place to live, humanity will take a giant step towards protecting the fragile ecosystems of our planet.

Chapter 6

Chemicals and the
Management of Waste

The use of chemicals is essential in today's world. Their use is vital in the development process and for the promotion of human well-being. Chemicals are extensively used by all societies, irrespective of their stage of development. However, if not handled properly, toxic chemical materials and by-products can have adverse effects on human health and harmful consequences for the environment. Hazardous chemical waste can contaminate soil and groundwater and find its way into the bottom sediments of rivers and lakes. Released as sewage, it can make poisonous, or kill, valuable living marine resources, either directly or by moving through the food chain. Radioactive waste can also be highly toxic and requires extremely secure handling and disposal. Over the years, the growing prevalence of these materials in industrial societies has not been matched by effective policies to deal with them appropriately. Occasionally, this has resulted in severe and devastating accidents.

Reducing the production of dangerous industrial wastes and improving their safe handling and proper disposal are vital if human health and the environment are to be protected. The safe handling and management of toxic, hazardous and radioactive wastes is critical at all stages, including production, transportation, recycling, treatment, storage and final disposal. The safe management of chemicals and waste will require collaborative action by governments, private industry and international organizations. Close cooperation is needed in assessing the dangers of hundreds of chemicals, sharing information about dangers internationally, establishing a consistent system of labelling substances and promoting safer alternatives to harmful chemical use.

Minimizing the dangers posed by the world's growing volume of radioactive waste requires ever more vigilance in enforcing international safety standards. To protect human health and the environment, safe management and disposal of radioactive waste should be an integral part of worldwide nuclear safety efforts. By 1995, some 481 billion cubic meters of low and intermediate-level radioactive waste will be generated annually. About two-thirds of this total will be produced in the industrialized countries of the United States, Western Europe and Japan, and one-third in Eastern Europe and the developing countries. The main sources for this radioactive waste are nuclear power generation, medical centers, research institutions, mines and industrial facilities.

The reduction of pollution and waste will require a transition to environmentally sound technologies in all areas of human activities. Efforts will need to be undertaken throughout the manufacturing, agriculture, energy and transportation industries to reduce the impact of chemical use on the Earth. In a number of cases, the cumulative effects of past pollution have highlighted the urgent need for actions to avoid permanent degradation and destruction of the environment. The industrialized countries, with their experiences and wide range of new and innovative waste minimization technologies, must forge new partnerships to ensure that the developing countries do not follow the historic path of inefficiency and mistakes in waste and chemical management.

Toxic Chemicals

The substantial use of chemicals is essential to meet the social and economic goals of the world community. Today's best practice demonstrates that they can be widely used in a cost-effective manner and with a high degree of safety. However, much remains to be done in order to ensure that the best practices in toxic chemical production, use and handling prevail. There are two major problems in the environmentally sound management of chemicals, particularly in developing countries. First, there is a general lack of sufficient scientific information regarding the risks entailed by the use of a great number of chemicals. Second, for those chemicals for which data is even available, there is a general lack of resources for their careful use.

Gross chemical contamination has, in recent years, been continuing within some of the world's most important industrial areas. This contamination is causing grave damage to human health, human genetic structures, human reproduction and the environment. Restoration of these areas will require major investments and the development of new techniques. The long-range effects of such pollution are only recently being grasped. The importance and extent of those effects, extending even to the fundamental chemical and physical processes of the Earth's atmosphere and climate, is also only recently being recognized.

The broadest possible awareness of chemical risks is a prerequisite for achieving chemical safety. The principle of the right of the community and of workers to know those risks must be recognized. However, the right to know the identity of hazardous ingredients should be balanced with industry's right to protect confidential business information. Industry must apply acceptable standards of operation in all countries of the world in order not to damage human health and the environment. The introduction of chemicals and chemically-related industries into developing countries that lack sufficient infrastructure and trained personnel for chemical safety is also of concern.

A prerequisite for the environmentally sound management of toxic chemicals is a reliable assessment of health and environmental risks. There is also a need for national and local emergency response capabilities to deal with chemical accidents. Training courses and direct public information campaigns are important in this respect to build awareness about the problems of chemical safety.

Safe chemical use mandates the need for a universal system for the classification and labelling of chemicals. Adequate labelling of chemicals is the simplest and most efficient way of indicating how to handle and use them safely. Governments should also promote the exchange of information on toxic chemicals and chemical risk, covering scientific, technical, economic and legal dimensions.

Effective chemical control and risk management urgently require increased international cooperation. To reduce unacceptable or unreasonable chemical risks as much as is economically possible, governments should establish risk reduction programs that employ a broad-based approach and involve a wide range of options. Governments should also work to replace toxic chemicals with less hazardous substitutes. By the year 2000, all countries should introduce national systems for the environmentally sound management of chemicals, including legislation and enforcement.

There is mounting international concern that part of the international movement of toxic products is being carried out in violation of existing national and international law. Such illegal trade poses grave threats to the environment and public health of all countries, particularly developing countries. The United Nations General Assembly has requested international cooperation in the prevention of the illegal traffic in toxic and dangerous products and wastes.

All the above-mentioned issues are closely linked. Their successful implementation requires intensive international work and the improved coordination of current international activities. A considerable number of international bodies are currently involved in work on chemical safety. In many countries, programs for the promotion of chemical safety are in place. Such programs have important international implications, as chemical risks do not respect national boundaries. However, national and international efforts need to be increased in order to attain the environmentally sound management of chemicals on a worldwide basis. In the area of toxic chemical use, six program areas are proposed: assessing the risks of chemical use, the classification and labelling of chemicals, chemical information exchange, risk reduction programs, the safe management of chemicals and illegal trade in toxic chemicals.

Assessing the Risks of Chemical Use

The environmentally sound management of toxic chemicals is essential, not only to undo the mistakes of the past but also to harness the use of chemicals for sustainable development. Of the approximately 100,000 commercial chemical substances and the several thousand more chemical substances of natural origin, many are dangerous and have polluted and contaminated food, other products and the environment.

Fortunately, human exposure to most toxic chemicals has been limited, as most are used in small amounts. Over 95 percent of the world's chemical production involves some 1500 chemicals. However, the lack of crucial data for risk assessment for many high volume production chemicals poses a serious problem. This situation is further exacerbated by the lack of resources to assess those chemicals for which data is even available.

Assessing the environmental hazards and human health risks a particular chemical may cause is a prerequisite to planning for its safe and beneficial use. Careful assessment of chemical risks is expensive and resource-intensive. It can be made more cost-effective by strengthening international cooperation and encouraging better coordination throughout the chemical industry. Such cooperation would make the best use of available resources and avoid unnecessary duplication of efforts. However, each nation must have its own technical staff with experience in toxicity testing and exposure analysis, two of the most important components of chemical risk assessment.

The objective of this program area is to strengthen international chemical risk assessment. By the year 2000, the goal is to assess several hundred priority chemicals or groups of chemicals, including major pollutants and contaminants of global significance. A further goal is to produce guidelines for acceptable exposure levels for a greater number of toxic chemicals.

Programs and Activities

- Programs relating to chemical risk assessment within the United Nations system should be expanded. These include programs under the auspices of the United Nations Environment Programme, The World Health Organization and the Food and Agriculture Organization of the United Nations.

- Mechanisms to increase collaboration between governments, industry, academia and private organizations should be developed. All groups which are involved in aspects of risk assessment of chemicals should work in cooperation. In particular, research activities to improve understanding of the actions of toxic chemicals should be coordinated.

- Procedures should be developed for the national exchange of chemical assessment reports.

- The chemical industry must participate actively. For all substances produced, industry should provide all of the data which is necessary for the assessment of potential risks to human health and the environment.

- Such data should be made available to relevant national authorities and international bodies and other interested parties involved in hazard and risk assessment. To the greatest possible extent, this information must be made available to the public, taking into account any legitimate claims of confidentiality.

- Criteria must be developed by which to set priorities for the assessment of toxic chemicals which are of global concern.

- In order to control and prevent risk in the manufacture and use of toxic and hazardous chemicals, technical cooperation and financial support should be given to activities aimed at expanding and accelerating chemical assessment and risk control.

- In order to enable decision-makers to adopt adequate measures to reduce risks posed by chemicals, major research efforts should be launched. This research should seek to improve current methods of predicting the effects of chemicals on human health and the environment.

- Research efforts should also include an investigation of safe alternatives to toxic chemicals that pose an unreasonable and otherwise unmanageable risk to the environment or human health. In particular, alternatives need to be found for chemicals that are toxic, persistent, accumulative in food chains or cannot be adequately controlled.

- In an effort to reduce the use of animals for testing purposes, research should be conducted into methods to find alternatives to the use of test animals in chemical research.

- Epidemiological studies should be conducted with a view to establishing a cause-and-effect relationship between exposure to chemicals and the occurrence of certain diseases.

- Toxicological studies must be conducted in an effort to assess the risks of chemicals to the environment.

- The results of chemical risk assessment must be widely disseminated in an understandable fashion. Training and education projects involving women and children should be given the highest priority.

Financing

Most of the data and methods for chemical risk assessment are developed in the industrialized countries of the world. A global expansion and acceleration of the chemical risk assessment will require a considerable increase in research and safety testing by industry and research institutions. The cost projections in this area only address the need to strengthen the capacities of relevant United Nations bodies. It should be noted that there are considerable costs, often not possible to quantify, that are not included. These include the costs to industry and governments of generating the safety data underlying the assessments. The estimated average total annual cost of implementing the activities of this program are about $30 million from the international community.

Classification and Labeling of Chemicals

Adequate labelling of chemicals and the dissemination of written safety materials on the health and environmental hazards of chemicals are the simplest and most efficient way of indicating how to handle and use chemicals safely. For the safe transportation of dangerous chemicals, a comprehensive strategy is currently in use. This system primarily takes into account the acute hazards of chemicals. A standardized global hazard classification and labelling system is not yet available to promote the safe use of chemicals in the workplace or in the home. Classification of chemicals can be made for different purposes and is a particularly important tool in establishing labelling systems. Building on progress already made in this field, there is a need to develop standard hazard classification and labelling systems.

By the year 2000, the objective is to have in place a standardized global hazard classification and labelling system. Such a system should include material safety data sheets and easily understandable symbols.

Programs and Activities

- Governments and industry should work together to launch a project to establish a classification and labelling system for chemicals for use in all United Nations official languages. Such a system should also include adequate pictograms.

- Care must be taken so that such a labelling system does not lead to the imposition of unjustified trade barriers.

- The new system should draw on current systems to the greatest extent possible. It should be developed in steps and should address the subject of chemical compatibility with labels for various types of applications.

- An international coordinating group should be established to evaluate and study existing hazard classification and information systems to establish general principles for a standardized global system.

- Such a coordinating group should draft proposals for standardization of hazard communication terminology and symbols. This effort should be directed toward the translation of information into the language level of the actual users of chemicals.

- Governments, scientific institutions and private organizations should launch training courses and information campaigns to aid in the understanding and use of a new standardized classification and labelling system for chemicals.

Financing

The technical assistance costs related to this program are included in estimates provided for the safe management of chemicals later in this chapter. The estimated average total annual cost for strengthening international organizations to handle this task is about $3 million from the international community.

Chemical Information Exchange

It is essential that there be a free and full global flow of information relating to both the risks and benefits of chemical use. The activities in this area are aimed at enhancing the sound management of toxic chemicals through the exchange of scientific, technical, economic and legal information. The London Guidelines for the Exchange of Information on Chemicals in International Trade are a set of procedures which have been adopted in order to increase chemical safety through the worldwide exchange of information.

The export to developing countries of banned or severely-restricted chemicals has been the subject of mounting concern. Special provisions have been included in the London Guidelines regarding the exchange of information on banned and severely restricted chemicals. Without an adequate infrastructure for controlling the importation, distribution, storage and disposal of chemicals, some importing countries lack the ability to ensure the safe use of hazardous chemicals. Knowledge and information on restricted or banned chemicals is essential for enabling importing countries to make informed decisions on whether to import and how to handle such chemicals.

To address this issue, provisions for Prior Informed Consent were introduced into the London Guidelines and into international guidelines on the importation of pesticides. These procedures require direct communication between exporting and importing countries when dealing with trade in hazardous chemicals which have been prohibited for reasons of safety and health in the exporting country. Within the General Agreement on Tariffs and Trade (GATT) framework, a binding international agreement is being sought on trade restrictions for products which have been banned or severely restricted in the exporting country.

In addition to the importance of restrictions on trade in banned chemicals, the free exchange of information on all chemicals is necessary. The objectives of this program area are to promote the increased exchange of information on chemical safety, use and emissions globally. By the year 2000, world-wide participation in information exchanges regarding banned or restricted chemicals is sought, including possible mandatory restrictions through legally binding agreements.

Programs and Activities

- Governments and the chemical industry should act to create national centers for chemical information. The creation of national chemical information systems in developing countries should also be a priority.

- Databases on toxic chemicals should be developed. This must include training in the use of relevant software, hardware and other facilities. It is also vital that all international information material on toxic chemicals be available in all official languages of the United Nations.

- Technical cooperation and information should be provided to all countries, especially those with shortages of technical expertise. Such assistance should include training in the interpretation of relevant

technical data regarding the safety, environmental health and carcino-
genic risks of chemicals.

- In order to assure that importing countries are fully informed of the
risks of using products which have been banned or restricted in the
exporting country, Prior Informed Consent procedures should be implemented world-wide as soon as possible.

- Efforts should continue toward providing legally-binding agreements
regarding restrictions on the exportation of banned and restricted
chemicals.

Financing

The estimated average total annual costs (1993-2000) of implementing
the activities of this program are about $10 million from the international
community in the form of grants or aid.

Risk Reduction Programs

There are often harmless alternatives to toxic chemicals which are currently in use. Risks associated with toxic chemical use can frequently be
reduced simply by using other safer chemicals or even non-chemical
technologies. Establishing pollution prevention procedures and setting
standards for chemical use in food, water and consumer goods are other
examples of risk reduction. In a wider context, risk reduction involves
broad-based approaches to toxic chemical use which take into account
the entire life cycle of the chemicals.

Broad-based approaches to reducing the risks of chemical use encompass the use of cleaner products and technologies, product labelling, direct limitations on chemical use, economic incentives for safe use and
regulations for safe handling and exposure. The phasing out or banning
of chemicals that pose unreasonable risks to human health and the environment is another important aspect of reducing the risk of chemical use.
Restrictions on chemicals that are toxic, persistent and accumulate in
food chains are also necessary.

In the agricultural area, pest management which uses biological control agents instead of toxic pesticides is one approach to risk reduction.
Other areas of risk reduction encompass the prevention of chemical

accidents, the prevention of poisoning by chemicals and the clean-up and rehabilitation of areas damaged by toxic chemicals.

The objective of this portion of *AGENDA 21* is to eliminate unacceptable risks and reduce risks posed by toxic chemicals by employing a wide range of risk reduction options.

Programs and Activities

- All countries should consider adopting policies based on chemical producer liability principles. Such policies need to cover the manufacture, trade, transportation, use and disposal of chemicals.

- Measures to identify and minimize exposure to toxic chemicals by replacing them with less toxic substitutes should be developed.

- Chemicals that pose unreasonable risks to human health and the environment and those that are toxic, persistent, accumulate in food chains and whose use cannot be adequately controlled should be phased out in all countries.

- Policies and regulations for the prevention of chemical accidents should be adopted. These policies should include land-use planning, permit systems and accident-reporting requirements.

- National poison control centers should be established or strengthened to ensure prompt and adequate diagnosis and treatment of poisonings. National centers for chemical accident response should also be established.

- Manufacturers, importers and others handling toxic chemicals should be required to develop emergency response procedures for chemical accidents.

- Guidelines and policies should be developed which require manufacturers, importers and others using toxic chemicals to disclose information declaring risks and emergency response arrangements for toxic chemicals.

- The global overdependence on the use of agricultural chemicals should be reduced through alternative farming practices, integrated pest management and other appropriate means.

- Pesticides whose previous acceptance was based on criteria which is now recognized as insufficient or outdated should be reviewed. Their replacement with other pest control methods should be stipulated, particularly in the case of pesticides that are toxic, persistent or accumulate in food chains.

- Risks from the storage of outdated chemicals should be eliminated as much as possible by environmentally sound disposal practices.

- The chemical industry should be encouraged to develop an internationally agreed-upon code of principles for the management of trade in chemicals. Such a code should recognize the necessity for information on potential risks when the chemicals become waste products. Information on environmentally sound disposal practices must also be included in such a code.

- A "responsible care" approach by chemical manufacturers which takes into account the total life cycle of chemical products must be developed and implemented.

- At the national level, communication guidelines on chemical risks should be developed to provide information to the public for a comprehensive understanding of risks.

- Community "right-to-know" programs must be developed which include the sharing of information on the causes of accidental and potential releases of toxic chemicals. Such programs should also provide information on means of preventing chemical accidents and methods for reporting annual routine emissions of toxic chemicals.

- Large industrial enterprises, including transnational corporations, should be encouraged to introduce policies demonstrating their commitment to the environmentally sound management of toxic chemicals.

- Such companies should be induced to adopt standards of operation that are equivalent to those existing in the countries of their origin.

- Small and medium-sized industries should also be encouraged to develop procedures for risk reduction in their activities.

- Measures and regulations should be adopted to prevent the export of chemicals that are banned or severely restricted for health or environmental reasons. Such regulations should have an exception for instances in which prior written consent for the export has been received from the importing country.

- The chemical industry must be encouraged to phase out any banned chemicals that are still in stock. Such chemical must be disposed of in an environmentally sound manner.

Financing

Most costs related to this program are included in the estimates for funding provided in the activities for assessing the risks and the safe management of chemicals. Requirements for training and strengthening emergency and poison control centers are estimated to be about $4 million annually from the international community.

The Safe Management of Chemicals

Many countries lack national systems to cope with chemical risks. Most countries lack the scientific means of collecting evidence of chemical misuse and of judging the impact of toxic chemicals on the environment. There are many difficulties involved in the detection and tracking of certain types of chemicals. Significant new uses of chemicals are creating potential hazards to human health and the environment in developing countries.

The basic elements for the safe management of chemicals are effective legislation and enforcement, adequate information, the establishment of risk management policies, the capacity for the rehabilitation of contamination, emergency response capabilities and effective education programs. The goal is to have national systems for environmentally sound management of chemicals in place in all countries by the year 2000.

Programs and Activities

- Nations should establish and strengthen a national liaison for all parties involved in chemical safety (for example, agriculture, environment, education, industry, labor, health, transportation, police, civil defence, economic affairs, research institutions and poison control centers).

- Networks of emergency response centers, including poison control centers should be developed. In cooperation with the chemical industry, national and local capabilities to prepare for and respond to accidents should be developed, including regularly tested and updated emergency plans which identify the means and equipment necessary to reduce the impact of accidents.

- Direct information programs which provide information about chemical stockpiles, environmentally safe alternatives and emission inventories should be used to increase the awareness of the general public to problems of chemical safety.

- The manufacturing, distribution, transportation and disposal of toxic chemicals should be carefully monitored and controlled in all countries to ensure compliance with safety rules and provide accurate reporting of relevant data.

- Chemical safety legislation and community "right-to-know" regulations should be enacted. Chemical safety information should be translated into all languages.

- All nations need to work with all relevant international organizations to develop effective and standardized chemical management policies and guidelines.

- National laboratories should be developed in all countries to ensure the availability of adequate national control of the importation, manufacture and use of chemicals.

- Technical training programs and research into the management of chemicals should be established and promoted by the use of grants and fellowships for studies at recognized research institutions with active chemical safety programs.

- In cooperation with industry and trade unions, training programs in the management of chemicals, including emergency response, should be established.

- In all countries, the basic elements of chemical safety principles should be included in the primary education curricula.

Financing

The estimated total annual cost to implement all of the activities in this area is about $600 million, including $150 million from international grants or aid.

Illegal Trade in Toxic Chemicals

There is currently no global agreement on traffic in toxic and dangerous products. Toxic and dangerous products are those that are banned, severely restricted, withdrawn or not approved for use or sale by governments in order to protect public health and the environment. There is mounting international concern that illegal international traffic in these products is causing growing public health and environmental problems, particularly in developing countries. The concern relates both to trade in toxic chemicals in violation of a country's laws and to traffic which is not carried out in accordance with international safety guidelines. Activities under this program area are intended to improve the ability to detect and halt any illegal attempt to introduce toxic and dangerous products into any country.

Programs and Activities

- Legislation intended to prevent the illegal import and export of toxic and dangerous products is necessary in all countries. Appropriate penalties must be included in such legislation to deter violations. Enforcement programs to monitor compliance with such legislation is also necessary.

- All nations should develop national alert systems to assist in detecting illegal traffic in toxic and dangerous products. Local communities should be involved in the operation of such a system.

- There should be increased cooperation in the exchange of information on illegal movements of toxic and dangerous products. In conjunction with this, a network for the continuous monitoring of illegal traffic in toxic products should be established.

- Research into the environmental, economic and health implications of illegal trade in hazardous chemicals should be conducted.

Financing

No additional financing estimates were included in *AGENDA 21* for activities related to halting the illegal international traffic in toxic chemicals.

Hazardous Wastes

The sound management of hazardous wastes is another area which is of paramount importance for proper health, environmental protection and natural resource management. Hazardous wastes are often indiscriminately dumped into rivers, abandoned along roadsides and poured directly into oceans. They threaten the health and safety of all people. Millions of tons of potentially hazardous wastes cross national borders each year on their way for recycling or disposal. Despite new laws, many countries lack the ability to enforce their legal requirements. They often have little or no record of how much or what types of wastes are being produced and have no adequate facilities to manage wastes in an environmentally sound manner. The problem of hazardous waste management involves not only the waste generated today, but also the legacy of wastes inappropriately disposed of in the past.

The environment and human health are threatened by the increasing amount of hazardous wastes produced and improperly managed. Many countries have inadequate infrastructure, insufficient training and education programs and a lack of information on environmental contamination and the health risks from exposure. A general lack of criteria for monitoring and identifying hazardous wastes hampers the efforts to prevent the illegal movement of hazardous wastes.

An international strategy should be developed for the environmentally sound management of hazardous wastes. This involves essentially four priorities. The first is to minimize hazardous wastes through a change in industrial processes and consumer patterns. Processing wastes into useful recycled material should feature prominently in this strategy. The second aim is to promote and strengthen the general capacities to deal with hazardous waste and improve knowledge about the health and environmental impacts of hazardous waste. The third priority is to provide for cooperation in the management of international movements of hazardous wastes. The final program is to prevent the illegal international traffic in hazardous wastes. The activities outlined in this area are very closely related to and have implications for many of the program areas described in other chapters.

Prevention and Reduction

Human health and environmental quality are undergoing continuous damage by the increasing amount of hazardous wastes being produced. There are progressive direct and indirect costs to society and to individual citizens in connection with the generation, handling and disposal of such wastes. It is crucial to understand the economic value of preventing and minimizing hazardous wastes, including the employment and environmental benefits. A full understanding of the economic benefits of reducing hazardous waste will ensure that the necessary capital investment is made available through economic incentives.

One of the first priorities in hazardous waste management must be minimizing the absolute amount of waste produced. This must take place as part of a broader approach to changing industrial processes and consumer patterns. To effectively reduce the amount of hazardous waste, cleaner production processes must be introduced into all industries wherever feasible. Among the most important elements in this effort is the recovery of hazardous wastes and their transformation into useful materials. The application and development of new low-waste and recycling technologies is a central focus of hazardous waste minimization. An intermediate goal should be to stabilize the quantity of hazardous waste generated at current levels. Long-term targets should be established for reducing the amount of hazardous waste produced per unit of manufacture. The reduction in the hazardous quality of waste products should also be an objective.

Programs and Activities

- Major efforts should be made to establish or modify standards or purchasing specifications to avoid discrimination against recycled materials. Care must be taken, however, to ensure that the recycled materials are themselves environmentally sound.

- Governments should develop economic or regulatory incentives to stimulate industrial innovation in cleaner production methods. Economic incentives should also be used to encourage industry to invest in waste prevention and recycling technologies.

- Governments should encourage industry to treat, recycle, reuse and dispose of wastes at the source of generation. These efforts should be taken only when the generation of hazardous wastes is unavoidable.

- In order to identify options for minimizing the generation of hazardous wastes, environmental impact assessments should be conducted, taking into account the cradle-to-grave approach to the management of hazardous wastes. Environmental audits should also be used in this regard.

- Research and development should be intensified on cost-effective alternatives to processes and materials that currently result in particularly dangerous hazardous wastes. Emphasis should be given to alternatives that will be economically feasible for developing countries. Research into the use of biotechnologies to prevent or minimize waste should also be conducted.

- The goal should be the ultimate phase-out of those substances that present an unreasonable risks and that pose particular problems for environmentally sound disposal or treatment.

- Domestic facilities to handle hazardous wastes of domestic origin should be established.

- Governments of industrialized countries should promote the transfer of environmentally sound technologies and know-how on clean technologies and low-waste production to developing countries.

- There should be substantial increases in the funding for transfer of cleaner technologies to developing countries. Small and medium-sized business enterprises should be included in such plans.

- In order to identify technology transfer and hazardous waste management needs, inventories of hazardous waste production should be developed in all countries.

- Governments should cooperate with industry trade associations to develop guidelines and codes of conduct on cleaner production.

- Governments should promote cleaner production through the establishment of centers to provide training and information on environmentally sound technologies.

- In order to identify where cleaner production methods are needed, industry should establish environmental management systems, including environmental auditing of its production or distribution sites.

- Efforts must be taken to develop guidelines for estimating the costs and benefits of various approaches to cleaner production and waste minimization. Such estimates should include the costs of rehabilitating contaminated sites.

• Governments should enact regulations that establish that industry has the ultimate responsibility for the environmentally sound disposal of the hazardous wastes that their activities generate.

• Information clearing-houses and networks should be established that are easy for government institutions, industry and private organizations to access and use.

• A comprehensive survey should be undertaken to determine the effectiveness of economic regulations and incentives for hazardous waste management and prevention.

• Industries must be encouraged to be forthright in their operations and provide information to the communities that might be affected by the generation, management and disposal of hazardous wastes.

• Industrial training programs which incorporate hazardous waste prevention and minimization techniques should be developed. These should include demonstration projects at the local level to develop "success stories" in cleaner production.

Financing

It has been estimated that the average total annual costs of implementing the activities of this program are about $750 million, all of which is required from the international community on grant or aid terms.

Hazardous Waste Management

Many countries lack the capacity to handle and manage hazardous wastes. This is primarily due to inadequate infrastructure, lack of regulation, insufficient training and a lack of coordination between different agencies involved in waste management. In addition, there is a general lack of knowledge about environmental contamination and the associated health risks of human exposure to hazardous waste. Steps need to be taken immediately to identify those populations around the world that are at high risk from their exposure to toxic waste. One of the main priorities in ensuring environmentally sound management of hazardous waste is to provide awareness, education and training programs covering all levels of society. There is also a need to undertake research programs to understand the nature of hazardous wastes, to identify their potential environmental effects and to develop technologies to safely handle those wastes. Finally, there is a need to strengthen the capacities of institutions that are responsible for the management of hazardous wastes.

Programs and Activities

- Surveillance systems for the purpose of identifying hazardous wastes and their treatment and disposal sites should be established. Contaminated sites that require rehabilitation should be identified.

- The risks to human health and the environment should be identified and the measures required to clean up disposal sites determined. Industry should be compelled to make the necessary information available.

- In conjunction with such inventories, notification systems and registries of exposed populations and of adverse health effects should be developed.

- Exposure and health assessments of populations residing near uncontrolled hazardous waste sites should be conducted immediately. Necessary remedial measures should be initiated as soon as possible.

- The clean-up of hazardous waste sites should be conducted in cooperation with industry and international organizations. The technology, expertise and financing for this purpose should be provided by the application of the "polluter pays" principle.

- Guidelines and easy-to-implement methods for the classification of hazardous wastes should be developed. Practical technical guidelines for the prevention, minimization, safe handling and disposal of hazardous wastes are also necessary.

- Training and research programs related to the evaluation, prevention and control of hazardous waste health risks should be developed. Research is necessary on the health effects of hazardous wastes in developing countries, including the long-term effects on children and women. The dissemination of technical and scientific information dealing with the various health aspects of hazardous wastes must be greatly expanded.

- Expanded technological research on environmentally sound hazardous waste handling, storage, transportation, treatment and disposal is essential. The focus should be on identifying relevant and improved technologies for the safe control of hazardous wastes.

- Public awareness of hazardous waste issues must be increased. The development and dissemination of hazardous waste information that the general public can understand is a high priority. Educational materials concerning hazardous wastes and their effects on the environment and human health should be developed and distributed for use in schools, by women's groups and by the general public.

- Hazardous waste management programs must include participation by the general public, particularly women. This should include participation at grass-roots levels.

- The establishment of combined treatment/disposal facilities for hazardous wastes in small and medium-sized industries should be encouraged. Research aimed at the needs of small and medium-sized industries should also be conducted.

- The feasibility of establishing and operating national and regional hazardous waste treatment centers should be studied. Such centers should be used for education and training, as well as for the promotion of the transfer of technologies for the environmentally sound management of hazardous wastes.

- Wherever they operate, transnational corporations and other large-scale enterprises should be encouraged to make commitments to adopt standards of hazardous waste generation and disposal that are equivalent to standards in the country of their origin.

- Environmental audits of existing industries should be conducted to improve in-plant systems for the management of hazardous waste.

- Industry-based institutions for dealing with hazardous wastes should be established, along with service industries for handling hazardous wastes.

- In developing countries, government regulators, labor and industrial management staff must be trained in the use of technologies to minimize and manage hazardous wastes in an environmentally sound manner.

- Governments should require that their military establishments conform to their national environmental norms in the treatment and disposal of hazardous wastes.
- Hazardous waste disposal in the country of origin should be encouraged to the extent that it is environmentally sound and feasible. International movement of waste should take place on sound environmental, economic and legal grounds.

Financing

Average total annual costs for implementing the activities of this program are about $18.5 billion on a global basis with about $3.5 billion related to activities in developing countries and the bulk related to activities in industrialized countries. Approximately $500 million of the amount required for projects in developing countries should be provided from the international community.

International Cooperation

The objectives of this program area are to increase international cooperation in the environmentally sound management of hazardous wastes—particularly in the control and monitoring of international movements of such wastes. Efforts should be made to develop international criteria to identify and classify hazardous wastes and to standardize international legal agreements. The export of hazardous wastes to countries that do not have the capacity to deal with those wastes in an environmentally sound way should be prohibited globally.

Programs and Activities

- Various important procedures for the safe handling and disposal of hazardous waste have been developed regionally. The Basel and Bamako Conventions incorporate many of these procedures. Such procedures should be followed or adopted by all countries. Governments are urged to ratify the Basel Convention and the Bamako Convention.
- Clear criteria and guidelines for environmentally and economically sound resource recovery, recycling, reclamation and direct or alternative uses of hazardous wastes should be developed.

- Acceptable recovery practices should be developed for the purpose of preventing abuses and falsification in the above operations.
- Appropriate rules and procedures for liability and compensation for damage resulting from the international movement and disposal of hazardous wastes should be developed.
- In order to minimize damage from accidents arising from international movements of hazardous wastes, provisions for temporary emergency financial assistance should be developed.
- National and regional systems for the monitoring and surveillance of international movements of hazardous waste should be developed.
- Guidelines for the identification and environmentally sound treatment of hazardous wastes should be developed. Safety standards for managing hazardous wastes in an environmentally sound manner should be standardized and implemented.
- Appropriate methods for testing, characterizing and classifying hazardous wastes should be adopted.

Financing

Because this program area covers a relatively new field of operation and because of the lack of adequate studies on the costs of activities under this program, no cost estimate is available at present. However, the costs for some of the activities in this area have been covered under the funding estimates for hazardous waste management earlier in this chapter.

Illegal Traffic in Hazardous Waste

Illegal traffic of hazardous wastes can cause serious threats to human health and the environment and impose abnormal burdens on the countries that receive such shipments. The prevention of such illegal traffic will benefit the environment and public health in all countries, particularly developing countries. Successful prevention requires effective monitoring and the enforcement and imposition of appropriate penalties. The objectives of this program are to allow countries to detect and halt any illegal attempt to traffic in hazardous wastes.

Programs and Activities

- All countries should implement legislation to prevent the illegal import and export of hazardous wastes. To deter violations, appropriate penalties must be included in such legislation.

- To monitor compliance with such legislation, national enforcement programs should be implemented. Special attention should be given to those persons who are known to have conducted illegal traffic in hazardous wastes and to those hazardous wastes that are particularly susceptible to illegal traffic.

- Governments should develop an information network and alert system to assist in detecting illegal traffic in hazardous wastes. Local communities should be involved in the operation of such a network.

- Governments should cooperate in the exchange of information on illegal movements of hazardous waste and should make such information readily available.

- The environmental, economic and health implications of the illegal traffic in hazardous wastes should be assessed on a continuing basis.

Financing

No financing estimates were prepared for the activities in this program area.

Solid Waste Management

The General Assembly of the United Nations has noted that the environmentally sound management of solid wastes is among the environmental issues of major concern in maintaining the quality of the Earth's environment. Solid wastes include all domestic refuse and non-hazardous wastes such as commercial and institutional wastes, street sweepings and construction debris. In some countries, the solid waste management system also handles human wastes such as night-soil, ashes from incinerators, septic tank sludge and sludge from sewage treatment plants. Program areas included in this section of *AGENDA 21* are closely related to the following other program areas: Consumption and Human Health in Chapter 2, Fresh Water Resources in Chapter 3 and Human Settlements in Chapter 5.

Environmentally sound waste management must go beyond the mere safe disposal or recovery of wastes and address the root cause of the problem by attempting to change unsustainable patterns of production and consumption. This implies the application of a life cycle management concept. Four major areas are the focus of activities in this section: minimizing wastes, maximizing waste reuse and recycling, environmentally sound waste disposal and treatment, and extending waste service coverage. These four areas are interrelated and mutually supportive and must be developed within a comprehensive and environmentally responsive framework for managing municipal solid wastes.

Minimizing Waste

Unsustainable patterns of production and consumption are increasing the quantities and variety of solid waste at unprecedented rates. This trend will significantly increase the quantities of wastes produced—by four- to five-fold by the year 2025. A preventive waste management approach which focuses on changes in lifestyles and in production and consumption patterns offers the best chance for reversing these current trends. The objective is to stabilize or reduce the production of waste, based on the weight, volume and composition of waste. Waste separation should also be encouraged in order to facilitate waste recycling and reuse. Policies should be developed which use economic penalties and incentives to induce modifications of production and consumption patterns. Waste prevention and minimization should be the principal objective of national waste management programs.

Programs and Activities

- By the year 2000, all industrialized countries should have programs in place to stabilize or reduce the production of wastes which are destined for final disposal. The goal is to limit waste to current levels. Developing countries should also work towards that goal without jeopardizing their development prospects.

- By the year 2000, all countries, and in particular the industrialized countries, should have programs to reduce the production of agricultural chemical wastes, containers and packaging materials.

- In order to reduce losses which result in solid waste, procedures for the efficient transportation and storage of agricultural products, food-stuffs and other perishable goods should be developed.

- Private organizations and consumer groups should be encouraged to participate in such programs.

- Research should be encouraged into the design of environmentally sound technologies and into the development of measures to reduce wastes to a minimum.

- Economic incentives to reduce unsustainable patterns of production and consumption should be developed. Regulations and incentives should be used to encourage industry to change product design and reduce industrial process wastes through cleaner production tech-nologies and good housekeeping practices. Both industry and con-sumers must be encouraged to use types of packaging that can be safely reused.

- Monitoring is a key prerequisite for keeping track of changes in waste quantity and quality and their impact on health and the environment. Country-level waste monitoring programs should be implemented.

- Information networks on clean technologies and waste minimization should be established and strengthened.

- The effectiveness of all waste minimization techniques should be re-viewed. Successful waste minimization technologies and procedures will need to be identified and widely disseminated. In particular, new techniques with high potential should be identified.

- Particularly in developing countries, the transfer of waste-reduction technologies to industry must be encouraged.

- Concrete national standards for effluents and solid waste should be established.

- Education programs must be developed to raise the consciousness of industry, concerned groups and the public in general. The principles and practices of preventing and minimizing wastes should be incorporated within school curricula at all levels. Material on the envi-ronmental impacts of waste must also be made widely available.

Financing

It is suggested that industrialized countries consider investing in waste minimization the equivalent of about 1 percent of their national expenditures on solid wastes and sewage disposal. At current levels, this would amount to about $6.5 billion annually, including about $1.8 billion related to minimizing municipal solid wastes.

Reuse and Recycling

The exhaustion of traditional disposal sites, stricter environmental controls over waste disposal and increasing quantities of more persistent wastes have all contributed to a rapid increase in the cost of waste disposal services. These costs could double or triple by the end of the decade. Additionally, certain current disposal practices pose an immediate threat to the environment. As the economics of waste disposal services change, waste recycling and resource recovery are becoming inreasingly cost-effective. Future waste management programs must take maximum advantage of resource-efficient approaches to the control of wastes. To support this approach to waste management, it is important that markets for products from reclaimed materials be identified and developed.

Programs and Activities

- By the year 2000, national and local waste reuse and recycling programs should be in place in all industrialized countries. By the year 2010, such programs should be in use in all developing countries.

- Priority should be given to waste reuse and recycling. Existing purchasing standards or specifications should be reviewed to avoid discrimination against recycled materials, taking into account the saving in energy and raw materials.

- Information and research is required to identify promising socially-acceptable and cost-effective forms of waste reuse and recycling which are relevant to each country. Potential markets for recycled products should be identified.

- An extensive review should be conducted of the options and techniques for the reuse and recycling of all forms of municipal solid wastes.

- The extent and types of waste reuse and recycling operations currently in operation should be identified. Ways by which the effectiveness of these operations could be increased should be determined.

- Funding for research pilot programs to test various options for reuse and recycling should be increased. Such programs should include small-scale cottage-based recycling industries; compost production; treated waste-water irrigation and energy recovery from wastes.

- The development and improvement of existing waste recycling and reuse technologies should be continued. The transfer of such technology should be supported. Machinery for reusing plastics, rubber and paper should be the subject of technology transfer projects.

- Special research grants should be made available on a competitive basis for innovative research projects on recycling techniques.

- National waste policies should be reformed to provide incentives for waste reuse and recycling. Incentive options should be used to encourage industry, institutions, commercial establishments and individuals to recycle wastes instead of disposing of them.

- Incentives to local and municipal authorities that recycle the maximum proportion of their wastes can be adopted. Specific mechanisms such as deposit/refund systems should be developed as incentives for reuse and recycling. Economic incentives to improve the marketability of recyclable waste should be adopted.

- Various economic measures and regulations, including tax incentives, can be used to support the principle that generators of wastes must pay for their disposal. Legal and economic conditions to encourage investments in waste reuse and recycling should be developed.

- The use of recyclable materials, particularly in packaging, should be encouraged. The separate collection of recyclable parts of household wastes should be encouraged.

- Training will be required to reorient current waste management practices to include waste reuse and recycling. Waste reuse and recycling training should be included as an integral component of in-service urban management training programs.

- The advantages and civic obligations of waste reuse and recycling should be included in all school curricula and relevant general educational courses. Public education and awareness programs to promote the use of recycled products should be developed and implemented.

- Private organizations, community-based organizations and women's, youth and public interest groups should act to mobilize community support for waste reuse and recycling through focused community-level campaigns. Consumer, women's and youth groups should launch pilot programs to demonstrate waste reuse and recycling.

- Local and municipal authorities should act to mobilize community support for waste reuse and recycling by involving and assisting independent and small-scale waste reuse and recycling operations.

- Programs to support small communities' waste reuse and recycling industries in developing countries should be developed.

Financing

It is suggested that funding for recycling activities be based on a proportion of municipal waste expenditures. If the equivalent of 1 percent of waste-related municipal expenditures was devoted to safe waste reuse schemes, worldwide expenditures for this purpose would amount to $8 billion. Total annual costs of implementing the activities of this program area in developing countries are approximately $850 million.

Solid Waste Disposal

Even when wastes are minimized or recycled, some wastes will still remain. Even after treatment, all discharges of wastes have some residual impact on the environment. There are strong environmental and health reasons for improving waste treatment and disposal practices. In developing countries, the problem is of a more fundamental nature: less than 10 per cent of urban wastes receive some form of treatment and only a small proportion of treatment is in compliance with any acceptable quality standard. Because of the potential threat to human health, fecal matter treatment and disposal should be given the highest priority. The objective in this area is to effectively treat and safely dispose of increasing proportions of solid waste.

Programs and Activities

- By the year 2000, waste treatment and disposal standards should be in place in all countries. Also by the year 2000, waste-related pollution monitoring and surveillance programs should be used in all countries.

- By the year 1995, at least 50 per cent of all sewage, waste waters and solid wastes in industrialized countries should be treated or disposed of in conformance with environmental and health guidelines. By 2005, this goal should be met in all developing countries.

- By the year 2025, the disposal of *all* sewage, waste waters and solid wastes should be done in conformity with national or international environmental quality guidelines.

- Programs should be launched to improve the control and management of waste-related pollution. These programs should act to encourage countries to seek waste disposal solutions within their own territory and as close as possible to the origin of the waste.

- Standard setting and monitoring are two key elements essential for gaining control over waste-related pollution. Scientific evidence and the pollution impacts of wastes in the environment should be assembled and analyzed in order to formulate scientific guidelines for the environmentally sound management of solid wastes.

- Monitoring equipment and training in its use must be included in any technical assistance programs.

- Training programs for waste-related pollution monitoring and enforcement should also be developed. Pollution control agencies must have the necessary legal mandate and resources to effectively carry out their duties.

- An information clearing-house to collect and disseminate information on all aspects of waste management should be established. Such efforts should be directed towards the review of recent developments and the dissemination of information on the effectiveness of techniques for safe waste disposal.

- Specific research is necessary on low-cost, low-maintenance wastewater treatment systems; safe sludge disposal options; industrial waste treatment; and low-technology, ecologically safe waste disposal options.

- In cooperation with business and industry, the transfer of industrial waste treatment technologies is necessary.

- The rehabilitation, operation and maintenance of existing facilities should also be a focus of efforts. Technical assistance on improved maintenance practices and on the planning and construction of new waste treatment facilities is also required.

- Programs to segregate and safely dispose of the hazardous components of municipal solid waste are vital to protecting environmental and human health.

- Investments in waste disposal facilities should be equal and parallel to investments in water services.

- Both formal and in-service training should be provided which focuses on pollution control, waste treatment, disposal technologies and the operation and maintenance of waste-related facilities.

Financing

Safe waste disposal programs are relevant to both industrialized and developing countries. In industrialized countries, the focus is on improving facilities to meet higher environmental quality standards. In developing countries, considerable investment is required to build new treatment facilities. The average total annual cost of implementing the activities of this program in developing countries is estimated to be about $15 billion, including about $3.4 billion from the international community on grant or aid terms. No financing estimates are provided for activities in industrialized countries.

Extending Waste Service

By the end of the century, over 2.0 billion people will be without access to basic sanitation and an estimated half of the urban population in developing countries will be without adequate solid waste disposal services. As many as 5.2 million people—including 4 million children under five years of age—die each year from waste-related diseases. The health impacts are particularly severe for the urban poor. The health and environmental impacts of inadequate waste management result in water, land and air pollution. Extending and improving waste collection and safe disposal services is crucial to gaining control over this form of pollution. The overall objective of this program area is to provide healthy, environmentally safe waste collection and disposal services to all people.

Programs and Activities

- By the year 2025, the goal is to provide all humanity with adequate waste services and sanitation. To achieve this goal, financing mechanisms for waste service development in deprived areas must be developed. The "polluter pays" principle should be applied by setting waste management charges at rates that reflect the actual costs of providing the services. This will ensure that those who generate the wastes pay the full cost of disposal in an environmentally safe way.

- Given the ever-increasing numbers of unserved urban poor and the urgent need to address the problem of solid waste disposal, new mechanisms are essential to ensure accelerated development of urban waste disposal services. An international clearing-house should be established on solid waste management. Systematic reports on progress in providing waste services to those without such services should be undertaken.

- Governments should act to launch aggressive programs in different parts of the developing world to extend waste services to unserved populations, particularly the urban and rural poor.

- Policy changes at national and local levels should enhance the rate of waste service coverage. These changes should include using low-cost options for waste management.

- A high priority should be assigned to the extension of waste services to all settlements, particularly urban slums, regardless of the legal status of such settlements. Revisions should be made to existing codes and regulations to permit the use of the full range of low-cost alternative technologies for waste disposal.

- Information on the application of innovative and low-cost alternatives for waste disposal should be distributed to targeted audiences. Training on the planning and construction of low-cost waste collection and disposal options should be implemented.

- Research should be conducted to find solutions and equipment for managing wastes in areas of concentrated populations and on small islands. In particular, there is a need for cost-effective and hygienic human waste collection and disposal systems. The transfer of technologies, especially technologies for such high-density settlements, is vital.

- Campaigns should be launched to encourage active community participation in the management of waste, particularly household waste. Community participation should be encouraged in planning and implementing procedures for solid waste management.

- Improvements in management techniques are likely to yield the greatest returns in terms of improving waste management service efficiency. The skills of management-level personnel in waste management agencies should be upgraded.

Financing

The estimated average total annual cost of implementing the activities of this area are about $7.5 billion, including about $2.6 billion from the international community on grant or aid terms.

Radioactive Wastes

Radioactive wastes are generated in the production of nuclear energy as well as in nuclear applications in medicine, research and industry. The safety risks from radioactive wastes vary from very small in short-lived, low-level wastes up to very large for high-level wastes. Annually about 200,000 cubic meters of low-level and intermediate-level waste and 10,000 cubic meters of high-level waste is generated worldwide from nuclear power production. These volumes are increasing as more nuclear power units are placed in operation, current nuclear facilities are decommissioned and the use of radionuclides increases. High-level waste contains about 99 percent radionuclides and presents the greatest health risk. Waste volumes from industrial and medical nuclear applications are generally much smaller, typically some tens of cubic meters or less per year per country.

Given their particular characteristics, the safe and environmentally sound management of radioactive wastes is of vital importance to humanity. Safe management includes the minimization of waste and their transportation and disposal. In most countries with a substantial nuclear power program, technical and administrative measures have been taken to implement a radioactive waste management system. In many other countries where national nuclear programs are still only in development or where only industrial or medical nuclear applications are in use, such systems are critically needed. The objective is to ensure that radioactive wastes are safely managed, transported, stored and disposed of in a manner which protects human health and the environment.

Programs and Activities

- All nations should take practical measures to minimize and limit the generation of radioactive wastes and provide for their safe processing, conditioning, transportation and disposal.

- Radioactive waste safety standards and guidelines for the safe and environmentally sound management and disposal of radioactive wastes should be developed on an international basis.

- In order to promote the safe storage, transportation and disposal of radioactive wastes, the transfer of relevant technologies must be encouraged. The return to the supplier of radiation sources after their use should also be a method for management of radioactive waste.

- Environmental impact assessments should be adopted for the management of radioactive waste. Emergency procedures and storage, transportation and disposal standards should be implemented.

- The Code of Practice on the Transboundary Movements of Radioactive Waste should be adopted by all countries.

- Studies must be completed on replacing the current voluntary moratorium on the disposal of low-level radioactive wastes at sea by a total ban.

- The storage or disposal of high-level, intermediate-level and low-level radioactive wastes should be prohibited near the marine environment unless scientific evidence shows that such storage or disposal poses no unacceptable risk to people or the marine environment or does not interfere with other legitimate uses of the sea.

- The export of radioactive wastes to countries that prohibit the import of such wastes should be halted immediately.

- Research and development should be conducted into methods for the safe and environmentally sound treatment, processing and disposal of high-level radioactive waste. These efforts should include deep geological disposal.

- Research concerned with evaluating the health and environmental impact of radioactive waste disposal should also be conducted.

- Trained personnel and facilities for the handling, processing, storage and disposal of wastes generated from nuclear applications are also needed in all countries which use nuclear materials in medicine or industry.

Financing

The costs at the national level of managing and disposing of radioactive wastes are considerable and will vary depending on the technology used for disposal. The estimated average total annual cost to international organizations to implement the activities of this program is about $8 million.

* * *

The advancement of human civilization in the past century has been based, to a large extent, upon the use of increasing amounts of chemicals. Most chemicals are safely produced, used and disposed of. However, there are great risks associated with the improper use and disposal of certain substances, particularly materials which are hazardous to human health and the environment. The world community must cooperate to ensure that the use of chemicals to enhance the quality of human life is conducted in a manner which is profoundly safe.

The very nature of human society and industrial development produces enormous quantities of waste products. A cooperative global effort must be undertaken to guarantee that this waste is properly managed. Greater levels of efficiency can be achieved through efforts to minimize the generation of waste and through increased efforts to recycle waste into useful products. Before the waste problems of humanity reach catastrophic proportions, the world community has a critical opportunity to correct the mistakes of the past and move forward in implementing bold measures to confront the issue of waste.

Chapter 7

Sustainable Economic Growth

The world's financial, trade and governmental systems have all contributed to unprecedented global economic growth in this century. However, this economic growth has often been achieved with insufficient consideration of important environmental and social realities. This short-sighted approach has led to conditions which now threaten future development and human progress. Over the years, the international economic system has favored the over-exploitation of raw materials, often at serious environmental cost, particularly in developing countries. The same system has also made the fragile economies of developing countries highly vulnerable to changes in world economic conditions—changes over which these developing countries have little control. In recent years, largely as a result of the demands of repaying international debt, there has been a net transfer of money from the developing to the industrialized world. This has left the developing world with little resources for combating poverty or arresting further environmental degradation.

These patterns highlight the need to integrate environmental and developmental considerations throughout the decision-making process at all levels, including international economic relations. It is critical that international relations between nations be conducted on a basis that is both

233

environmentally responsible and equitable, particularly with regard to financing, trade, investments and access to science and technology.

The transition to sustainable development requires a much more effective use of the Earth's resources. It will also require accountability for the environmental and economic impacts of such use. More realistic economic values must be placed on the environment and our natural resources. The operation of market forces can be a powerful ally in providing the incentives to change. At the same time, economic growth in developing countries is essential for sustainable development and cannot be overly restrained. International policies that control trade and the flow of global finances have a major impact on sustainable development. Agricultural and other commodities, the most important income sources for developing countries, are among the products most protected by the trade restrictions of industrialized countries. The international trading system must act to reduce tariffs and phase out non-tariff barriers to trade.

The economic valuation of natural resources on the sole basis of their extraction and distribution costs has often resulted in inadequate incentives to develop sustainable resource uses. The failure to include full environmental costs in the valuation of resources has also led to the over-consumption of resource-based products and ensuing environmental degradation. Developing accounting methods which value all of the environmental costs of resource use is an important measure, not only with respect to trade and consumption patterns, but also with respect to such resources as oceans, fresh water and forests.

The economic policies of individual countries and international economic relations both have great relevance to sustainable development. The transition to a global economic system which fosters sustainable growth will necessitate new ideas and the innovative use of pricing policies, economic instruments and a wide range of regulatory measures. The urgent need to accelerate sustainable development calls for a global partnership to ensure that new international and national policies are used to bring about fundamental changes in the world economic system. Concern for the environment must be included in the development of all such policies and environmental costs must be included at all levels of accounting.

The worldwide drive for sustainable development will not gather momentum if the developing countries are weighted down by external indebtedness, if development financing is inadequate, if barriers restrict access to markets or if commodity prices and the terms of trade remain depressed. The record of the 1980's was essentially negative on each of these counts and needs to be reversed. New policies and measures are needed to create an international environment that is strongly supportive of national sustainable development efforts. International cooperation in this area should be designed to complement and support—not diminish—sound domestic economic policies in both industrialized and developing countries.

The international economy should provide a supportive global climate for achieving environment and development goals. Four major areas are highlighted: international trade policies, making trade and environment mutually supportive, financial resources for developing countries, and economic policies to support sustainable development. In view of the acute environmental and developmental problems of the least developed countries, particular efforts are warranted in implementing all of the activities in this chapter.

Later in this chapter, additional related areas will be addressed. These include integrating environment and development issues into decision-making, creating a legal and regulatory framework that is supportive of sustainable development, using economic instruments and market incentives, creating environmental/economic accounting systems, promoting the transfer of environmentally sound technology to developing countries and encouraging international cooperation in sustainable development efforts.

International Trade Policies

International economic relations, such as trade and financial flows, have a significant influence on the ability of developing countries to achieve economic growth in a manner consistent with the sound management of natural resources. World trade today is of the order of $6 trillion per year, the majority of it being accounted for by the industrialized economies. The conditions governing international trade are of particular importance to the developing countries, since trade plays a crucial role in their drive towards structural transformation and growth.

Trade in commodities dominates the economies of many developing countries in terms of production, employment and export earnings. In the 1980's, there were very low and declining prices for most commodities in international markets. This led to a substantial decrease in commodity export earnings for many producing countries. The deterioration of terms of trade and the use of protectionist barriers which limit exports to industrialized-country markets tends to impair the ability of developing countries to mobilize the resources needed for sustainable development. Agricultural subsidies and high tariffs on processed products are particular obstacles to the export trade of developing countries. As the trade system provides for the exchange of goods and services and can modify patterns of production and consumption, it can be used to create both a positive and negative impact on the environment. An open trading and financial system would be beneficial to all trading partners.

In some cases, international trade can provide the additional resources needed for economic growth and development while also providing significant investment for improving environmental quality. However, in most cases, domestic resources will be the main component of national investment. A sound environment can, in turn, provide the resources needed to sustain growth and underpin a continuing expansion of national and international resource use.

Financial investment is critical for developing countries to achieve the economic growth needed to improve the welfare of their populations and to meet their basic needs in a sustainable and environmentally sound manner. Many developing countries have experienced a decade-long trend of negative net transfer of financial resources. During the 1980's, the payments that many of these countries had to make (in particular, interest payments on international debt) exceeded their income. As a result, vital domestic resources had to be transferred abroad instead of invested locally for sustainable economic development. The debt crisis continues to impair the functioning of the international financial system and prevents it from fulfilling its vital role in providing funds to support development and trade.

An open, equitable and predictable trading system that is consistent with the goals of sustainable development will be of benefit to all trading partners. Improving market access for the exports of developing countries would have a positive environmental impact and, therefore, make an important contribution towards sustainable development. Experience has shown that sustainable development requires a commitment to sound economic policies and management, and an effective and predictable public administration. The integration of environmental concerns into decision-making and progress towards democratic government are also essential components of sustainable development.

There must be substantial and progressive reductions made in the support and protection of agriculture and industry. These changes must cover internal administration, market access and export subsidies. In agriculture and industry, there is much room for initiatives aimed at liberalizing trade policies on a global basis in order to make production more responsive to environment and development needs.

The international trading environment has been affected by a number of developments that have created new challenges and opportunities, and have made international economic cooperation of even greater importance. World trade has continued to grow faster than world output in recent years. However, the expansion of world trade has been unevenly distributed and only a limited number of developing countries have been able to achieve significant growth in their exports. Protectionist pressures continue to endanger the functioning of an open global trading system. In recent years, a growing number of developing countries have adopted courageous policy reforms involving ambitious trade liberalization. Far-reaching reforms and profound restructuring processes are taking place in Central and Eastern European countries, paving the way for their integration into the world economy and the international trading system. Increased attention is being devoted to enhancing the role of business enterprises and promoting competitive markets. The Generalized System of Preferences has proved to be a useful trade policy instrument, although its objectives have yet to be fulfilled. Trade strategies relating to electronic data interchange have also been effective in improving trading efficiency.

Efforts are underway, through the Uruguay Round of trade negotiations, to bring about the further liberalization and expansion of world trade. These efforts are also directed at enhancing the trade and development possibilities of developing countries and providing greater security and predictability to the international trading system. In the years ahead, governments should strive to promote an open and equitable global trading system that will enable all countries to improve their economic structures and standards of living through sustained economic development.

Programs and Activities

- The international community should find ways of achieving a better functioning of commodity markets. The functioning of commodity markets must be improved and consistent commodity policies must be enacted at national and international levels.

- In order to reduce dependence on commodity exports, efforts should also be taken to provide for greater diversification in the commodity trade of developing economies.

- In order to encourage diversification efforts, compensation mechanisms for shortfalls in commodity export earnings of developing countries should continue to be applied.

- All countries should implement efforts to halt and reverse protectionism. Trade barriers that restrict imports of primary and processed commodities should be eliminated.

- Greater efforts must be made to expand market access, particularly to developing countries.

- There must be substantial and progressive reductions in those types of government support that induce uncompetitive production, such as production and export subsidies for agricultural commodities.

- Developing countries should act to create domestic environments that have an optimal balance between production for the domestic and export markets. Efforts must be undertaken to improve the efficiency of export and import trade as well as the functioning of domestic markets.

- Developing countries must expand processing, distribution and marketing practices in the commodity industry.

- Commodity prices should be structured to reflect the environmental, social and resource costs of commodity production.

- There should be much greater cooperation between producers and consumers. The exchange of views and information on investment plans, prospects and markets for individual commodities should be increased. In this regard, particular attention should be paid to achieving international agreements on cocoa, coffee, sugar and tropical timber.

- Assistance should be provided to developing countries in the design and implementation of commodity policies and the use of information on commodity markets.

- Occupational health and safety matters, technology transfers and environmental considerations should be taken into account in all matters of international trade.

- An international trade dispute settlement process should be developed to ensure that environment-related standards are not used as non-tariff barriers to trade. This should promote multilateral agreements rather than unilateral action.

- For trade liberalization to be successful, it is necessary to ensure positive net cash flows to developing countries. This can be achieved by increasing official development assistance. Substantially reducing the debts and debt-service requirements of developing countries will also be necessary.

- The continued clearing of outstanding balances would restore the ability of the international financial system to contribute to growth and development. At the same time, coordinated action could substantially reduce the debt owed to private banks and official creditors. Debt owed to official creditors by low-income debtors should continue to be written off.

- An increase in domestic savings in industrialized countries would be a complement to policies to restrain consumption on environmental grounds.

Financing

The estimated average total annual cost of implementing the activities in this program area is about $8.8 billion from the international community on grant or aid terms.

Making Trade and Environment Mutually Supportive

Environment and trade policies should be mutually supportive. An open global trading system makes possible the more efficient allocation and use of the Earth's resources. This will contribute to an increase in production and incomes and to a lessening of humanity's demands on the environment. Increased global economic activity will provide additional resources that are needed for economic growth and development and improved environmental protection. A sound environment, on the other hand, provides the ecological and other resources needed to sustain growth and underpin a continuing expansion of trade. An open, trading system supported by sound environmental policies will have a positive impact on the environment and contribute to sustainable development.

International cooperation in the environmental field is growing. In a number of cases, trade provisions in international environment agreements have played a role in tackling global environmental challenges. Trade measures have been used in certain specific instances to enhance the effectiveness of regulations for the protection of the environment. In order to not provide unjustified restrictions on trade, such regulations should address the root causes of environmental degradation. The challenge is to ensure that trade and environment policies are consistent and that they both reinforce the process of sustainable development. However, consideration must be given to the fact that environmental standards which are valid for industrialized countries may have unwarranted social and economic costs in developing countries. Governments should strive to make international trade and environmental policies mutually supportive.

Programs and Activities

- Efforts must be undertaken to encourage international productivity and competitiveness and to encourage a constructive role on the part of industry in dealing with environment and development issues.

- The General Agreement on Tariffs and Trade (GATT), the U.N. Conference on Trade and Development (UNCTAD) and other economic institutions should undertake adequate studies for the better understanding of the relationship between trade and environment.

- In those cases when trade measures related to environment are used, efforts should be taken to deal with the root causes of environment and development problems in a manner that avoids the adoption of environmental measures which result in unjustified restrictions on trade.

- Efforts must be taken to avoid the use of trade restrictions as a means to offset differences in cost arising from differences in environmental standards and regulations. The application of this type of restriction could lead to trade distortions and increase protectionist tendencies.

- Great care must be taken to ensure that environment-related regulations, including those related to health and safety standards, do not constitute a means of arbitrary or unjustifiable discrimination or a disguised restriction on trade.

- Factors which affect environment and trade policies in the developing countries must be borne in mind in the application of environmental standards, as well as in the use of any trade measures.

- Unilateral actions to deal with environmental challenges outside the jurisdiction of the importing country should be avoided. Environmental measures addressing global environmental problems should, as far as possible, be based on an international consensus.

- Domestic measures targeted to achieve certain environmental objectives may need trade measures to render them effective. Should trade policy measures be found necessary for the enforcement of environmental policies, certain principles and rules should apply.

- These should include the principle of non-discrimination and the principle that the trade measure chosen should be the least trade-restrictive necessary to achieve the objectives.

- Adequate notification of national regulations should be provided to all countries which the regulations will affect.

Financing

No financing requirements are provided for the program activities in this area of *AGENDA 21*.

Financial Resources for Developing Countries

Investment is critical to the ability of developing countries to achieve the necessary economic growth to improve the welfare of their populations and to meet their basic needs. The efforts to achieve this economic growth must be undertaken in a sustainable manner without deteriorating or depleting the resource base that underpins the development. Sustainable development requires increased investment for which domestic and external financial resources are needed. Foreign private investment and the return of domestic capital are an important source of financial resources. These resources depend on a healthy investment climate. Many developing countries have experienced a decade-long net loss of financial resources, during which their incomes were exceeded by payments they had to make, in particular for interest payments on debts. As a result, domestic resources had to be transferred abroad instead of being invested locally.

External indebtedness has emerged as a main factor in the economic stalemate in the developing countries. For many developing countries, the acceleration of development will not take place without an early solution to the problems of external indebtedness. The burden of debt payments on these countries has imposed severe restrictions on their ability to accelerate growth and eradicate poverty. This burden has led to a contraction in imports, investment and consumption. In this context, additional financial resources for developing countries and the efficient utilization of such resources is essential.

Programs and Activities

- The international community encourages countries with heavy debts to private banks to continue to negotiate commercial bank debt reduction plans with their creditors. The parties to such negotiations should take due account of both the medium-term debt reduction and new money requirements of the debtor country.

- With regard to debt owed to official creditors, recent measures have been taken by the Paris Club to provide more generous terms of relief to the poorest most-indebted countries. Efforts to implement these terms in a way that gives additional support to their economic reform efforts are welcomed.

- Many low-income countries with substantial debt burdens have taken significant actions to service their debt and safeguard their credit-worthiness. These actions are commended. Particular attention should be paid to the resource needs of these countries. Other debt-distressed developing countries which are making great efforts to continue to service their debt and meet their external financial obligations also deserve due attention.

- Growth-oriented solutions to the problem of developing countries with serious debt-servicing problems must be developed. Particularly in the case of low-income countries in the process of economic reform, the support of the financial institutions is necessary. Measures by financial institutions in the refinancing of interest are noted with appreciation.

Financing

The costs and specific *AGENDA 21* details and requirements relating to financing are included under the Financing section in Chapter 8: Implementing *AGENDA 21*.

Economic Policies to Support Sustainable Development

The unfavorable global financial environment which faces developing countries makes the efficient use of domestic financial resources all the more important. In a number of countries, policies are necessary to correct misdirected public spending and large budget deficits. Restrictive investment policies and distortions in exchange rates also need to be corrected. Obstacles to entrepreneurship need to be removed in all countries. In industrialized countries, increased savings rates would help generate resources to support the transition to sustainable development both domestically and in developing countries. Effective, efficient, honest and accountable public administration is an essential element for sustainable economic development. All countries should increase their efforts to eliminate the mismanagement of public and private affairs, including corruption.

Many indebted developing countries are undergoing structural adjustments relating to debt rescheduling or new loans. While such programs are necessary for improving these countries balance-of-payments, in some cases they have resulted in adverse social and environmental effects. In certain instances, such restructuring has resulted in cuts in spending for health care, education and environmental protection. It is important to ensure that such structural adjustment programs do not have negative impacts on the environment and social development. It is necessary to establish economic policy reforms that promote the efficient planning and use of resources for sustainable development. It is also necessary to foster entrepreneurship and the incorporation of social and environmental costs in resource pricing.

Programs and Activities

- The industrialized countries should encourage a stable and predictable international economic environment, particularly with regard to monetary stability, rates of interest and exchange rates.

- The industrialized countries should take substantial steps to stimulate savings and reduce fiscal deficits.

- Developing countries should implement sound economic policies to maintain the monetary discipline required to promote price stability. They should take steps to ensure realistic exchange rates and raise domestic savings and investment.

- All countries should develop policies that improve efficiency in the allocation of resources and take full advantage of the opportunities offered by the changing global economic environment.

- In particular, countries should remove the barriers to progress caused by bureaucratic inefficiencies, administrative strains, unnecessary controls and the neglect of market conditions.

- All countries should encourage entrepreneurship by improving facilities for enterprise creation and market entry. The essential objective should be to simplify or remove the restrictions, regulations and formalities that make it more complicated, costly and time-consuming to set up and operate business enterprises in many developing countries.

- Opportunities should be provided for farm and non-farm small-scale enterprises and for indigenous populations and local communities to contribute fully to the attainment of sustainable development.

- Governments of industrialized countries should enhance their efforts to provide developing countries with increased technical assistance in the design and implementation of economic policies.
- Assistance in the design and operation of efficient tax systems, accounting systems and a financial industry should also be provided.
- Stronger economic cooperation between developing countries has long been accepted as an important component of efforts to promote economic growth in the developing world. The efforts of the developing countries to promote economic cooperation among themselves should be enhanced and supported by the international community.
- These policy modifications must involve substantial changes in public administration, central banking, tax administration, savings institutions and financial markets of developing countries.

Financing

It is estimated that the average total annual cost of implementing the activities in this area will be about $50 million from the international community.

Environment and Development in Decision-Making

Economic development has received the world's priority attention. During the last two decades, however, there has been increasing concern about its adverse effects on the environment. To correct this, environmental policies have been formulated, but rarely have they been fully integrated with economic policies. It is now clear that sustainable development requires the integration of environmental and economic factors.

Prevailing systems for decision-making in many countries tend to separate economic, social and environmental factors at the policy, planning and management levels. This influences the actions of all groups in society, including governments, industry and individuals. A fundamental reshaping of decision-making processes is necessary if environment and development are to be put at the center of economic and political decision-making. This section consists of the following program areas: environment and development at the policy, planning and management

245

levels; legal and regulatory frameworks; economic instruments and market incentives; and environmental and economic accounting systems.

Policy and Management

In recent years, some governments have begun to make significant changes in the institutional structures of government in order to enable a more systematic consideration of the environment. The environment must be taken into account when decisions are made on economic, social, fiscal, energy, agricultural, transportation, trade and other policies. New methods are also being developed for achieving better coordination between national and local government, industry, the scientific community, environmental groups and the public in the process of developing effective approaches to environment and development. The responsibility for bringing about these changes lies with governments acting in close partnership with the private industry and organizations.

The exchange of experiences between countries can also be significant. National plans, goals and objectives, and national rules, regulations and laws must be understood by all countries. In this context, it must be remembered that environmental standards may pose severe economic and social costs if they are uniformly applied in developing countries. The overall objective in this area is to restructure the decision-making process to include full consideration of economic and environmental issues.

Programs and Activities

- All countries should work to ensure the integration of economic, social and environmental considerations in decision-making at all levels and in all ministries.

- They should adopt a domestic policy framework that reflects a long-term perspective with a consideration of connections between various political, economic, social and environmental issues.

- Regular reviews should be conducted of the state of economic and social conditions and the state of the environment and natural resources in every country.

- The use of data and information at all stages of planning and management must be improved in order to make systematic and simultaneous use of social, economic, developmental and ecological data.

- Comprehensive analytical procedures for the assessment of the economic, social and environmental impacts of decisions need to be adopted. A broad range of analytical methods should be encouraged in order to provide various points of view.
- Flexible planning approaches need to be used that allow the consideration of multiple goals and changing needs.
- Legal, regulatory and economic tools should be utilized for planning and management. These should be regularly reviewed and adapted to ensure that they continue to be effective.
- The delegation of planning and management responsibilities to the lowest level of public authority should be the goal.
- Effective and equitable opportunities for participation by women should be promoted at all levels.
- Procedures for involving local communities in contingency planning for environmental and industrial accidents should be implemented. An open exchange of information on local hazards must be provided.
- Countries should develop systems for the monitoring and evaluation of progress towards achieving sustainable development by adopting indicators that measure changes in economic, social and environmental dimensions.
- Every country should adopt a national strategy for sustainable development based on *AGENDA 21*. This strategy should build upon and harmonize the various economic, social and environmental policies and plans that are operating in the country. The experience gained through previous efforts, such as preparation of national reports for the Earth Summit, should be incorporated into this strategy.
- The goals should be to ensure socially responsible economic development while protecting the resource base and environment for the benefit of future generations. The strategy should be developed through the widest possible public participation.
- Research should be undertaken with the explicit objective of assisting policy decisions and providing recommendations on improving management practices.
- Efforts should be made to improve education and technical training, particularly for women and girls, by including interdisciplinary approaches in technical, vocational, university and other curricula.

- There should also be efforts to undertake systematic training of government personnel, planners and managers on a regular basis.
- All countries, in cooperation with private groups and the media, should promote public awareness of the importance of considering environment and development in an integrated manner.
- Mechanisms for facilitating a direct exchange of information and views with the public should be developed.

Financing

The average total annual cost for the activities of this program is about $50 million, all of which will be necessary from the international community.

Legal and Regulatory Framework

Laws and regulations are among the most important instruments for transforming environment and development policies into action. Although the volume of legal texts in this field is steadily increasing, much of the law-making in many countries seems to be ad-hoc and piecemeal or has no effective enforcement to back it up. While there is continuous need for improved laws in all countries, many developing countries do not have adequate environmental laws and regulations. It is essential to develop and implement enforceable and effective laws and regulations that are based upon sound social, ecological, economic and scientific principles. It is equally critical to develop workable programs to enforce compliance with the laws, regulations and standards that are adopted. Technical support will be needed for many countries to accomplish these goals. Technical cooperation in this field should include legal information, advisory services and specialized training.

The enactment and enforcement of laws and regulations is also essential for the implementation of most international agreements in the field of environment and development. A survey of existing agreements was undertaken in preparation for the Earth Summit. This survey has indicated that many countries are failing to comply with international treaties by not enacting or enforcing required laws. The overall objective is to promote environment and development policies through appropriate legal and regulatory policies and enforcement mechanisms.

Programs and Activities

- The laws and regulations which have been enacted and the related administrative machinery which has been established should be periodically reviewed. Such a review should be directed at ensuring that the laws and regulations are effective in actual practice.

- The effectiveness of laws and regulations can be increased with the promotion of public awareness and the preparation and distribution of educational material.

- Specialized training, including workshops, seminars, education programs and conferences, should be developed for public officials who design, implement, monitor and enforce laws and regulations.

- Effective judicial and administrative procedures for actions affecting the environment and development should be established. Care should be taken to provide access to individuals, groups and organizations with a recognized legal interest.

- Assistance in the preparation of comprehensive inventories and reviews of national legal systems should be provided to developing countries. Past experience has demonstrated the usefulness of combining such legal information services with legal expert advice.

- A cooperative training network for sustainable development law should be developed and implemented.

- Especially for students from developing countries, academic institutions should cooperate to provide postgraduate programs and in-service training facilities in environment and development law.

- Such training should address the effective application and progressive improvement of applicable laws. Educational efforts should also develop the related skills of negotiating, drafting and mediation and the training of trainers.

- Private organizations already active in this field should cooperate with related university programs to develop curriculum and to offer a maximum range of options to interested governments and potential sponsors.

- Each country should develop strategies to maximize compliance with its own laws and regulations. These strategies should include sanctions which are designed to punish infractions, obtain restitution and deter future violations. Methods for regularly reviewing compliance and for detecting violations must be implemented.

- Mechanisms for the involvement of individuals and groups in the development and enforcement of laws and regulations on environment and development should be developed.

- Countries which have signed international agreements should improve their procedures for collecting information on the legal and regulatory measures taken to comply with the agreements.

- This program relies essentially on a continuation of ongoing work on legal issues. Closer cooperation between existing databases may be expected to lead to improved standardization and compatibility of legal data.

Financing

It is estimated that the average total cost of implementing the activities of this program through the year 2000 will be about $6 million per year. All of this funding will be required from the international community.

International Legal Instruments

In a separate but related area, various vital aspects of the international treaty-making process should be taken into account. There should be further development of international law on sustainable development, with special attention to the delicate balance between environmental and developmental concerns. There is also a need to clarify the relationship between existing international environmental agreements and relevant social and economic agreements. Many existing international legal agreements in the field of environment were developed without adequate participation of developing countries. These agreements will need to be reviewed in order to reflect the concerns and interests of developing countries. The overall objective should be to evaluate the effectiveness of international law relating to the environment and development.

All nations agree that environmental policies should deal with the root causes of environmental degradation and not result in unnecessary restrictions to trade. Domestic measures targeted to achieve certain environmental objectives may need trade measures to render them effective. However, trade policy measures for environmental purposes should not be used as a means of arbitrary or unjustifiable discrimination or as a disguised restriction on international trade. Unilateral actions to deal with environmental challenges outside the jurisdiction of the importing country should be avoided. Environmental measures which address international environmental problems should, as far as possible, be based on an international consensus.

Programs and Activities

- An effort should be made to identify and prevent actual or potential conflicts, particularly between environmental and economic agreements. The broadening and strengthening of the United Nations system should be considered in order to facilitate the identification, avoidance and settlement of international disputes in the field of sustainable development.

- At periodic intervals, efforts should be undertaken to review and assess both the past performance and effectiveness of existing international agreements as well as the priorities for future law-making on sustainable development.

- This may include an examination of the feasibility of elaborating the general rights and obligations of all nations in the field of sustainable development.

- In the area of avoidance and settlement of disputes, further study should be undertaken to broaden and make more effective the range of techniques currently available. This may include procedures for the exchange of data and information, and methods for notification and consultation regarding situations that might lead to disputes with other nations in the field of sustainable development.

- In times of armed conflict, measures should be considered to address large-scale destruction of the environment that cannot be justified under international law. The specific competence and role of the International Committee of the Red Cross should be taken into account.

- In view of the vital necessity to ensure safe and environmentally sound nuclear power, and in order to strengthen international cooperation in this field, efforts should be made to conclude the ongoing negotiations for a nuclear safety convention in the framework of the International Atomic Energy Agency.

- The parties to international agreements should consider procedures and mechanisms to promote and review their effective, full and prompt implementation. In this regard, efficient and practical reporting systems on the implementation of international legal instruments should be established.

- In all these activities, the effective participation of all countries, in particular developing countries, should be ensured through appropriate provision of technical assistance and financial assistance.

- Developing countries should be given "headstart" support in their national efforts to implement international agreements.

- Support should include assistance in building expertise in international sustainable development law and in assuring access to the necessary reference information and scientific and technical expertise.

Financing

No cost estimates were developed for the implementation of the programs and activities in the area of international agreements on sustainable development.

Economic Instruments and Market Incentives

Environmental laws and regulations are important but alone they cannot be expected to deal with the all of the problems of environment and development. Prices, markets and fiscal and economic policies also play a complementary role in shaping attitudes and behavior towards the environment. During the past several years, many nations have been increasing the use of market-oriented economic approaches to environment and development problems. This has taken place primarily in industrialized countries, but it is also occurring in Central and Eastern Europe and in some developing countries. Examples of this approach include the "polluter-pays" principle and the more recent "natural-resource-user-pays" concept.

Within a supportive economic and legal context, market-oriented approaches can enhance a country's capacity to deal with the issues of environment and development. This type of approach can provide cost-effective solutions, promote technological innovation and influence environmental behavior.

What is needed is an international effort to explore and make more effective and widespread the use of economic and market-oriented approaches. This will involve a reorientation of policies on the part of governments. It will also require cooperation between economic and environmental organizations and agencies with expertise in this area, including transnational corporations.

There are two fundamental objectives in this area. The first is to incorporate environmental costs into the decisions made by producers and consumers. There must be an international effort to reverse the tendency to treat the environment as a "free good" and pass environmental costs on to other parts of society, other countries or future generations. The second objective is to move towards the integration of social and environmental costs into all economic activities, so that prices will appropriately reflect the relative scarcity and total value of natural resources.

Programs and Activities

- All governments should act to establish effective combinations of economic, regulatory and voluntary (self-regulatory) approaches to environmental and sustainable development problems. Efforts must be made to remove or reduce any government subsidies that do not conform with sustainable development objectives. Existing economic and fiscal incentives must also be revised to meet environmental and developmental objectives.

- A policy framework should be developed that encourages the creation of new markets in pollution control and environmentally sound resource management.

- Product pricing which is consistent with sustainable development objectives should be encouraged.

- Governments, in cooperation with business and industry, should undertake studies to determine how economic instruments and market mechanisms can be used effectively in the following areas: energy, transportation, agriculture and forestry, water, wastes, health and tourism.

- A special effort should be made to develop economic instruments and market mechanisms which are geared to the particular needs of devel-

253

oping countries and countries with economies which are in transition to market-based systems.

- Economic and environmental organizations and research institutes should provide technical support to developing countries on issues relating to the application of such economic instruments and market mechanisms. Regional seminars should be encouraged and regional centers of expertise should be developed.

- Given that the use of economic instruments and market mechanisms is relatively recent, the exchange of information about different countries' experiences with such approaches should be actively encouraged.

- Governments should encourage research and analysis on effective uses of economic instruments and incentives. Such research should focus on such key issues as the role of environmental taxation, the implications of economic incentives on competitiveness and international trade, and the possible social implications of using various economic instruments.

- The theoretical advantages of using pricing policies to support sustainable development need to be better understood. Business, industry, large enterprises and transnational corporations need to explore the practical implications of pricing that includes environmental costs. Much more research needs to be conducted into the actual methodologies used for valuing environmental costs.

- Institutions of higher learning need to review their curricula and strengthen studies in sustainable development economics.

- Economic and research organizations with expertise in this area need to provide training sessions and seminars for government officials.

- Business and industry, including large industrial enterprises and transnational corporations with expertise in environmental matters, also need to organize training programs in the areas of environmental accounting and natural resource valuation.

Financing

The estimated average total annual cost of implementing the activities of this program is about $5 million from the international community on grant or aid terms.

Environmental and Economic Accounting

A first step towards the integration of the concept of sustainability into economic management is to establish a better method to measure the crucial role of the environment as a source of natural capital and as a sink for by-products generated by human activities. As sustainable development encompasses social, economic and environmental dimensions, it is important that national accounting procedures are not restricted to measuring the production of goods and services that are bought and sold conventionally. A common framework needs to be developed whereby the environmental and social contributions that are not currently included in conventional national accounts will be incorporated in such accounts in the future. A program to develop national systems of integrated environmental and economic accounting in all countries is proposed. The main objective is to expand existing systems of national economic accounts in order to integrate environment and social dimensions in the accounting framework. This should include systems of accounts for natural resources in all nations. The resulting systems of integrated environmental and economic accounting should be seen as a complement to, rather than a substitute for, traditional national accounting practices for the foreseeable future.

Programs and Activities

- Policies will have to be designed to foster changes in the way the environment is perceived in relation to the economy and provision of goods and services. Policies should be developed to promote more appropriate production and consumption patterns. Measures should be adopted to encourage shifts in technology use and economic management that anticipate and prevent the depletion of resources and irreversible environmental degradation.

- All nations should obtain the SNA Handbook on Integrated Environmental and Economic Accounting from the The Statistical Office of the United Nations Secretariat. Efforts must be taken to develop, test, refine and standardize the concepts and methods proposed by the SNA Handbook.

- At the national level, integrated economic and environmental accounting systems should be adopted by the agencies dealing with national accounts, in close cooperation with environmental statistics and natural resource departments. The purpose must be to assist national economic analysts and decision-makers in their national economic planning efforts.

- Unpaid productive work such as domestic work and child care should be included in national accounts and economic statistics. Time-use surveys should be a first step in the process of developing these accounts.

- Governments should seek to identify and consider measures to correct price distortions arising from environmental programs which affect land, water, energy and other natural resources.

- Governments should encourage corporations to provide relevant environmental information through open and complete reporting to shareholders, creditors, employees, governmental authorities, consumers and the public.

- Corporations must also be encouraged to develop and implement methods and rules for accounting for sustaining development.

- Major efforts should be made to augment the capacity to collect and analyze environmental data and information and to integrate it with economic data.

- International donor agencies should consider financing the development of data banks to help ensure that national planning for sustainable development is based on precise, reliable and effective information.

- The exchange of international experience in the establishment of integrated economic and environmental accounting systems should be encouraged, particularly in connection with the valuation of non-marketed natural resources. The cooperation of business and industry, including large industrial enterprises and transnational corporations with experience in valuation of such resources, should also be sought. Guidelines and mechanisms should be developed for the adaptation and diffusion of information technologies to developing countries. State-of-the-art data management technologies should be adopted.

- The training of national accountants, environmental statisticians and national technical staff must be undertaken for the establishment and development of national integrated economic and environmental accounting systems.

- This should include technical training of those involved in economic and environmental analysis, data collection and national accounting, as well as training decision-makers to use such information in a pragmatic and appropriate way.

Financing

The average total annual cost of implementing the activities of this program is estimated to be about $2 million from the international community.

Transfer of Environmentally Sound Technology

Environmentally sound technologies protect the environment, are less polluting, use all resources in a more sustainable manner, recycle more of their wastes and products and handle residual wastes in a more acceptable manner. In the context of processing and production, environmentally sound technologies are those that generate low or no waste. "End of the pipe" technologies for the treatment of pollution after it has been generated are also considered environmentally sound technologies. Environmentally sound technologies are not just individual technologies, but total systems which include know-how, procedures, goods, services and equipment, as well as organizational and managerial procedures.

The use of such new and efficient technologies will be essential to achieve sustainable development, maintain the world's economy, protect the environment and alleviate poverty and human suffering. Particularly in developing countries, there is a need for favorable access to environmentally sound technologies. Such access should be encouraged by measures that promote technology cooperation and encourage the transfer of necessary technological, economic and managerial knowledge. Technology cooperation will involve joint efforts by business, research and development facilities and governments. The activities proposed in this chapter are aimed at improving conditions for the transfer of technology, including state-of-the-art technology. Inherent in these activities is the need to improve or replace the technology currently being used in many areas.

Concepts for assuring access to environmentally sound technologies in developing countries must be developed. A large body of useful technological knowledge lies in the public domain and is not covered by patents . There is a need to enhance the access of developing countries to such technologies. Developing countries also need to have access to the know-how and expertise required for the effective use of these technologies. Consideration must be given to the role of patent protection and intellectual property rights.

Proprietary technology is available through commercial channels and international business is an important vehicle for technology transfer. Tapping this pool of knowledge and combining it with local innovations to generate alternative technologies should be pursued. The effective transfer of environmentally sound technologies also involves innovative incorporations of such technologies into the local or national culture. The impact of patent protection on the access to and transfer of environmentally sound technology to developing countries should also be examined.

Improved access to information is also crucial to enable countries, in particular developing countries, to make more rational technology choices. With relevant and current information, these countries will be better able to assess the need for environmentally sound technologies prior to their transfer. Research and development capacity is crucial to the effective use of environmentally sound technologies. Education and training programs should work to produce specialists who are literate in environmentally sound technology with an interdisciplinary outlook. Achieving this capability involves the training of craftspersons, technicians and middle-level managers, scientists, engineers and educators.

The objectives in this area are to help to ensure worldwide access to state-of-the-art environmentally sound scientific and technological information, to promote and finance the transfer of environmentally sound technologies and expertise on favorable terms, to promote environmentally sound indigenous technologies that may have been neglected, and to promote long-term technological partnerships between holders of environmentally sound technologies and potential users.

Programs and Activities

- Information systems should be developed and linked through national and international clearing-houses in the fields of agriculture, industry and energy. Such a network should include national and regional patent offices that are equipped to produce reports on state-of-the-art technology. The clearing-house networks should disseminate information on available technologies, their sources, their environmental risks and the terms under which they may be acquired. They should operate on an information-demand basis and focus on the information needs of the end-users.

- These clearing-houses should take the initiative in helping users to identify their needs and in disseminating information that meets those needs. Existing news, public information and communication systems should be used for this purpose. The information should highlight and detail concrete cases where environmentally sound technologies were successfully developed and implemented. In order to be effective, the clearing-houses need to provide not only information, but also referrals to other services, including sources of advice, training, technologies and technology assessment. The clearing-houses should facilitate the establishment of joint ventures and partnerships of various kinds.

- An inventory of existing clearing-houses or information exchange systems should be undertaken. The existing sources should be strengthened and improved when necessary.

- Governments and international organizations should promote and encourage private industry to develop effective methods for access to and transfer of environmentally sound technologies.

- Policies and programs should also be developed for the effective transfer of environmentally sound technologies that are publicly owned or in the public domain.

- Favorable conditions should be created by governments to encourage public and private innovation, marketing and use of environmentally sound technologies.

- Existing subsidy and tax policies and other regulations should be examined to determine whether they encourage or impede the access to and transfer of environmentally sound technologies.

- Barriers to the transfer of privately owned environmentally sound technologies should be reduced and specific incentives, fiscal or otherwise, should be developed for the transfer of such technologies. This should include measures to prevent the abuse of intellectual property rights.

- Industrialized countries should take steps to enhance the access to and transfer of patent-protected environmentally sound technologies, in particular to developing countries. There should be efforts to expand rules for the acquisition of patent-protected technology through compulsory licensing that includes provisions for equitable and adequate compensation to the patent-holder.

- The purchase of patents and licenses on commercial terms for their transfer to developing countries on non-commercial terms should be considered as part of development assistance.

- Financial resources should be made available to developing countries to allow them to acquire technology to implement measures to promote sustainable development.

- National capacities to assess, develop, manage and apply new technologies should be developed. This will require the strengthening of existing institutions, the training of personnel at all levels and the education of the end-user of the technology.

- A collaborative network of national and international research centers on environmentally sound technology should be established.

- Support should be provided for programs of cooperation and assistance in the areas of research and development, training, maintenance, national technology needs assessments, environmental impact assessments and sustainable development planning.

- Support should also be provided for programs of scientific research and the wide dissemination of technology development information. This should include developing links among facilities to maximize their efficiency in understanding, disseminating and implementing technologies for sustainable development.

- Plans and studies supporting these programs should provide the basis for potential financing of technology transfers by development banks, private interests and non-governmental organizations.

- On a voluntary basis, qualified experts from developing countries in the field of environmentally sound technologies who are currently working in industrialized countries should be assisted in any efforts to return to their home countries.

- Training must be provided in the management of environmentally sound technology, including the preparation of environmental impact and risk assessments.

- Long-term collaborative arrangements should be promoted between enterprises of industrialized and developing countries for the development of environmentally sound technologies.

- Multinational companies, as repositories of scarce technical skills needed for the protection and enhancement of the environment, have a special role in promoting cooperation in technology transfer. They are important channels for such transfer and they are an important asset for building a trained human resource pool.

- Joint ventures should be promoted between suppliers and recipients of technologies. Together with direct foreign investment, these ventures can constitute important channels for transferring environmentally sound technologies.

Financing

The estimated average total annual costs of implementing the activities of this program area are between $450 million and $600 million. All of this funding will be required from the international community on grant or concessional terms.

* * *

The success of all of the far reaching programs of *AGENDA 21* depends on the ability to effectively integrate environmental concerns into the fabric of international economic activity. Environmental matters must become a standard component of international trade policies, of legal decisions, of economic accounting procedures and of the political process. To accomplish this integration, there must be enormous international cooperation on all levels of economic decision-making. The goal of sustainable development of the Earth provides a central principle around which such cooperation can revolve.

As important as international efforts are in this area, it will be individual efforts which ensure the success of *AGENDA 21*: the efforts of business people to consider environmental costs in their personal day-to-day enterprises, the attempts by consumers to change their long-standing patterns of economic behavior and the struggles by decision-makers to balance the environmental dangers with the economic costs. The outcome of these and countless other personal actions will be the true measure of the success of *AGENDA 21*.

Chapter 8

Implementing AGENDA 21

In order to effectively implement the all of the programs proposed in *AGENDA 21*, major efforts will be needed to increase the participation of all social groups in sustainable development activities. To achieve a deep and genuine global involvement, enormous strides must be made in providing accurate and relevant information to the public and to decision-makers at all levels.

Human society is immeasurably rich in diverse social communities and experiences that can assist governments in the quest for environmentally sound and sustainable development. Building environmental and economic security requires a social partnership that makes use of the contributions of all peoples and assures that each will share in the benefits. Implementing any successful action plan for environmentally sound and sustainable development will require greater popular participation by all levels of society.

One of the fundamental prerequisites for the achievement of sustainable development is broad public participation in decision-making. This includes the need for individuals, groups and organizations to directly participate in environmental impact assessments and to know about and participate in decisions which potentially affect the communities in which they live and work. Individuals, groups and organizations must have open access to all information which is relevant to environment and development, including information on products and activities that are likely to have a significant impact on the environment.

Education is perhaps the single most important influence in changing human attitudes and behavior. It is vital for promoting economic growth and raising the quality of life by providing the knowledge and skills that produce jobs and increase productivity. It is essential to incorporate sustainable development concepts into all levels of education for all groups of society.

The various program areas in this chapter address the means for moving towards a true social partnership in support of the common goal of the sustainable development of Earth. Activities to strengthen participation by all major social groups are included. Programs to provide increased access to accurate information are also detailed.

The Role of Women

The international community has endorsed several plans of action for the full and equal integration of women into all environmental and developmental activities. Several agreements have also been adopted to end gender-based discrimination and ensure that women have access to land, other resources, education and safe and equal employment. Effective implementation of these plans will depend on the active involvement of women in economic and political decision-making and will be critical to the successful implementation of Agenda 21.

Efforts must be undertaken to increase the proportion of women decision-makers, planners, technical advisers, managers and extension workers in all environment and development fields. By the year 2000, a strategy should be developed to eliminate all constitutional, legal, administrative, cultural, behavioral, social and economic obstacles to women's full participation in sustainable development and in public life. In this regard, clear governmental policies and national plans should be developed for the achievement of equality in all aspects of society. As a matter of urgency, measures to ensure that women and men have the same right to decide freely and responsibly the number and spacing of their children must be implemented. All necessary legal, administrative, social and educational measures to eliminate violence against women in all its forms must be adopted and enforced.

Programs and Activities

- Plans should be developed to increase the proportion of women involved as decision-makers, planners, managers, scientists and technical advisers in programs for sustainable development.

- Measures to eliminate illiteracy among females and to expand the enrollment of women and girls in educational institutions should be adopted. The goal is universal access to primary and secondary education for girl children and increased educational and training opportunities for women and girls in sciences and technology, particularly at the post-secondary level.

- Programs should be developed to promote the reduction of the heavy workload of women and girl children at home and outside through the establishment of more and affordable nurseries and kindergartens by governments, local authorities, employers and other organizations.

- Efforts should be made to promote the sharing of household tasks by men and women on an equal basis and to promote the provision of environmentally sound technologies which have been designed and developed in consultation with women.

- Programs are necessary to support and strengthen equal employment and pay opportunities for women. These must be supported by adequate day-care facilities and parental leave and by equal access to credit, land and other natural resources.

- Efforts should be made to establish rural banking systems to increase rural women's access to credit.

- Consumer awareness programs must be implemented which emphasize the crucial role which women play in achieving the changes which will be necessary to reduce or eliminate unsustainable patterns of consumption and production. Such programs should also encourage investment in environmentally sound activities.

- Programs are needed to eliminate persistent negative images, stereotypes, attitudes and prejudices against women in the media, advertising and education.

- Countries must take urgent measures to avert the ongoing rapid environmental and economic degradation in developing countries which dramatically affects the lives of women and children in rural areas. The effects of drought, desertification, deforestation, armed hostilities, natural disasters, toxic waste and the use of unsuitable agricultural chemical products must be counteracted.

- Research is needed into the impact of cut-backs in social services, food and fuel subsidies, education and health services on women. Research should also continue on the integration of the value of unpaid work, including work that is currently designated "domestic", in accounting systems in order better to represent the true value of the contribution of women to the economy.

- Gender impact assessments should be included as a necessary step in the development of environmental and developmental programs.

Financing

The estimated average total annual cost of implementing the activities of this section will be about $40 million from the international community on grant and aid terms.

The Role of Youth

Youth, those adolescents over the age of twelve, comprise nearly 30 percent of the world's population. The majority of the over 1.2 billion youth in developing countries face a difficult future, since often their very basic needs as children have not been met, leaving them unprepared for adult life. For example, a mere 23 percent of the world's youth complete secondary education. Only 9 percent of those who live in developing countries do so. In the industrial world, youth unemployment has increased faster than any other group in society, presently reaching levels well over 28 percent in some countries.

Youth, who are destined to inherit the world, need to be accorded the right to a secure and healthy future. The involvement of today's youth in environmental and developmental decision-making will be critical to the long-term success of *AGENDA 21*. In addition to their intellectual contribution and their ability to mobilize support, they bring unique perspectives that need to be taken into account. Each country should establish a process to promote dialogue between the youth community and government at all levels. Youth need access to information and an opportunity to present their perspectives on government decisions.

Immediate efforts should be undertaken to combat human rights abuses against young people, particularly young women and girls. Youth must have access to education, training and employment to enable them to lead better lives and contribute to environmental protection and sustainable economic and social development. Increasing consideration should be given to providing all youth with the legal protection and support necessary for them to fulfill their personal and economic aspirations and potentials.

Programs and Activities

- Procedures should be established that allow for the participation of youth of both genders in the environmental decision-making process.
- Efforts must be made to ensure access for all youth to all types of education. By the year 2000, more than 50 percent of youth should be enrolled in secondary education or equivalent vocational training programs. All education should incorporate the concepts of environmental awareness and sustainable development throughout the curricula.
- Innovative education methods should be used which are aimed at increasing practical skills, such as environmental scouting.
- Initiatives must be begun to reduce current levels of youth unemployment. Alternative employment opportunities and job training must be provided for young men and women.
- Educational and awareness programs specifically targeted to the youth population must be developed. National and local media, private organizations and businesses should assist in this effort.

Financing

The average total annual cost of implementing the activities of this program area is about $1.5 million from the international community.

The Role of Children

Children will inherit the responsibility of looking after the Earth. In many developing countries they comprise nearly half the population. Children in both developing and industrialized countries are highly vulnerable to the effects of environmental degradation. They are also highly aware of environmental problems and are vocal supporters of environmental thinking. In order to safeguard the future, the specific interests of children need to be taken fully into account in the development of all programs on environment and sustainable development.

Programs and Activities

- Governments should take active steps to implement programs for children which are designed to achieve progress in the areas of health, nutrition, education, literacy and the alleviation of poverty.

- Efforts must be taken to expand educational opportunities for children, including education for environmental and developmental responsibility. Overriding attention must be paid to the education of girl children.

- Procedures should be established to incorporate children's concerns into all relevant policies and strategies for environment and development at all levels.

Financing

Financing requirements for most of the activities in this area are included in estimates for other *AGENDA 21* programs.

The Role of Indigenous People

Indigenous people have an historical relationship with their lands and are generally the descendants of the original inhabitants of such lands. Indigenous people represent a significant percentage of the global population. Over many generations, they have developed a holistic traditional scientific knowledge of their lands, natural resources and environment. Indigenous people must enjoy the full measure of human rights and fundamental freedoms without hindrance or discrimination. As a result of economic, social and historical factors, their ability to participate fully in sustainable development practices on their own lands has tended to be limited. Some of the goals of this program area are already contained in such international legal instruments as the Indigenous and Tribal Peoples Convention and are being incorporated into the Universal Declaration on Indigenous Rights which is being prepared by the United Nations. 1993 is the International Year for the

World's Indigenous People and this presents a timely opportunity to mobilize further international technical and financial cooperation.

There must be global recognition that the lands of indigenous people should be protected from activities that are environmentally unsound and actions that the indigenous people concerned consider to be socially and culturally inappropriate. In this regard, there must also be recognition that traditional dependence on renewable resources and ecosystems, including sustainable harvesting, continues to be essential to the cultural, economic and physical well-being of indigenous people. Some indigenous people may require greater control over their lands and more opportunity for the self-management of their resources, including participation in the establishment and management of protected areas.

Programs and Activities

- Policies should be adopted that will protect indigenous intellectual and cultural property and protect the right to preserve customary practices and administrative systems.

- Efforts must be made to incorporate the values, views and knowledge of indigenous people into resource management and other programs that may affect them.

- Indigenous people should be informed, consulted and allowed to participate in national decision-making.

- Technical and financial assistance should be provided for programs that support the sustainable self-development of indigenous people and their communities.

- Research and education programs must be developed for the purpose of achieving a better understanding of indigenous people's environmental knowledge and experiences and applying this information to contemporary development challenges.

- Efforts should be made to increase the efficiency of indigenous people's resource management systems, for example, by promoting the use of suitable technological innovations.

- National arrangements to consult with indigenous people should be increased in order to incorporate their values and traditional practices into national policies in the field of natural resource management and conservation.

- Governments should incorporate the rights and responsibilities of indigenous people into the legislation of each country.

- International development agencies and governments should commit financial and other resources to education and training for indigenous people to develop their capacities to achieve sustainable self-development. Particular attention should be given to strengthening the role of indigenous women.

Financing

The estimated average total annual cost of implementing all of the activities of this section will be about $3 million from the international community on grant or aid terms.

The Role of Private Organizations

Private organizations play a vital role in the shaping and implementation of participatory democracy. Their credibility lies in the responsible and constructive role they play in society. Formal and informal organizations, as well as grass-roots movements, are essential partners in the implementation of *AGENDA 21*. The nature of the independent role played by private organizations within a society provides for real participation. Their independence is a major attribute of private organizations and is the precondition of real participation.

One of the major challenges facing the world community as it seeks to achieve environmentally sound and sustainable development is the need to activate a sense of common purpose on behalf of all levels of society. The chances of forging such a sense of purpose will depend on the willingness of all groups to participate in genuine social partnership and dialogue.

Private organizations, including non-profit organizations, possess well-established and diverse experience and expertise in fields which will be of particular importance to the implementation of *AGENDA 21* programs. The community of private organizations offers a global network that should be tapped in support of efforts to achieve these common goals.

To ensure that the full potential contribution of private organizations is realized, the fullest possible communication and cooperation between international organizations, national and local governments and private organizations should be promoted. Private organizations will also need to foster cooperation and communication among themselves to reinforce their effectiveness.

Programs and Activities

- Methods should be developed to enhance existing procedures by which private organizations contribute to decision-making, implementation and evaluation of environmental and sustainable development programs.

- Levels of financial and administrative support for private organizations and the extent and effectiveness of their involvement should be reviewed.

- An open and effective means of achieving the participation of private organizations in the implementation of *AGENDA 21* at all levels should be designed.

- Private organizations and their self-organized networks should be allowed to contribute to the review and evaluation of all *AGENDA 21* programs.

- Private organizations should have full access to accurate and timely data and information in order to allow for their effective contribution to research and the design, implementation and evaluation of *AGENDA 21* programs.

- Efforts should be made to encourage partnerships and dialogue between local private organizations and local authorities in activities aimed at sustainable development.

- Private organizations should be allowed to be involved in national procedures which are established to carry out *AGENDA 21*, especially in the fields of education, poverty alleviation and environmental protection and rehabilitation.

- The findings of private monitoring and review should be taken into account in the design and evaluation of policies concerning the implementation of *AGENDA 21*.

- Private organizations should be assisted in their efforts to develop their own training programs.

271

- Legislative measures are necessary to ensure the right of private organizations to protect the public interest through legal action.

Financing

Increased financial and administrative support will be needed for private organizations and their networks, in particular those based in developing countries. Private organizations will require significant additional funding, but these costs cannot be reliably estimated on the basis of existing information. Relatively limited but unpredictable costs will be involved at the international and national levels.

The Role of Farmers

Agriculture occupies one-third of the land surface of the Earth and is the central activity for much of the world's population. Rural activities take place in close contact with nature, adding value to it by producing renewable resources. "Farmers", as used in this section, includes all rural people who derive their livelihood from activities such as farming, fishing and forest harvesting. The rural household and the family farmer, a substantial number of whom are women, have long been the stewards of much of the Earth's resources. Farmers must conserve their physical environment as they depend on it for their sustenance. Over the past 20 years there has been an impressive increase in total agricultural production. Yet, in some regions, this increase has been outstripped by population growth, international debt or falling commodity prices.

The natural resources that sustain farming activity need proper care, and there is a growing concern about the sustainability of current agricultural production systems in many parts of the world. A farmer-centered approach is the key to the attainment of sustainability in both industrialized and developing countries. A significant proportion of the rural population in developing countries depends primarily upon small-scale, subsistence-oriented agriculture which is based on family labor. However, these crucial family farming units have limited access to resources, technology or means of production. As a result, they are often forced into the overexploitation of marginal lands and natural resources.

The key to the successful implementation of *AGENDA 21* lies in the motivation and attitudes of individual farmers. Success is also dependent on government policies that provide incentives to farmers to manage their natural resources in an efficient and sustainable manner.

Programs and Activities

- Efforts should be made to ensure the implementation of the all of the *AGENDA 21* programs relating to sustainable livelihoods, agriculture and rural development.

- Pricing mechanisms, trade policies and fiscal incentives must be developed that positively affect individual farmer's decisions about an efficient and sustainable use of natural resources.

- Farmers and their representative organizations must be allowed to participate in the formulation of agricultural policy.

- Women's access to tenure and the use of land must be protected. Women's property rights, access to credit, technology and training must be enhanced and expanded.

- The formation of farmers' organizations must be supported by providing adequate legal and social conditions.

- National and international research centers should cooperate with farmers' organizations in developing environment-friendly farming techniques and agricultural development projects for specific areas.

- Efforts must be undertaken to document local knowledge, practices and experiences so that the lessons of the past affecting farming, forests and fishing will not be lost.

- Networks should be established for the exchange of experiences that help to conserve land, water and forest resources, minimize the use of chemicals and reduce or re-utilize farm wastes.

- Efforts should be undertaken to develop environmentally sound farming technologies that enhance crop yields, maintain land quality, recycle nutrients, conserve water and energy, and control pests and weeds.

- Studies of high-resource and low-resource agriculture should be made in order to compare their productivity and sustainability.

- Research should be undertaken on mechanization that would optimize human labor and animal power. The use of new and efficient hand-held and animal-drawn equipment that can be easily operated and maintained should also be studied.

- Governments should develop curricula for agricultural colleges and training institutions that would integrate ecology into agricultural science. Interdisciplinary programs in agricultural ecology are essential to the training of a new generation of agricultural scientists and field-level extension agents.

- Legal mechanisms to ensure effective land tenure to farmers is vital. The absence of legislation indicating land rights has been an obstacle in taking action against land degradation in many farming communities in developing countries.

- Locally managed credit systems, local production and distribution facilities, small-scale processing units, and marketing and distribution systems should be developed and supported in all countries.

- There must be increased access for farmers to agricultural training, credit and the use of improved technology, in particular, for women and farmers from indigenous groups.

Financing

The financing needed for this program area is estimated in Chapter 3 under Agriculture and Rural Development. The costs shown under Chapters 2 and 3 on Combating Poverty, Desertification and Mountain Ecosystems are also relevant for this area.

The Role of Local Authorities

Because so many of the problems and solutions addressed by *AGENDA 21* have their roots in local activities, the participation and co-operation of local authorities will be essential for its success. Local authorities develop and operate the economic, social and environmental infrastructure. They also oversee planning processes, establish local environmental policies and regulations, and assist in implementing national environmental policies. As the level of governance closest to people, local authorities play a vital role in educating, mobilizing and responding to the public.

Programs and Activities

- Each local authority should enter into a dialogue with its citizens, local organizations and private enterprises and adopt a "local" *AGENDA 21.*

- Local authorities should learn from citizens and local, civic, community, business and industrial organizations the information needed for formulating the best strategies. This process of consultation will also increase household awareness of sustainable development issues.

- Partnerships should be fostered among the United Nations Center for Human Settlements (Habitat), the World Bank, regional banks, the International Union of Local Authorities, the World Association of the Major Metropolises, Summit of Great Cities of the World, the United Towns Organization and other relevant partners.

- Representatives of associations of local authorities are encouraged to establish processes to increase the exchange of information, experience and mutual technical assistance among local authorities.

Financing

It has been estimated that the average total annual cost for implementing the activities in this area will be about $1 million.

The Role of Workers and Unions

Efforts to implement sustainable development will involve changes and opportunities at all levels of society. Individual workers will be foremost among those affected by these changes. As their representatives, trade unions are a vital component in achieving sustainable development. The experience of unions in addressing industrial change and the extremely high priority that they give to protection of the working environment and the related natural environment provides them with a sound basis from which to become fundamental partners in the global transition to sustainable development. Their historic promotion of socially responsible economic development also provides a useful background. The existing network of collaboration among trade unions and their extensive membership provides important channels through which the concepts and practices of sustainable development can be supported.

The overall objective is the alleviation of poverty and the achievement of full and sustainable employment in safe, clean and healthy environments. Workers should be full participants in the implementation and evaluation of activities related to *AGENDA 21*.

Programs and Activities

- For workers and their trade unions to play a full role in sustainable development, governments and employers should provide full protection for the rights of individual workers to freely associate and of their right to organize.

- Governments, business and industry should promote the active participation of workers and their unions in decisions on the design, implementation and evaluation of policies and programs on environment and development. This should include input into employment policies, industrial strategies, labor programs and technology transfers.

- Employer/worker/government collaborative efforts at the workplace, community and national levels should be established to deal with safety, health and environmental issues.

- Governments and employers should ensure that workers and their representatives are provided with all relevant information to enable their effective participation in these decision-making processes.

- Trade unions and employers should establish the framework for joint environmental policies and set priorities to improve the overall environmental performance of business.

- Trade unions should seek to ensure that workers are able to participate in environmental audits and environmental impact assessments in the workplace.

- Workers should have access to adequate training to augment environmental awareness, ensure their safety and health, and improve their economic and social welfare. Workers and their representatives should be involved in the design and implementation of worker training programs conducted by employers and governments.

Financing

The estimated average total annual cost of implementing the activities of this area is about $300 million from the international community on grant or concessional terms.

The Role of Business and Industry

Business and industry, including transnational corporations, play a crucial role in the social and economic development of a country. Business and industry is interpreted to include all manufacturing, mining, utilities, services and commerce, both private and public, and operating nationally or internationally. Increased global prosperity, a major goal of the development process, is primarily achieved by the activities of business and industry. Stable government policies encourage business and industry to operate responsibly and efficiently and to implement long-term strategies. Business enterprises, whether large or small and formal or informal, provide major trading, employment and livelihood opportunities world-wide. Increasingly, business opportunities are being made available to women. These opportunities are contributing towards women's professional development, strengthening their economic role and transforming social systems. Business and industry should be full participants in the implementation and evaluation of activities related to *AGENDA 21*.

Through more efficient and cleaner production processes throughout product life cycles, the policies and operations of business and industry can play a major role in reducing impacts on the environment. Technological innovations, industrial development and the transfer of technology are, to a very large extent, within the province of business and industry.

Business and industry must recognize environmental management as among the highest corporate priorities and as a key determinant for the success of sustainable development. Some enlightened business leaders are already implementing "responsible care" and product stewardship programs. These pacesetters are also fostering openness and dialogue with their employees and the public and are carrying out environmental audits. As innovators in business and industry, they are increasingly implementing voluntary initiatives, enacting self-regulations and taking greater responsibility in ensuring that their activities have minimal impacts on human health and the environment. The growing consciousness of consumers and the general public has contributed to this increased awareness of environmental concerns in business and industry.

The improvement of production systems through technologies and processes that utilize resources more efficiently and produce less waste is an important pathway towards sustainability for business and industry. Similarly, the encouragement of inventiveness, competitiveness and voluntary initiatives is necessary for stimulating more efficient and effective options. Two program areas are included in this section: cleaner production and entrepreneurship.

Cleaner Production

There is increasing recognition that production that uses resources inefficiently creates residues and wastes that have adverse impacts on human health and the environment. Good engineering and management practices can minimize waste throughout the product life cycle. The concept of cleaner production implies striving for optimal efficiency at every stage of a product's life cycle. The result will nearly always be an improvement in the overall competitiveness of the enterprise.

Programs and Activities

- Governments should implement laws, standards and economic measures that promote the use of cleaner production. Voluntary private initiatives should also be encouraged.

- Governments, business and industry, academia and international organizations should work towards the internalization of environmental costs into accounting and pricing mechanisms.

- Business and industry should be encouraged to report annually on their environmental records, as well as on their use of energy and natural resources.

- They should also adopt and report on the implementation of codes of conduct for promoting the best environmental practice, such as the International Chamber of Commerce's Business Charter on Sustainable Development and the chemical industry's responsible care initiative.

- Governments should promote technological cooperation between businesses, encompassing research and development, management, marketing and the application of cleaner production.

- Industry should incorporate cleaner production policies in its operations and investments, taking into account its influence on suppliers and consumers.

- Industry and business associations should encourage individual companies to undertake programs for improved environmental awareness and responsibility at all levels.
- In collaboration with industry and academia, private organizations should increase education, training and awareness activities relating to cleaner production.

Financing

No financing costs were included in *AGENDA 21* for this program.

Entrepreneurship

Business entrepreneurship is one of the most important driving forces for environmentally sound technological innovations. Competition inspires entrepreneurs to increase efficiency and respond to challenges and opportunities in the marketplace. Small and medium-sized entrepreneurs, in particular, play a very important role in the social and economic development of a country. Often, they are the major means for rural development, increasing off-farm employment and providing the transitional means for improving the livelihoods of women. Responsible entrepreneurship can play a major role in improving the efficiency of resource use, reducing hazards, minimizing wastes and safeguarding environmental qualities.

Programs and Activities

- Governments should encourage the establishment and operation of sustainably managed businesses. Measures for such encouragement should include regulations and economic incentives.
- Administrative procedures to approve applications to operate business enterprises should be streamlined in order to facilitate investment decisions.
- In cooperation with private business, governments should encourage the establishment of venture capital funds for sustainable development projects and programs.

- In collaboration with business, industry, academia and international organizations, governments should support training in the environmental aspects of business management.
- Efforts should be made to develop and enhance apprenticeship programs for youth.
- Business and industry, including transnational corporations, should be encouraged to establish worldwide corporate policies on sustainable development.
- To encourage the transfer of technology, business and industry should arrange for environmentally sound technologies to be available to affiliates in developing countries without extra external charges.
- Companies should encourage overseas affiliates to modify their procedures in order to reflect local ecological conditions and to openly share experiences with local authorities, governments and international organizations.
- Large business and industry, including transnational corporations, should consider establishing partnerships with small and medium-sized enterprises to help facilitate the exchange of experience in managerial skills, market development and technological know-how.
- Business and industry should establish national councils for sustainable development and help promote environmentally sound entrepreneurship. The inclusion of women entrepreneurs should be accelerated.
- Business and industry, in collaboration with academia and the scientific/engineering community, should increase research and development of environmentally sound technologies and environmental management systems.
- Business and industry should ensure responsible and ethical management of products and processes from the point of view of health, safety and environmental aspects.
- Financial aid institutions should continue to encourage and support small- and medium-scale entrepreneurs engaged in sustainable development activities.
- International organizations should increase support for research and development on improving the technological and managerial

requirements for sustainable development, in particular for small and medium-sized enterprises in developing countries.

Financing

The activities included under this program area are mostly changes in the orientation of existing activities and additional costs are not expected to be significant. The cost of activities by governments and international organizations are already included in other program areas.

The Role of the Scientific and Technological Community

The global scientific and technological community, including engineers, architects, industrial designers, urban planners and other professionals, will play a vital role in implementing the actions proposed by *AGENDA 21*. This section focuses on how to enable them to make a more open and effective contribution to decision-making processes concerning environment and development. It is important that the role of science and technology in human affairs be more widely known and better understood, both by decision-makers who help determine public policy and by the general public. The cooperative relationship existing between the scientific and technological community and the general public should be extended and deepened into a full partnership. Improved communication and cooperation between the scientific and technological community and decision-makers will facilitate greater use of scientific and technical information in the development of policies and programs.

Decision-makers should create more favorable conditions for improving training and independent research in sustainable development. Existing efforts will have to be strengthened and new approaches developed to provide policy makers and the general public with current information and practical know-how on the concept of sustainable development. The public should be assisted in communicating their sentiments to the scientific and technological community concerning how science and technology might be better managed to benefit their lives. By the same token, the independence of the scientific and technological community to investigate, exchange and publish their findings without restriction must be assured.

281

The adoption of international ethical guidelines and codes of practice will enhance the professionalism of the scientific and technological community. This will also increase the recognition of the value of its contributions in the areas of environment and development.

Two program areas are included in this section: cooperation with decision-makers, and guidelines and codes of practice. Additional information regarding sustainable development and science is contained later in this chapter.

Cooperation with Decision-Makers

The scientific and technological community and policy-makers must increase their interaction in order to implement strategies for sustainable development on the basis of the best available knowledge. Decision-makers should provide the necessary framework for rigorous research and for the full and open communication of the findings of such research. Decision-makers must also develop ways in which research results can be effectively communicated to decision-making bodies to better link scientific and technical knowledge with strategic policy.

Programs and Activities

- Governments should review how national scientific and technological activities could be more responsive to sustainable development needs. There must be major efforts to ensure that the full range of national needs for scientific and technological programs are communicated to governments and the public.

- Cooperative mechanisms to address regional needs for sustainable development must be developed. Such regional efforts could be facilitated through public/private partnerships and provide support to governments, industry, educational institutions and other private organizations.

- Efforts must be made to improve and expand scientific and technical advice to the highest levels of all governments, the United Nations and other international institutions.

- Programs for disseminating research results of universities and research institutions must be greatly strengthened. This requires greater support for the scientists, technologists and teachers who are engaged in communicating and interpreting scientific information for policy makers, professionals in other fields and the general public.

- Such support requires the full and open sharing of data and information among scientists and decision-makers. The publication of national scientific research reports and technical reports that are understandable would also improve cooperation between scientists and decision-makers.

- Efforts must be made to improve the links between official and independent research institutes and industry so that the latest research will become an important element of industrial strategy.

Financing

The average total annual cost of implementing the activities of this program is estimated to be about $15 million from the international community on grant or concessional terms.

Guidelines and Codes of Practice

As professionals and members of disciplines devoted to the search for knowledge, scientists and technologists have a special set of responsibilities. Increased ethical awareness in environmental and developmental decision-making should help ensure that the functioning of the natural world is properly valued by present and future societies. A strengthening of the codes of practice and guidelines for the scientific and technological community would increase environmental awareness and contribute to the acceptance of the concept of sustainable development. It would enhance the level of esteem and regard for science and technology and improve the accountability of the scientific and technological community. To be effective in the decision-making process, such codes of practice and guidelines must not only be agreed upon by the scientific and technological community, but also recognized by society as a whole.

Programs and Activities

- Efforts must be taken to strengthen national and international cooperation to develop codes of practice and guidelines regarding environmentally sound and sustainable development. The goal should be to develop a common framework between the scientific and technological community and society as a whole.

- Education and training in developmental and environmental ethical issues should be expanded to integrate such objectives into education curricula and research priorities.

- National and international environment and development legal agreements should be amended to ensure that appropriate codes of practice and guidelines are incorporated into such regulatory machinery.

Financing

The average total annual cost of implementing the activities of this program will be about $5 million from the international community.

* * *

Providing Information

The availability of accurate and timely information to decision-makers and the general public is an essential element in efforts towards sustainable development. The knowledge base by which humanity can understand and conquer the major problems of today is developed, in large measure, by the scientific community. Education is the social institution entrusted with the main responsibility for passing on to succeeding generations the wisdom, knowledge and experience gained from the past. It represents a guided path which helps individuals to understand their own societies and to take their place in them.

Central to the success of *AGENDA 21* is the provision of information regarding the sustainable development of the Earth to both the public and decision-makers at all levels. The next sections deal with two vital areas: the use of science to develop the knowledge necessary to foster sustainable development and the use of education to spread such knowledge. Both of these areas are indispensable for enabling people to adapt to a swiftly changing world and to develop an ethical awareness which is consistent with the sustainable use of natural resources.

Science for Sustainable Development

This section focuses on the role and the use of the sciences in supporting the management of the environment and the future development of humanity. The four program areas in this section are intended to support the specific scientific requirements identified in other *AGENDA 21* programs.

Scientists are continually improving their understanding of climatic change, resource consumption, demographic trends and environmental degradation. Changes in these and other areas need to be taken into account in working out long-term strategies for global development. An essential role of the sciences is to provide information for the formulation of environment and development policies. A first step towards improving the scientific basis for these strategies is a better understanding of land, oceans, atmosphere and their interlocking cycles. This is essential if more accurate estimates are to be provided concerning the carrying capacity of planet Earth and of its resilience to the stresses placed upon it by human activities. The sciences can provide this understanding through increased research into the underlying ecological processes and through the application of modern and effective tools that are now available. These innovative and efficient tools include remote-sensing devices, robotic monitoring instruments and new computing and modelling capabilities.

The sciences are increasingly being understood as an essential component in the search for feasible pathways towards sustainable development. The sciences play an important role in emphasizing the fundamental significance of the Earth as a life support system. The sciences should continue to play an increasing role in improving the efficiency of resource use and in finding new development practices, resources and alternatives. There is a constant need for the sciences to promote less intensive uses of energy in industry, agriculture and transportation.

In the face of threats of irreversible environmental damage, lack of full scientific understanding should not be an excuse for postponing actions which are justified in their own right. Precaution should be the global approach for policies relating to complex systems that are not yet fully understood and whose consequences cannot yet be predicted. Scientific knowledge should be applied to articulate and support the goals of sustainable development, through scientific assessments of current conditions and future predictions of life on Earth. Such assessments should be used at all levels in the decision-making process. Of crucial importance is the need for scientists in developing countries to participate fully in international scientific research programs dealing with the global problems of environment and development. This will allow all countries to participate on equal footing in negotiations on global environmental and developmental issues.

There are four programs which are outlined in this area: science and sustainable management, increasing scientific understanding, long-term scientific assessment and enhancing scientific capabilities.

Science and Sustainable Management

Sustainable development requires long-term perspectives and the integration of the environmental effects of global change into the development process. To achieve this, it will be necessary to use the best scientific and traditional knowledge available. To ensure that human impact upon the Earth is minimized, the development process must be constantly re-evaluated in light of the latest findings of scientific research. Good environmental and developmental management must be scientifically robust, seeking to keep open a range of options to ensure a flexibility of response.

Often, there is a communication gap between scientists, policy makers and the public. Much better communication of scientific information is required. The primary objective is for each country to identify the state of its scientific knowledge and its research needs in order to achieve, as soon as possible, substantial improvements in scientific understanding at all levels of society.

Programs and Activities

- All countries should prepare an inventory of their natural and social science data which is relevant to sustainable development. They should also identify their research needs and priorities in the context of international research efforts.
- Current research should be broadened to include more involvement of the public in establishing long-term societal goals.

- The scientific community must develop and apply new tools for quality-of-life indicators covering health, education, social welfare, the state of the environment and the economy.

- Science must also strive to develop innovative economic approaches to environmentally sound development and new and improved incentive structures for better resource management.

- In order to improve knowledge of the costs and benefits of different development policies, the collection and analysis of data on the connections between the condition of ecosystems and the health of human communities must be increased.

- Science must improve its capabilities for determining scientific research priorities at the national, regional and global levels to meet the needs of sustainable development. This is a process that involves scientific judgements regarding short-term and long-term benefits and possible long-term costs and risks. This process should be carried out in an open, honest and "user-friendly" manner.

- Efforts must be made to develop methods to link the findings of the established sciences with the indigenous knowledge of different cultures.

Financing

The estimated average total annual costs of implementing the activities of this program are about $150 million, including about $30 million from the international community on grant or aid terms.

Increasing Scientific Understanding

In order to promote sustainable development, more extensive knowledge is required of the Earth's carrying capacity, including the processes that could either impair or enhance its ability to support life. The global environment is changing more rapidly than at any time in recent centuries. As a result, substantial surprises may be expected. The next century could see significant environmental changes. At the same time, the human consumption of energy, water and non-renewable resources is increasing, on both a total and a per/capita basis. Critical shortages of all of these vital items may ensue in many parts of the world if environmental conditions remain unchanged.

Human social processes both affect and are influenced by these changing environmental conditions. Human factors are key driving forces in these intricate sets of relationships and exert their influence directly on global change. Study of the human dimensions of the causes and consequences of environmental change is essential. One key objective is to improve the fundamental understanding of the connections between human and natural environmental systems. Another goal is to improve the analytical and predictive tools required to better understand the environmental impacts of human development options.

Programs and Activities

- An expanded global network should be developed to monitor various natural cycles. Such a network should be used to test hypotheses regarding their behavior and improve research into the interactions among the various global cycles.

- Observation and research programs should be expanded in global atmospheric chemistry and the sources and sinks of greenhouse gases. It is also absolutely vital that the results of such research are presented in a publicly accessible and understandable form.

- Research programs on marine and terrestrial systems must be expanded. Global databases of their components must be strengthened.

- Efforts in predictive modelling of the Earth system and its subsystems must be expanded. These computer modelling efforts should include the functioning of these systems assuming different intensities of human impact.

- There must be greater coordination of satellite missions and of the networks, systems and procedures for processing and disseminating their data.

- The capacity must be developed for predicting the responses of terrestrial, freshwater, coastal and marine ecosystems to short- and long-term changes in the environment.

- There must be intensive efforts to further develop the science of restoration ecology.

- Further studies must be conducted into the role of biodiversity and the impact of the loss of species on the functioning of ecosystems and the global life-support system.

• A global observing system for the rational management of coastal and mountain zones must be developed. Freshwater quantity/quality monitoring systems must be significantly expanded, particularly in developing countries.

• In order to understand the Earth as a system, Earth observation systems from space must be developed which will provide continuous and long-term measurements of the interactions of the atmosphere, hydrosphere and lithosphere. A distribution system for such data must be developed.

• The engineering sciences must develop technology that can automatically collect, record and transmit information, in order to monitor marine, terrestrial and atmospheric processes and provide advance warning of natural disasters.

• Research must be intensified in the physical, economic and social sciences to better understand the impacts of economic and social behavior on the environment. Such research should also strive to understand the impact of environmental degradation on local and global economies.

• Research must be conducted on the human, economic and social responses to global change.

• Efforts must be made to increase the use of appropriate new technologies to support sustainable development. These technologies include supercomputers, space-based observational technology, Earth- and ocean-based observational technologies, data management and database technologies.

• The development of new "user-friendly" technologies that provide understandable information and knowledge for decision-makers and the general public is vital.

Financing

The average total annual cost of implementing the activities of this program is estimated to be about $2 billion, including about $1.5 billion from the international community.

Long-Term Scientific Assessment

Meeting scientific research needs in the environment/development field is only the first step in the support that the sciences can provide for sustainable development. The knowledge acquired may then be used to provide scientific assessments of the current status of the Earth and for prediction of possible future global conditions.

Although many of the long-term environmental changes that are likely to affect people and the biosphere are global in scale, key changes can often be made at the national and local levels. At the same time, human activities at the local and regional levels often contribute to global threats. Thus, scientific assessments and projections are required at the global, regional and local levels. Many countries and organizations already prepare reports on the environment and development which review current conditions and indicate future trends. Regional and global assessments should make full use of such reports but should be broader in scope and include the results of detailed studies of future conditions. The primary objective is to provide assessments of the current status and trends in major environmental issues in order to develop alternative long-term strategies.

Programs and Activities

- Existing data- and statistics-gathering systems which are relevant to developmental and environmental issues must be coordinated. This will allow for the preparation of long-term scientific assessments. These assessments should be based on data on resource depletion, import/export flows, energy use, health impacts, demographic trends and other factors.

- The assessments which are made must be widely distributed in a form that is responsive to public needs and can be easily understood.

- National and regional environmental and developmental audits and a five-year global audit should be carried out on a regular basis. The results of these audits should be made available to the general public.

- Standardized audits should help to refine the pattern and character of development and the capacities of global and regional life-supporting systems to meet the needs of human and non-human life forms.

- Such audits will also be useful in identifying areas and resources which are most vulnerable to further degradation.
- The preparation of such audits will involve the integration of all relevant sciences at the national, regional and global levels, and should be organized by governmental agencies, private organizations, universities, research institutions and the United Nations.

Financing

It has been estimated that the average total annual cost of implementing the activities of this program area will be about $35 million, including about $18 million from the international community.

Enhancing Scientific Capability

In view of the increasing role that the sciences have to play in dealing with the issues of environment and development, it is essential to increase the scientific capabilities in all countries, particularly in developing countries. This is necessary to enable them to participate fully in the generation and application of the results of scientific research and development concerning sustainable development. There are many ways to enhance scientific and technological capacity. Some of the most important of these are education and training in science and technology, improvements in research and development infrastructures, development of incentives to encourage research and development and greater utilization of research results in industry. Such capacity-building will also form the basis for the improvement of public awareness and understanding of the sciences.

Programs and Activities

- Efforts should be undertaken to promote the education and training of scientists, not only in their own individual disciplines, but also in their ability to identify, manage and incorporate environmental considerations into research and development projects.
- Education in all sciences must ensure that a sound knowledge base in natural systems, ecology and resource management is provided.

- Curricula must be developed to train specialists who are capable of working in interdisciplinary programs related to environment and development, including the field of applied social sciences.

- The scientific infrastructure in schools, universities and research institutions must be strengthened, particularly those in developing countries. This may be accomplished by the provision of adequate scientific equipment and access to current scientific literature.

- National scientific and technological databases must be developed which can process data in unified formats and systems.

- Full and open access must be provided to the depository libraries of regional scientific and technological information networks.

- The submission of scientific and technological information and databases to global or regional data centers and network systems must be encouraged and promoted.

- Global scientific and technological information networks which are linked to national scientific and technological databases must be developed.

- Activities to reduce information barriers due to language differences must be expanded.

- Particularly in developing countries, the applications of computer-based retrieval systems must be expanded in order to cope with the growth of scientific literature.

- Mechanisms for the sharing of basic research, data and information must be expanded and encouraged. Such mechanisms should be designed to enhance professional cooperation among scientists in all countries and to establish strong alliances between industry and research institutions.

- Existing networks of natural and social scientists and universities must be expanded.

- Information on indigenous environmental and developmental knowledge should be compiled, analyzed and published. The communities that possess such knowledge should be assisted in efforts to benefit from the information.

- Efforts must be taken to create conditions (e.g., salaries, equipment, libraries) to ensure that scientists can work effectively in their home

292

countries. Efforts must also be made to recruit more women in research and research training.

- Scientific and technological information networks must be funded so that they will be able to function effectively and efficiently in satisfying the scientific needs of developing countries.

Financing

The estimated average total annual costs of implementing the activities of this program are about $750 million, including about $470 million from the international community on grant or aid terms.

Education, Public Awareness and Training

All education, including formal education, public awareness and training, should be recognized as a process by which human beings and societies can reach their fullest potential. Education, the raising of public awareness and training are linked to virtually all areas in *AGENDA 21*. The program areas which are described in this section are: reorienting education, increasing public awareness and promoting training.

Reorienting Education

Education is critical for promoting sustainable development and improving the capacity of people to address environment and development issues. While basic education provides the underpinning for environmental and developmental education, the latter needs to be incorporated as an essential part of learning.

Both formal and non-formal education are indispensable to changing people's attitudes. Both are also critical for achieving environmental and ethical awareness of the values, attitudes and behavior which will be necessary for sustainable development of the Earth to succeed. To be effective, environment and development education should deal with the dynamics of the physical, biological, social, economic and spiritual environment. Information regarding all of these aspects should be integrated into all disciplines.

The main objective is to ensure universal access to basic education for all children and to achieve primary education for at least 80 percent of girls and boys of primary school age. A further goal is to reduce the global adult illiteracy rate to at least half of its 1990 level. Efforts should focus on increasing the literacy and basic education of women.

Beyond these fundamental educational goals, there must be a global effort to achieve environmental and developmental awareness in all levels of society.

Programs and Activities

- All countries should prepare national strategies for meeting basic learning needs of their citizens. This must include providing universal and equal access to education for girls and boys, women and men.

- Private organizations can make an important contribution in designing and implementing educational programs.

- Governments should strive to prepare strategies aimed at integrating environment and development issues into education at all levels within the next three years. This should be done in cooperation with all segments of society.

- A thorough review of curricula should be undertaken to ensure that there is a multidisciplinary approach which encompasses environment and development issues and their social and cultural aspects.

- Countries are encouraged to set up national advisory environmental education coordinating bodies with representatives of various environmental, developmental, educational and gender organizations.

- These bodies should help mobilize different population groups and communities to assess their own needs and to develop the necessary skills to create and implement their own environment and development initiatives.

- Educational authorities, with assistance from community groups or private organizations, are recommended to set up pre-service and in-service training programs for all teachers and administrators which address the nature and methods of environmental and development education. Such training programs should make use of the wide experiences and information available from private organizations.

- Every school should be assisted in designing environmental activity work plans, with the participation of students and staff.

- Schools should involve school-children in local and regional studies on environmental health, including safe drinking water, sanitation, food and ecosystems.

- School-based activities should be implemented which link these studies with information on national parks, wildlife reserves, ecological heritage sites, etc.

- Within two years, the United Nations, with the assistance of governments and private organizations, should establish a program to integrate *AGENDA 21* into all existing United Nations educational materials.

- Regional organizations and national authorities should be encouraged to elaborate similar parallel programs.

- Countries should cooperate with each other to prepare educational tools that include regional environment and development issues and initiatives.

- All countries should support university activities and networks for environmental and development education. Cross-disciplinary courses should be made available to all students. Programs at a post-graduate level should include specific courses for the further training of decision-makers.

- Countries should strengthen or establish national centers of excellence in education in environmental and developmental sciences, law and the management of specific environmental problems.

- Non-formal education activities should be encouraged at the local, regional and national levels by support for the efforts of non-formal educators and other community-based organizations.

- Public and scholastic forums should discuss environmental and development issues and suggest sustainable alternatives to policy-makers.

- Educational authorities, with the assistance of private organizations, should promote all types of adult education programs for continuing education in environment and development. These authorities and industry should encourage business, industrial and agricultural schools to include such topics in their curricula.

- Corporations should also include sustainable development in their education and training programs.

- Priority should be given to the education of young females and to programs promoting literacy among women. Governments and educational authorities should foster opportunities for women in nontraditional fields and eliminate gender stereotyping in curricula. This could be done by improving enrollment opportunities, reforming entrance and teacher staffing policies and providing incentives for establishing child-care facilities.
- Governments should affirm the rights of indigenous peoples to use their experience and understanding of sustainable development to play a part in education and training.
- Training and public awareness activities related to the environment should be given a high priority in budget allocations and should be protected from budget cutting requirements.
- Allocations within existing education budgets should be shifted to favor primary education, with a focus on environment and development.
- Efforts should be made to create conditions where a larger share of educational costs are borne by local communities, with rich communities assisting poorer ones.
- Debt for education swaps should be developed and encouraged.
- Restrictions on private schooling should be lifted.
- The more effective use of existing facilities should be promoted. These should included multiple school shifts and the development of open universities and other long-distance teaching.
- Low-cost or no-cost use of mass media for the purposes of education should be encouraged and developed.

Financing

It has been estimated that the average total annual cost of implementing this program will be from $8 billion to $9 billion, including about $3.5 billion to $4.5 billion from the international community.

Public Awareness

There is still a significant lack of awareness of the interrelated nature of human activities and the environment. Developing countries, in particular, lack clear information regarding these vital issues. In all countries, there is a crucial need to increase public sensitivity to environment and development problems and to cultivate a sense of personal environmental responsibility. Individual motivation and commitment to sustainable development must be fostered among all people. The objective is to promote broad public awareness of the concepts of sustainable development.

Programs and Activities

- Advisory bodies should be established or strengthened for public environment and development information. Activities of these bodies should be coordinated with private organizations and important media. Such bodies should encourage public participation in discussions of environmental policies and assessments.

- The United Nations system should improve its outreach and public awareness activities to promote greater involvement in all parts of the system.

- Public environmental and developmental information services should be implemented in all countries for raising the awareness of all groups, particularly decision-makers.

- Educational materials of all kinds and for all audiences should be based on the best available scientific information, including the natural, behavioral and social sciences.

- A cooperative relationship with the media, popular theater groups, and the entertainment and advertising industries should be developed. The goal should be to initiate discussions to mobilize their experience in shaping public behavior and consumption patterns. Such information should be distributed by making wide use of their most effective methods. Such cooperation will also increase active public participation in the debate on the environment.

- UNICEF should make child-oriented material available to media as an educational tool, ensuring close cooperation between out-of-school public information services and primary level school curriculum.

- Universities should enrich pre-service curricula for journalists on environment and development topics.

- All countries, in cooperation with the scientific community, should establish ways of employing modern communication technologies for effective public outreach.

- National and local educational authorities should expand the use of audio-visual methods. This is especially vital in rural areas through the use of mobile units.

- Such activities should include producing television and radio programs for developing countries which involve local participation, employ interactive multimedia methods and integrate advanced methods with folk media.

- All nations should promote environmentally sound leisure and tourism activities which make use of museums, heritage sites, zoos, botanical gardens, national parks and other protected areas.

- All countries should encourage private organizations to increase their involvement in environmental and development problems.

- Efforts should be undertaken to increase interaction with and include indigenous people in the management, planning and development of their local environment. Traditional and socially learned knowledge should be distributed through means based on local customs and, if appropriate, with electronic media.

- All organizations should develop support programs to involve young people and children in environment and development issues.

- Both men and women should be targeted for awareness campaigns which stress the role of the family in environmental activities.

- Public awareness should be heightened regarding the negative impacts of violence in society.

Financing

The average total annual cost of implementing the activities of this program is estimated to be about $1.2 billion, including about $110 million from the international community.

Training

Job training is one of the most important tools to develop human resources and accelerate the transition to a more sustainable world. It should be aimed at filling gaps in knowledge and skills that will help individuals find employment and become involved in environmental and development work. At the same time, training programs should promote a greater awareness of environment and development issues. Universal access to training opportunities, regardless of social status, age, gender, race or religion, should be an objective in this area. Job training should also strive to ensure that environmental and human ecological considerations are included at all management, marketing, production and finance levels.

Programs and Activities

- Efforts must be undertaken worldwide to identify workforce training needs and assess measures to meet those needs.

- National professional associations are encouraged to develop and review their codes of conduct to strengthen their environmental commitment. The training components of programs sponsored by professional bodies should ensure that information on sustainable development is included.

- Educational institutions should integrate environmental and developmental issues into all existing training curricula and promote the exchange of their methodologies and evaluations.

- Industry, universities, governments and private and community organizations should include an environmental management component in all training activities. The emphasis should be to immediately incorporate environmental concerns into in-plant vocational and management training programs.

- Environmental management training capacities should be strengthened. Specialized "training of trainers" programs should be established.

- New training approaches for existing environmentally sound practices should be developed that create employment opportunities and make maximum use of local resource-based methods.

- All nations should strengthen or establish practical training programs for graduates from vocational schools, high schools and universities to enable them to meet labor market requirements.

- Training and retraining programs should be established to meet environmental adjustments to the job market which have an impact on employment and skill qualifications.

- Governments are encouraged to consult with people in isolated situations (whether geographically, culturally or socially) to determine their needs for training to develop sustainable work practices and lifestyles.

- Governments, industry, trade unions and consumers should all promote an understanding of the interrelationship between good environment and good business practices.

- Particularly in deprived urban and rural areas, countries should develop a service of locally trained and recruited environmental technicians able to provide local people and communities with the services they require.

- Countries should enhance the public's ability to gain access to and effectively use information which is currently available on environment and development.

- Environmental labor-market information systems should be developed that supply data on current environmental job and training opportunities.

- Environment and development training resource-guides should be prepared and updated. These should include information on training programs, curricula, methodologies and evaluation results.

- All aid agencies should strengthen their training programs in all development projects, emphasizing a multidisciplinary approach which promotes awareness of and provides the necessary skills for a transition to a sustainable society.

- Existing networks of employers' and workers' organizations, industry associations and private organizations should exchange information on training and awareness programs.

- All governments should develop and implement strategies to deal with environmental threats and emergencies. Such strategies should emphasize urgent practical training and awareness programs for increasing public preparedness.

Financing

The estimated average total annual cost of implementing the activities of this program will be about $5 billion, including about $2 billion from the international community.

Information for Decision-Making

Sustainable development requires the availability of accurate and timely information to help decision-makers and the general public make sound decisions. In the broad sense, in the context of sustainable development, everyone is a user and provider of information. The need for information arises at all levels, from that of senior decision-makers at the national and international levels to the grass-roots and individual levels. The following two areas need to be implemented to ensure that decisions are based increasingly on sound information: bridging the data gap and improving information availability.

Bridging the Data Gap

While considerable data already exists, more and different types of data need to be collected regarding the status and trends of the planet's ecosystems, natural resources, pollution and economy. The gap in the availability, quality, coherence and accessibility of data between the industrialized and the developing world has been increasing. This gap seriously impairs the ability of developing countries to make informed decisions about environment and development issues.

There is a general lack of capacity, particularly in developing countries, for the collection and assessment of data and for its transformation into useful information. There is also a need for improved coordination among environmental, demographic, social and developmental information activities. Commonly used indicators such as the gross national product (GNP) and measurements of individual resource or pollution flows do not provide adequate indications of sustainability. Current methods for assessing the interactions between environmental, demographic, social and developmental factors are not sufficiently applied.

Programs and Activities

- Indicators of sustainable development need to be developed for use in national and international accounting systems.

- A suitable set of sustainable development indicators needs to be developed for areas outside of national jurisdiction, such as the high seas, the upper atmosphere and outer space.

- These indicators should be used in common, regularly updated and widely accessible reports and databases.

- All nations should carry out inventories of environmental, resource and developmental data. They should determine the gaps and organize activities to fill those gaps.

- International data-collection activities, including those of Earthwatch and World Weather Watch, need to be strengthened, especially in the areas of urban air, freshwater, land resources, forests, rangelands, desertification, other habitats, soil degradation, biodiversity, the high seas and the upper atmosphere.

- The activities related to development data of agencies and institutions of the United Nations system should be more effectively coordinated, perhaps through a "Development Watch" program.

- Special attention also needs to be paid to such areas as demographic factors, urbanization, poverty, health and rights of access to resources, as well as special groups, including women, indigenous peoples, youth, children and the disabled and their relationships with environment issues.

- With the rapid evolution of data-collection and information technologies, it is necessary to develop guidelines and mechanisms for the rapid and continuous transfer of those technologies, particularly to developing countries.

- International cooperation for training in all areas and at all levels will be required, particularly in developing countries. That training will have to include technical training of those involved in data collection, assessment and transformation, as well as assistance to decision-makers concerning how to use such information.

- Countries and international organizations should make use of new techniques of data collection, including satellite-based remote sensing.

- As large quantities of data from satellite sources will need to be processed in the future, national and international information centers should set up continuous and accurate data-collection systems. Developing countries should be assisted in acquiring these technologies.

- Governments should consider undertaking the necessary institutional changes at the national level to achieve the integration of environmental and developmental information into all areas of governmental concern.

- All countries should establish mechanisms to provide local communities and resource users with the information and know-how they need to manage their environment and resources in a sustainable manner. This is particularly relevant for poor rural and urban populations, and indigenous, women's and youth groups.

Financing

The estimated average total annual cost of implementing the activities of this program will be about $1.9 billion from the international community on grant terms.

Improving Information Availability

There already exists a wealth of data and information that could be used for the management of sustainable development. Finding the appropriate information at the required time and at the relevant level is, however, a difficult task. Because of shortages of money and trained manpower and a lack of awareness of the value and availability of data, information within many countries is not adequately managed.

Even where information is available, it may not be easily accessible, either because of the lack of technology for effective access or because of high costs, especially for commercial information held outside a country. Existing national and international mechanisms for information processing and exchange need to be strengthened to ensure the effective and equitable availability of information.

Programs and Activities

- A major effort should be undertaken to transform existing information into forms which are more useful for decision-making. This effort should focus on providing information for different levels of use.

- Mechanisms should be established for transforming scientific, social and economic assessments into information which is suitable for both planning and public information. Both electronic and non-electronic formats should be used.

- Governments should support efforts to develop standards for the efficient exchange of information. This should include the development of standard access and dissemination formats and communication interfaces.

- All governmental and private organizations should document and share information about the sources of available information in their respective organizations. Existing programs in this regard should be reviewed and strengthened.

- Private organizations and business should be encouraged to strengthen the mechanisms for sharing their experiences and information on sustainable development.

- To support information sharing, electronic links to provide access to databases and other information sources should be encouraged. Such networks should be used to monitor the implementation of *AGENDA 21*, to transmit environmental alerts and to transfer technical data.

- Where necessary, new technology should be developed to permit participation of those not served at present by existing methods. Mechanisms should also be established for the transfer of information to and from non-electronic systems to ensure the involvement of those without access to electronic systems.

- Surveys should be undertaken of information available in the private sector on sustainable development and of present commercial distribution arrangements.

- Whenever economic or other constraints on supplying and accessing information arise, innovative schemes for subsidizing information access or removing the non-economic constraints should be considered.

- Research and development efforts in hardware, software and other aspects of information technology should be promoted, particularly in developing countries.

Financing

The estimated average total annual cost of implementing the activities of this program is about $165 million from the international community.

International Capacity-Building

The ability of a country to follow sustainable development paths is determined to a large extent by the capacity of its people and its institutions as well as by its ecological and geographical conditions. The need to strengthen national capacities is shared by all countries. Building the national capacity to implement *AGENDA 21* will require the efforts of the nations themselves, in partnership with the United Nations and all other countries. The international community, municipalities, private organizations, universities, research centers, business and industry must also assist in these efforts. It is essential for individual countries to identify their priorities and determine the means for building the capacity to implement *AGENDA 21*.

Technical cooperation, including that related to technology transfer, encompasses the whole range of activities to develop or strengthen individual and group capabilities. Technical cooperation is effective only when it is related to a country's own strategies and priorities on environment and development.

Programs and Activities

- Each country should review its capacity-building requirements for devising national sustainable development strategies, including those for implementing *AGENDA 21*.

- By 1997, the Secretary-General of the United Nations should submit to the General Assembly a report on the implementation of technical cooperation programs for sustainable development.

- Each country should seek consensus at all levels of society on specific policies and programs needed for capacity-building to implement

AGENDA 21. This consensus should result from a participatory dialogue of all relevant interest groups. This consensus should include an identification of skill gaps, institutional capabilities, technological and scientific requirements and resource needs.

- The United Nations Development Programme should assist in the identification of the requirements for technical cooperation for the implementation of *AGENDA 21.* An assessment should be made of existing activities in technical cooperation.

- The United Nations Development Programme should use its network of field offices to assist capacity-building at the country and regional levels. It should also make full use of the expertise of other bodies, in particular the United Nations Environment Programme, the World Bank and regional commissions and development banks.

- Countries desiring technical cooperation, including technology transfers, should formulate requests in the framework of long-term capacity-building strategies.

- Such strategies should address policy adjustments to be implemented, budgetary issues, cooperation and coordination among institutions, human resource requirements, and technology and scientific equipment requirements. They should cover public and private needs and consider strengthening scientific training and educational and research programs.

- There should also be greater use of long-term cooperative arrangements between municipalities, private organizations, universities, training and research centers and business. Programs such as the Sustainable Development Networks of the United Nations Development Programme should be assessed in this regard.

- The sustainability of development projects should be enhanced by including in the original project design a consideration of environmental impacts, institution-building costs, technology needs and financial and organizational requirements for operation and maintenance.

- Efforts should be made to assist countries, particularly the least developed countries, on matters relating to national environmental and developmental policies, human resource development, legislation, natural resources and environmental data.

- The United Nations Development Programme should continue to work to mobilize funds from the international community for capacity-building. These responsibilities may need to be accompanied by a strengthening of the United Nations Development Programme's own capacities.

- The national entity in charge of technical cooperation should establish a small group of key actors to steer the process, giving priority to the country's own strategies and priorities.

Financing

The annual cost of bilateral expenditures to developing countries for technical cooperation, including costs related to technology transfers, is about $15 billion, or about 25 per cent of total yearly official development assistance. The implementation of Agenda 21 will require a more effective use of these funds and additional funding in key areas. The estimated average total annual cost of implementing the activities of this section are between $300 million and $1 billion from the international community.

The Financing of AGENDA 21

Prior to the Earth Summit, the United Nations General Assembly decided that ways and means should be identified for providing new and additional financial resources for environmentally sound development programs and projects designed to solve environmental problems of global concern. It also sought ways to effectively monitor the provision of such new and additional financial resources. Various funding mechanisms, including voluntary ones, were considered. The possibility of a special international fund and other innovative approaches were examined.

This section deals with financing the implementation of *AGENDA 21*. For each of the other programs and sections, the secretariat of the Earth Summit has provided estimates of the total costs of implementation for developing countries and the requirements for financing which is needed from the international community. These indicate the need for a substantially increased effort both by countries themselves and by the international community.

Economic growth, social development and poverty eradication are the primary and overriding priorities in developing countries and are essential to meeting national and global sustainability objectives. In light of the global benefits to be realized by the implementation of *AGENDA 21* as a whole, the provision to developing countries of the necessary financial resources and technology will serve the common interests of humankind in general, including future generations. The cost of inaction could well outweigh the financial costs of implementing *AGENDA 21*. Inaction will significantly narrow the choices of future generations.

For dealing with the major environmental issues, special efforts will be required. Global and local environmental issues are interrelated. Economic conditions, both domestic and international, that encourage free trade and access to markets will help make economic growth and environmental protection mutually supportive for all countries, particularly for developing countries and countries undergoing the process of transition to a market economy. International cooperation for sustainable development should also be strengthened in order to support and complement the efforts of developing countries, particularly the least developed countries. All countries should assess how to translate *AGENDA 21* into national policies and programs through a process that will integrate environment and development considerations. National and local priorities should be established by means that include public participation and community involvement which promotes equal opportunity for men and women. For an evolving partnership among all countries of the world, sustainable development strategies and predictable levels of funding in support of longer term objectives are required. For that purpose, developing countries should articulate their own priority actions and needs for support and industrialized countries should commit themselves to addressing these priorities.

The implementation of the huge sustainable development programs of *AGENDA 21* will require the provision to developing countries of substantial new and additional financial resources. Grant or concessional financing should be provided according to sound and equitable criteria. The progressive implementation of *AGENDA 21* should be matched by the provision of the necessary financial resources. Full use and continuing improvement of funding mechanisms for the implementation of Agenda 21 should be sought.

Fundamentally, the activities of this section are related to the implementation of all the other chapters of *AGENDA 21*. In general, the financing for the implementation of *AGENDA 21* will come from a country's own public and private sectors. For developing countries, substantial new and additional funding will be required. Through *AGENDA 21*, industrialized countries reaffirm their commitments to reach the accepted United Nations target of 0.7 percent of their Gross National Product for official development assistance. To the extent that they have not yet achieved that target, all nations have agreed to augment their aid programs in order to reach that target as soon as possible. Some countries have agreed to reach the target by the year 2000. Those countries which have already reached the target are to be commended and encouraged to continue in their efforts. Other industrialized countries have agreed to make their best efforts to increase their level of official development assistance.

Funding for *AGENDA 21* should be provided in a way which maximizes the availability of new and additional resources and which uses all available funding sources and mechanisms. These sources include the multilateral development banks and funds and the International Development Association. The regional and subregional development banks and funds should play an increased and more effective role in providing resources on favorable terms needed to implement *AGENDA 21*.

The Global Environment Facility is managed jointly by the World Bank, the United Nations Development Programme and the United Nations Environmental Programme and is designed to provide additional funding for global environmental needs. This facility should cover the agreed incremental costs of relevant activities under *AGENDA 21*, in particular for developing countries. To meet this need, it should be restructured to encourage universal participation and have sufficient flexibility to expand its scope and coverage to relevant program areas of *AGENDA 21*. Its restructure should also ensure a governance that is open and democratic in nature, by guaranteeing a balanced and equitable representation of the interests of developing countries, as well as giving due weight to the funding efforts of industrialized countries.

Many relevant specialized agencies, other United Nations bodies and other international organizations have roles to play in supporting national governments in implementing *AGENDA 21*. Multilateral institutions for capacity-building and technical cooperation can provide necessary financial resources. Bilateral assistance programs will also need to be strengthened in order to promote sustainable development. Voluntary contributions through private non-governmental channels have been running at about 10 percent of official development assistance. Efforts can be undertaken to increase this level.

It is important to achieve durable solutions to the debt problems of low- and middle-income developing countries in order to provide them with the needed means for sustainable development. Measures to address the continuing debt problems of low- and middle-income countries should be kept under review. All creditors in the Paris Club should promptly implement the agreement to provide debt relief for the poorest heavily-indebted countries which are actively pursuing structural adjustment to their economies. Debt relief measures should be kept under review in order to address the continuing difficulties of those countries.

In order to achieve sustainability, a supportive international and domestic economic climate is important, particularly for developing countries. Mobilization of higher levels of foreign direct investment and technology transfers should be encouraged through national policies that promote investments and joint ventures. New and innovative ways of generating new public and private financial resources should be explored. In particular, various forms of debt relief should be pursued, including greater use of debt swaps. The use of economic and fiscal incentives and mechanisms should be examined. The feasibility of tradeable permits should be explored. New schemes for fund-raising and voluntary contributions must be developed. Finally, the reallocation of resources presently committed to military purposes can provide an enormous source of new resources for the implementation of *AGENDA 21*.

The secretariat of the Earth Summit has estimated the average annual costs (1993-2000) of implementing all of the activities in *AGENDA 21* in developing countries to be over $540 billion, including about $125 billion on grant or concessional terms from the international community. These are order-of-magnitude estimates only and have not been reviewed by individual governments. Actual costs will depend upon the specific strategies and programs which individual governments decide upon for implementation.

Industrialized countries and others in a position to do so should make initial financial commitments to give effect to *AGENDA 21*. Developing countries should also begin to draw up national plans for sustainable development to give effect to *AGENDA 21*. It will be important to monitor the adequacy of funding for *AGENDA 21* on a regular basis.

The Role of the United Nations

The mandate of *AGENDA 21* emanates from General Assembly resolution 44/228 which affirmed that the Earth Summit should elaborate strategies and measures to halt and reverse the effects of environmental degradation. These efforts were to be made in the context of increased national and international efforts to promote sustainable and environmentally sound development in all countries. Along with this, efforts were to be directed toward the promotion of economic growth in developing countries. The follow-up to the Earth Summit process will take place within the framework of the United Nations system, with the General Assembly being the supreme policy-making forum that will provide overall guidance. At the same time, governments have a responsibility to play an important role in the follow-up to the Earth Summit. Their commitments and actions should be supported by the United Nations system and international financial institutions. National and international efforts should mutually benefit and support each other.

The United Nations, with its extensive experience in various spheres of international cooperation in the field of environment and development, is uniquely positioned to help governments establish more effective patterns of economic and social development. All agencies of the United Nations system have a key role to play in the implementation of *AGENDA 21*. To ensure proper coordination and avoid duplication of effort, there should be an effective division of labor between various parts of the United Nations system. In fulfilling the mandate of the Earth Summit, there is a need to restructure and revitalize the United Nations. All bodies of the United Nations system should publish reports of their activities on the implementation of *AGENDA 21* on a regular basis. Serious and continuous reviews of their policies, programs, budgets and activities will also be required.

The continued active and effective participation of private organizations, the scientific community, business, industry, local groups and communities are also important for the implementation of *AGENDA 21*. There must also be an effective link between substantive action and financial support, and this requires close and effective cooperation be-tween the United Nations and international financial institutions. Effec-tive cooperation between the United Nations and the international finan-cial bodies must also be established to provide for the follow-up to *AGENDA 21*.

The overall objective of *AGENDA 21* is to integrate environment and development issues at all levels of decision-making—local, national, regional and international. Specific objectives are to ensure the implementation of every phase of *AGENDA 21*. To achieve this, the role and functioning of the United Nations system in the field of environment and development must be enhanced. All agencies, organizations and programs of the United Nations system should adopt concrete programs for the implementation of *AGENDA 21*.

Major efforts must be made to strengthen and encourage cooperation and interaction between the United Nations, governmental institutions and private organizations in the field of environment and development. Specific consideration should be given to allow private organizations which are committed to the implementation of *AGENDA 21* (particularly those related to major groups and women's groups) to have access to all relevant information available. This should include information, reports and other data produced within the United Nations system.

The General Assembly, as the highest level inter-governmental mech-anism on Earth, is the principal policy-making and appraisal organ on matters relating to the follow-up of the Earth Summit. The General As-sembly should organize a regular review of the implementation of *AGENDA 21*. In particular, the General Assembly should consider hold-ing a special session no later than 1997 for the purposes of an overall re-view and appraisal of *AGENDA 21*. The United Nations Economic and Social Council should assist the General Assembly in overseeing the im-plementation of *AGENDA 21*. In addition, the Council should undertake the task of coordinating all environmental and developmental aspects in United Nations' policies and programs.

In order to ensure the effective follow-up of the Earth Summit, as well as to enhance international cooperation on the implementation of *AGENDA 21*, a high-level Commission on Sustainable Development should be established in the United Nations. This Commission would report to the U.N. Economic and Social Council. This Commission should provide for the active involvement of all programs and organizations of the United Nations and international financial institutions. It should also actively encourage the participation of private organizations, including industry and the business and scientific communities. The first meeting of this Commission should be no later than 1993.

In the follow-up to the Earth Summit, in particular the implementation of *AGENDA 21*, all relevant programs and organizations of the United Nations will have an important role in supporting national efforts. There will be a need for an enhanced and strengthened role for the United Nations Environment Programme. Priority areas for this program should be as follows:

- promoting environmental activities throughout the United Nations;
- promoting international cooperation in the field of environment;
- developing and promoting the use of techniques such as natural resource accounting and environmental economics;
- promoting environmental monitoring and assessment;
- strengthening and making operational its early warning function;
- coordinating scientific research;
- disseminating environmental information and data;
- raising general awareness in the area of environmental protection through collaboration with the public and private entities;
- assisting in the further development of international environmental law;
- promoting the widest possible use of environmental impact assessments in connection with every significant economic development project or activity;
- developing an information exchange on environmentally sound technologies;
- providing technical, legal and institutional advice to governments; and
- developing assistance in cases of environmental emergencies.

In order for the United Nations Environment Programme to perform all of these vital functions, while retaining its role as the principal body within the United Nations system in the field of environment, it will require access to greater expertise and financial resources.

The United Nations Development Programme, like the United Nations Environment Programme, also has a crucial role to play in the follow-up to the Earth Summit. Its role will include the following:

- acting as the lead agency for United Nations efforts in capacity-building;
- mobilizing resources for capacity-building;
- strengthening its own programs in support of *AGENDA 21*;
- assisting countries in the establishment of national networks and activities for implementing *AGENDA 21*;
- assisting countries in coordinating domestic financial resources; and
- promoting and strengthening the role and involvement of women, youth and other major groups.

The United Nations Conference on Trade and Development will also play an important role in the implementation of Agenda 21. The role of the United Nations Sudano-Sahelian Office should be strengthened so that this body can participate effectively in the implementation of *AGENDA 21* provisions related to land resource management and combating drought and desertification. All United Nations specialized agencies and organizations have an important role to play in the implementation of relevant parts of *AGENDA 21*. The United Nations regional economic commissions, regional development banks and regional economic and technical cooperation organizations can all contribute to this process.

*   *   *

Every nation on Earth has an important role to play in the follow-up to the Earth Summit and the implementation of *AGENDA 21*. National efforts should be undertaken in a comprehensive manner so that both environment and development concerns are afforded the highest priority. All nations should prepare national action plans for the implementation of *AGENDA 21*. Each nation should set up a national coordination structure which is responsible for the follow-up of *AGENDA 21*. This structure would greatly benefit from the expertise of private organizations.

Private organizations and groups are important partners in the implementation of *AGENDA 21*. Relevant private organizations, including scientific, community and women's groups, should be given wider opportunities to make contributions in support of *AGENDA 21*. Support should be provided for developing countries' private organizations and their networks. Efforts should be made to design open and effective means to achieve the participation of private organizations in the process to review and evaluate the implementation of *AGENDA 21*.

Ultimately, the success of *AGENDA 21* will depend on the individual efforts of all members of humanity. Each person must share in the responsibility for the protection of life on Earth. The deep and abiding changes in human civilization which are envisioned in *AGENDA 21* are all based upon the premise that the Earth can be saved and that human civilization can achieve its collective potential.

Each of the program areas in *AGENDA 21* highlights a global consensus for strategies to confront and conquer the major problems that the world faces as it approaches the 21st century. In the past few years, substantial progress has been made in many of the areas elaborated in *AGENDA 21*. There is so much more to be done, however, that the tasks which lie ahead for humanity may sometimes seem overwhelming. The challenges are indeed daunting and the effort required will be enormous.

In the next few years, the basic tenets of *AGENDA 21* will begin to influence decision-making at every level of society. A deep understanding of the rationale behind the drive for sustainable global development will enable every person to contribute to the success of *AGENDA 21* programs. For the far-ranging programs of *AGENDA 21* to be successful, a concern for the environment must begin to be integrated into every human action and every personal decision. What we manufacture, what we buy, what we wear, how we travel, what we eat, who we choose as leaders: these and a myriad of other daily questions must begin to be answered with a recognition that every single human action has an impact upon both the environment and upon all other people. Humanity has reached the point in its history when it must begin the difficult and demanding task of taking responsibility for each and every one of its actions. The sheer numbers of human beings are now causing our collective actions to have an unprecedented effect upon the planet.

As humanity approaches the end of this century, it is poised at a cross-roads of unmatched magnitude. The very existence of human life on Earth may well depend upon the direction which is taken in the next few years. Without question, the character and quality of human life on this planet is at stake. The potential for catastrophe is huge. However, the possibilities for success are encouraging. *AGENDA 21* is itself a monu-ment to the ability of humanity to join together in a global effort to solve the major problems of civilization. We each now have the opportunity and responsibility to help shape the future of life on our fragile planet. The consequences of our collective decisions will be our heritage.

Index

317